Trübner's Oriental Series

EASTERN PROVERBS AND EMBLEMS

Trübner's Oriental Series

ANCIENT NEAR EAST
In 6 Volumes

I	The History of Esarhaddon *Ernest A Budge*
II	Studies in Biblical and Semitic Symbolism *Maurice H Farbridge*
III	A Talmudic Miscellany *Paul Isaac Hershon*
IV	Eastern Proverbs and Emblems *J Long*
V	Comparative Grammar of the Semitic Languages *De Lacy O'Leary*
VI	Comparative History of the Egyptian and Mesopotamian Religions *C P Tiele*

EASTERN PROVERBS AND EMBLEMS

ILLUSTRATING OLD TRUTHS

J LONG

Routledge
Taylor & Francis Group
LONDON AND NEW YORK

First published 1881 by
Trübner & Co Ltd

2 Park Square, Milton Park, Abingdon, Oxon OX14 4RN
711 Third Avenue, New York, NY 10017, USA

Routledge is an imprint of the Taylor & Francis Group, an informa business

First issued in paperback 2016

Transferred to Digital Printing 2007

British Library Cataloguing in Publication Data
A CIP catalogue record for this book
is available from the British Library

Eastern Proverbs and Emblems
ISBN 978-0-415-24459-6 (hbk)
ISBN 978-1-138-96817-2 (pbk)
Ancient Near East: 6 Volumes
ISBN 978-0-415-24284-4
Trübner's Oriental Series
ISBN 978-0-415-23188-6

EASTERN PROVERBS AND EMBLEMS

ILLUSTRATING OLD TRUTHS

BY

THE REV. J. LONG

MEMBER OF THE BENGAL ASIATIC SOCIETY, F.R.G.S.

LONDON

TRÜBNER & CO., LUDGATE HILL

1881

PREFACE.

THE materials from which this little work has been compiled are scattered over more than 1000 volumes, some very rare, and to be consulted only in libraries in India, Russia and other parts of the Continent, or in the British Museum. The field has been so wide and the materials so immense, that the work of condensation has been almost as difficult as that of collecting; many statements are, therefore, simply suggestive; amplification would require several volumes. The Author has spared neither time nor labour in collecting and classifying the treasures drawn from the rich and new storehouse of Eastern Emblems and Proverbs, with the view of helping those who have neither the means of collecting a large reference library nor the time to spend in the search.

This work, begun a quarter of a century ago in the jungles of India for the instruction of peasants and women, is designed to afford some help to the following classes—Orientalists, Lovers of Folk-Lore, Teachers, and Preachers. The former desire to open a vista into the recesses of Eastern thought on moral and religious subjects, especially in relation to women and the masses; the latter are anxious to fix in the school, the pulpit, or the press great spiritual truths by means of emblems and illustrations drawn from the depths of the popular mind. Those classes may, in the pithy and pointed *illustrations* of Proverbs, find a quarry out of which to draw some of their materials.

Orientalists are at last recognizing the truth that Proverbs are as deserving of their research as coins and inscriptions; and that whereas the latter refer chiefly to kings and the upper classes, Proverbs throw a light on the dark recesses of social life, on archaisms, old customs, history, and ethnology. Even the Zenana, barred to the stranger, opens its portals to let man have a peep in and spy out the thoughts and feelings of woman, who, in the East, depicts her feelings and thoughts in Proverbs and racy sayings.

The Proverbs selected in this book, though limited to those serving to illustrate *moral and religious subjects,* show how widely scattered nations under similar circumstances have come to similar conclusions; many of these resemblances arise from the identity of human nature, or are a portion of the spiritual heritage which men brought away with them from the cradle of the human race, and improved on by subsequent communication; by shewing the acute observation and sharp moral sensibility of the masses, they prove God has not left himself without witness in the human breast; they, therefore, form a basis for those who are labouring to bridge over the gulf between Eastern and Western thought.

The nineteenth century is pre-eminently distinguished for the attention it gives to elevating the masses by knowledge conveyed to them through the acceptable medium of parable and illustration. On this one point East and West concur—that, to tell on the minds of millions, we must make full use of illustrations from Nature and picturing by words. Buddhist preachers and Sufy teachers alike hoist the flag of Emblems, Parables, and Proverbs. Even the Divine Founder of Christianity Himself adopted the same method; for "without a parable spake He not to the people."

The modern missionary in the East, Spurgeon, Trench, and Ryle in England, bear, in their preaching and writings, testimony equally with the Buddhist and Biblical writings to the value of the Emblem, Parable, and Proverb. The following statement of Scarborough, in his "Chinese Proverbs," echoes the same sentiment from far-off Kathay:—

"Used as quotations, the value of proverbs in China is immense. So used in conversation, they add a piquancy and a flavour which greatly delights the Chinese, and makes mutual intercourse more easy and agreeable. But it is to the missionary that the value of an extensive acquaintance with Chinese proverbs is of the highest importance. Personal experience, as well as the repeated testimony of others, makes us bold to assert that even a limited knowledge of Chinese proverbs is to him of daily and inestimable value. A proverb will often serve to rouse the flagging attention of a congregation, or to arrest it at the commencement of a discourse. A proverb will often serve to produce a smile of good nature in an apparently ill-tempered audience, and so to call forth a kindly feeling which did not seem before to exist. And very often a proverb aptly quoted will serve to convey a truth in the most terse and striking manner, so obviating the necessity for detached and lengthy argument, whilst they fix at a stroke the idea you are wishing to convey."

The proverbs in this book have been selected for the *illustrations* they contain. Proverbs are not the productions of the book-worm or the midnight oil. *Proverbs* *were before books*—they come from the great books of Nature and common sense—from powers of observation, not blunted by book-cram; hence among the Proverbs in this book, though principally Eastern,* there are very few that are not intelligible to the European mind; like the Proverbs of Solomon, the Psalms, Bunyan's "Pilgrim's Progress," and the Arabian Nights, they speak in a language "understanded by the common people."

While illustrations by Emblem and Proverb are indispensable as media for conveying instruction in the East, they are highly valued in Europe also. The following observations of Archbishop Trench will find a response with all those who have aimed at winning the attention of the working classes, the peasantry, and "the Arabs of Society:"—

"Any one who by after investigation has sought to discover how much our rustic hearers carry away, even from sermons to which they have attentively listened, will find that it is hardly ever the course or tenor of the argument, supposing the discourse to have contained such; but if anything has been uttered, as it used so often to be by the best Puritan preachers, tersely, pointedly, epigrammatically, this will have stayed by them, while all the rest has passed away. Great preachers to the people, such as have found their way to the universal heart of their fellows, have ever been great employers *of proverbs*."

The Author will feel greatly obliged for any corrections or additions to this work forwarded for him to the Publishers.

* Many Russian Proverbs are given, which were collected by the Author in Moscow; but the Russians are a semi-Oriental people, and their Proverbs have an Eastern ring about them.

CONTENTS.

PART I.

PROVERBS AND EMBLEMS CHIEFLY MORAL.

PART II.

PROVERBS AND EMBLEMS MORAL AND RELIGIOUS.

PART III.

PROVERBS AND EMBLEMS RELIGIOUS.

EASTERN PROVERBS AND EMBLEMS.

PART I.

The Ant teaches the Sluggard.—Prov. 6. 6–8.

Animals teach us—thus the *ass* knowing his owner while man knows not God, Is. 1. 3; the *crow* having no barns, yet God provides for it; the *swallow* knowing his time to emigrate, but man forgets his time for departure from the world, Jer. 8. 7; and the ant here teaches. *Chanakyea* states, the lessons which the dog teaches us are—"of contentment with little—vigilant watching, gratitude and fortitude, the power of patience, indifference to cold and heat. The crow teaches providence for the future and agility; the cock—early rising, sharing food, and protecting women."

With respect to Ants, their uniform care and promptitude in improving every moment as it passes, the admirable order in which they proceed to the scene of action, the perfect harmony which reigns in their bands, the eagerness which they discover in running to the assistance of the weak and the fatigued, the readiness with which those that have no burden yield the way to their fellows that bend under their load, or when the grain happens to be too heavy, cut it in two, and take the half upon their own shoulders, furnish a striking example of industry, benevolence, and concord. The skill and vigour which they display in digging underground, in building their houses, in constructing their cells, and their prudence and foresight in making use of the proper seasons to collect a supply of provision sufficient for their purpose, are admirable.

Hebrew.—As rust comes on iron, so do weeds on a field unused.

Persian.—Water long stagnant becomes putrid.

Arab.—A well is not to be filled with dew.

Telugu.—Lame in the village, an antelope in the jungle.

"If you talk of work my body becomes heavy;
If you talk of dinner my body swells with delight."

Italian.—An idle brain is the devil's workshop.

Badaga.—The sluggard, like the peacock, is afraid of rain.

Tamul.—The horse opens the mouth when one says oats, shuts it when one says bridle.

Appearances Deceitful.—Gen. 13. 10–13.

Bengal.—How long does a dam of sand last?

Tamul.—A face like the moon, a mind of deadly poison.

Oriental.—Trust not to appearances—the drum which makes much noise is filled with wind.

Turk.—Be the pig white or black it is still a pig.

Russian.—The cow has a long tongue, but she is not allowed to speak.

Tamul.—While squatting a cat, when springing a tiger.

Turk.—The vessel leans, but her course is straight.

China.—You may draw a tiger's skin, not his bones. You may know a man's face, but not his mind.

Avoid the appearance of Evil.—1 Thess. 5. 22.

Japan.—In a field of melons do not pull off your shoes. Under a palm-tree do not adjust your cap.

Bengal.—Even a holy cow, if found in company with a stolen one, may be impounded.

Basque.—Cover yourself not with the skin of a wolf, if you would not be considered a wolf.

Telugu.—One associating himself with the vile will be ruined; it is like drinking milk under a palm-tree, *i.e.*, where, however innocent, it would be suspected he was drinking toddy.

The Angry Fool as a Bear robbed of her Whelps.

PROV. 17. 12.

The female bear is eminent for intense affection to her young, and dreadfully furious when deprived of them. Disregarding every consideration of danger to herself, she attacks, with intense ferocity, every animal that comes in her way, and, in the bitterness of her heart, will attack even a band of armed men. The Russians of Kamtschatka never venture to fire on a young bear when the mother is near; for, if the cub drop, she becomes enraged to a degree little short of madness, and, if she get sight of the enemy, will only quit her revenge with her life.

A she-bear destroyed the forty-two children who mocked the prophet, 2 Kings 2. 24. God's fury with the idolatrous Jews is compared to a bear bereaved, Hos. 13. 8. *David* had to defend himself against a bear, 1 Sam. 17. 34–36.

Saul, 1 Sam. 20. 30, and *Herod*, Mat. 2. 16, are striking examples of a fool in his wrath.

Jacob's sons, like a bear, for one man's faults destroyed a whole city, Gen. 24. *Saul* similarly destroyed the innocent priests, 1 Sam. 22. 11–19; so *Nebuchadnezzar* when he heated the furnace seven times, Dan. 3. 13–19.

Bengal.—Scratching the itch only produces a wound.
Telegu.—Pouring ghi on fire.
Gujerat.—Anger and water descend.
Tamul.—The irascible is like a man on horseback without a bridle.
Bengal.—A fire in the thatch is quickly kindled, so anger.
Badaga.—If a jackal howls, will my old buffalo die? If an angry man curses me, what shall I lose?
Tamul.—Like the man who would not wash his feet in the tank because he was angry with it.
Modern Greek.—The rancour of a camel is unforgiving.
Turk.—The torrent (anger) passes, the sand remains.

Man a Wild Ass's Colt.—Job 11. 12.

The wild asses commonly inhabit the deserts of *Great Tartary*, they migrate to feed in summer to the north and east of the Aral Sea, in winter they retreat towards India, they go also to Persia. Like wild horses, they are very shy; they will suffer the approach of man for an instant, and will then dart off with the utmost rapidity, fleet as the wind. The vast salt desert is their home, they scorn the multitude of the city; the wild ass *snuffeth up the wind* at her pleasure, Jer. 2. 24. The European ass is an emblem of obstinacy and immobility, not so the wild one. The Tartar asses exceed horses in speed, and are never caught alive, Job 39. 5–8.

Ishmael is called a wild man like an ass, Gen. 16. 12. *Ephraim* is compared to a wild ass, Hos. 8. 9, as he traversed the desert as earnestly in pursuit of idols as the wild untamed ass did in search of his mate, Jer. 14. 6. The asses snuff up the wind like dragons, *i.e.*, seek the air for want of water to cool their internal heat, Job 24. 5. *Robbers* are called wild asses, so the Bedouins; the desolate city, a joy of wild asses, Is. 32. 14. *Nebuchadnezzar* lived among wild asses, Dan. 5. 21.

The natural tenacity of sin is also compared to the Ethiopian's skin, Jer. 13. 23.

Turk.—In washing a negro we lose our soap.

Tamul.—Though he wash three times a day, will the crow become a white crane?

Kurd.—Out of a dog's tail you cannot get fat.

Veman.—No man's disposition will alter, neither can a dog's tail be made straight; the stubborn woman will even put her husband in a basket and sell him.

Veman.—If you take a bear-skin and wash it ever so long, will it, instead of its native blackness, ever become white? If you beat a wooden image, will it hence acquire any good quality?

Badaga.—Even if you give milk to a young snake, will it leave off its habit of creeping under the hedge?

Syriac.—If ye would be king (master of yourself) become a wild ass, *i.e.*, retire to solitude in the desert.

Beauty in the Ignorant as a Jewel in a Swine's Snout.—Prov. 11. 22.

A body may be beautiful, but the soul loathsome—such were Absalom and Jezebel.

Chanakyea.—A handsome youth of high family, but without learning, is like the palas (*Butea frondosa*) tree, fair to see, but without scent.

Hindu Dramatist.—Men are foolish in cherishing the gay blossoms of the palas, whilst they neglect the fruit-bearing amon, because its flowers are insignificant.

Drishtanta Shatak.—A bad person, though decorated, remains the same as cowdung, which, though it be fertilizing, does not become pleasing.

Bengal.—Outside smooth and painted, inside only straw—like Hindu idols stuffed with straw.

Russian.—A head without a mind is a mere statue.

Urdu.—The fruit of the colocynth is good to look at, not to taste.

Tamul.—An ignorant man is despised even by women.

Afghan.—My friend is black, but so is molasses black, *i.e.*, which is the best medicine for the wounded.

Persian.—The diamond fallen into the dunghill is not the less precious; the dust raised by high winds to heaven is not the less vile.

Malay.—Like a broom bound with a silk thread.

Arab.—Thorny trees produce gum.

Turk.—Man's perfection is interior; a beast's, exterior.

Sanskrit.—The beauty of the cuckoo is the voice; of women, chastity; of the deformed, learning; and of ascetics, patience.

Hebrew.—The bee is little among such as fly; her fruit is the chief of sweet things.

Beginning and Unable to Finish; not Counting the Cost.—Luke 14. 28.

Bengal.—The bird cannot fly, it flaps its wings in vain.

Panjabi.—A rat, too big for his hole, ties a blanket to his back

Panjabi.—A rat, having found a bit of turmeric, set up as a druggist.

Sanskrit.—In the fighting of she-goats, in the gathering of clouds at the dawn, in the squabble of husband and wife, the beginning is great and the doings small.

Bengal.—Digging for a worm, up rose a snake, *i.e.*, said when quarrels arise from jesting.

Telugu.—Make the hedge when you have sowed the seed.

The Glutton's God his Belly.—Phil. 3 19.

The Bengalis call a glutton one all belly. The Egyptians, on embalming a body, threw the belly into the river, as the cause of all sin. Meat itself is not sinful, but the inordinate desire of it, longing after delicacies, eating at unseasonable times, Ecc. 10. 16, 17, eating too much, Luke 21. 34, injuring the understanding, Prov. 23. 21. Solomon says put a knife to thy throat if thou be given to appetite, Prov. 23. 2. Isaac's appetite was a snare to him, Gen. 25. 28, 27. 4: so Esau's, Gen. 25. 30; Eli's sons, 1 Sam. 2. 12; Belshazzar, Dan. 5. 1; not so Daniel's, Dan. 1. 8–16.

Veman.—Why suffer anxiety for the belly? As to having a belly, the frog that lives in a rock is thy equal.

Tamul.—The epicure digs his grave with his teeth.

China.—His eyes are bigger than his stomach.*

Russian.—A full stomach is deaf to instruction.

Fool come to thrash—my stomach is aching.
Fool come to take wine—stop, let me take my caftan (coat) from the nail—

i.e., he is great at drinking, slow at work.

Talmud.—The lion roars, not in a crib full of straw, but in one full of flesh; *i.e.*, fulness of bread leading to pride.

Arab.—The belly of a man is his enemy.

Afghans express their belief that the evils of gluttony arise more from the man than the food, by the following: "Though the food was another's, the mouth is your own;" *i.e.*, you eat too much, and you throw the blame on the food.

Telugu.—He slipped, fell, and then said the ground was unlucky.

* We have the same in English—which was *the first* used?

Talmud.—Eight things are difficult to enjoy in abundance, but in moderation are good: Labour, sleep, riches, journeyings, love, warm water, bleeding, and wine.

Afghan.—The full stomach speaks Persian, *i.e.*, makes one proud. Persian as spoken only by the learned adds to their pride.

Book Cram.—2 TIM. 3. 7.

Mrichhakate.—Nature is woman's teacher, and she learns more sense than man, the pedant, gleans from books.

Talmud.—He is a box of books, *i.e.*, learning without judgment, or use of it.

Tamul.—He who is very learned is a learned fool.

Persian.—One pound of learning requires ten of common sense to acquire it.

Sanskrit.—Is the man possessed of books a pandit?

Sanskrit.—Women are instructed by Nature, the learning of men is taught by books.

Telugu.—Though he have read all that can be read, and be an acute disputant, never shall the hypocrite attain to final happiness. His meditations are like those of a dog on the dunghill.

Sanskrit.—Learning in the book is not learning, and money in the hand of another is not money, in a time of need.

Anger rests in the Fool's Bosom.—ECC. 7. 9.

The bosom is the seat of love, so Christ carries the lambs of the Church in his bosom, Is. 40. 11. The beggar rested in Abraham's bosom, Luke 16. 22.

Christ took on him our natural infirmities; he wept, and was angry, on the Sabbath question, Mark 3. 5, in driving away the money-changers, John 2. 13, 17, which shows there might be gall in a dove, passion without sin, fire without smoke, and motion without disturbance, for it is not bare agitation, but the sediment at the bottom which troubles and defiles the water, and when we see it windy and dusty, the wind does not make, but only raises, a dust; true anger, like the sword of justice, is keen but innocent, Eph. 4. 26; it sparkles like the coal on the altar with the fervour of pity. Anger passes through a wise man's heart, but does not rest in it, as it did with Cain, Gen. 4. 5–8, with Jacob's sons, Gen. 34. 7; and with Herod, Mat. 2. 16. A gust of anger puts holy feelings to flight, as with David, 1 Sam. 25, Elijah, 1 Kings 19. 4, Job, 3. 1, Jonah, 4. 4, Paul.

Telugu.—Getting angry with a rat and setting a house on fire.

Bengal.—Cutting off one's nose to hinder another's journey.

Bengal.—His anger exploded like gunpowder.

Bengal.—Should an angry man retire even to the forest there is no peace for him.

Malay.—Anger has no eyes.

Modern Greek.—Anger is the last that grows old.

Arab.—Three things are only known in the following way—a hero in war, a friend in necessity, and a wise man in anger.

Arab.—Anger is the fire of the heart. Prov. 25. 28.

Telugu.—A man ignorant of his own powers and those of his opponent, blustering in wrath, is like a bear performing the torch-dance, *i.e.*, in which of course he will be burnt.

Arab.—Cure your anger by silence.

Sanskrit.—A good man's anger lasts an instant, a meddling man's for two hours, a base man's a day and night, a great sinner's until death.

Braying a Fool in a Mortar.—Prov. 27. 22.

Veman compares the trying to produce good qualities in a crooked heart to pouring milk and sugar over bramble-berries, and boiling them, which will give no flavour. In Turkey great criminals were beaten to pieces in huge mortars of iron in which they usually pounded their rice. The Jews were in Babylon under captivity, yet were their proud hearts not humbled; God sent them messengers, but they ill-treated them; the Chaldeans came, yet they bound the Prophet Ezekiel, Ezek. 2. 3. The plough breaks the earth in many places, but does not better it if nothing is put in; if nothing be sown, thorns and thistles will come up: so afflictions may break our estate, yet if God do not sanctify these afflictions they yield only the harvest of tares. Mere affliction changes not the disposition, as the fire softens not a stone; pour vinegar from vessel to vessel it never becomes wine, Is. 1. 5.

Sanskrit.—Whoever treats kindly a bad man, ploughs the sky, paints a picture on water, and bathes the wind with water. Tit. 3. 10.

Telugu.—No man's disposition will alter, say what we may; neither can a dog's tail be made straight; the stubborn woman will put her husband in a basket and sell him.

Sanskrit.—It is possible to stop an elephant with a kick; for everything there is a remedy; but no cure for the headstrong.

The Shameless have a Brow of Brass.—Is. 48. 4.

Brass is a strong metal, hence the brazen serpent in the wilderness was made of it, Num. 21. 9; so were the gates of Babylon. The sinners' obstinacy is compared to a brow of brass; while the righteous, on the other hand, set their faces like a flint against sin: of the former were Pharaoh, Ex. 5. 1; Saul, 1 Sam. 15. 9–23; Jeroboam, 1 Kings 12. 28–33—of the latter, Jacob, Gen. 32. 24–28; David, 1 Sam. 17. 45; Stephen, Acts 7. 57.

Sinners are also said to have a hard or stony heart, a seared conscience, to be past feeling; they are likened to the deaf adder which will not hear the voice of the serpent-charmer. Such were Samuel's sons, 1 Sam. 2. 25, 6. 11; Jerusalem, Ez. 9. 9, 10.

Finnish.—The pig does not blush for its face.

Shánti Shatak.—Dogs delight to devour human bones, which are so disgusting, filled as they are with worms and moisture, and they eagerly lick the putrid juice as if it was palatable. Thus do mean people appear shameless when perpetrating vile actions, 2 Pet. 2. 22.

Deceitful Brethren as a Brook.—Job 6. 15.

Job lived in the barren dry desert of Arabia, where no river is, and water is scarce ; there are torrents in winter, swelling from the melting of the snow on the hills, as the Ganges does, *very noisy,* but in summer dried up or absorbed in the sand. The Arabs call a false friend a mirage, or a torrent, swelling, noisy in prosperity, but soon absorbed in the sand. Valleys in Arabia, that have a quarter of a mile wide of water in winter, are yet quite dry in summer.

Tyre trusted in its walls and port, and is now become only a place for fishermen to dry their nets on. The rich fool trusted in his wealth, Luke 12. 19, and it left him. Solomon states: "Confidence in an unfaithful man in time of trouble is like a broken tooth and a foot out of joint," Prov. 25. 19. That affection which is knit in God alone is indissoluble. The Jews trusted the Egyptians, who proved like a broken reed (Is. 36. 6), which not only fails the hand that leans upon it, but pierces and wounds it.

Bengal.—A loose tooth and feeble friend are equally bad.

Bengal.—A dam of sand and the love of the vicious have the same fate.

Chanak.—A wicked person, though sweet speaking, is not to be trusted; honey is on his tongue, but in his heart poison.

Busybody, as One taking a Dog by the Ears.—Prov. 26. 17.

From an idle whim or a foolhardy venture, a man thinks to show his prowess, fancying that he is able to master the dog which others scarcely dare come near. When he has taken it by the ears, he finds his folly, for, if he continues to hold it, his time is lost, and if he lets it go, it will fly at him before he can get beyond its reach. He has exposed himself both to pain and ridicule by a foolish attempt to get credit for courage and dexterity. Of the eleven Apostles, as Peter spoke most, he erred most, Mat. 16. 22, 26. 74. Paul condemns tattling women, 1 Tim. 5. 13.

Telugu.—Like a snake in a monkey's paw, *i.e.*, Jacko finds it difficult to hold it, and dangerous to let it go.

Bengal.—Oil your own wheel first.

English.—He that intermeddles with all things may go shoe the goslings.

Persian.—A babbler, a dog without a tail.

Bengal.—I bind him and he shrieks out, I loose him and he wants to fight with me.

Turk.—One rushing between two camels is kicked by both. To live in peace one must be blind, deaf, and mute.

Persian.—Whoever pats scorpions with the hand of compassion receives punishment.

Japan.—If dogs (busybodies) go about they must expect the stick.

China.—It is not as safe opening the mouth as keeping it shut.

Tamul.—Why should a man meddle with a hatchet lying on the road and hurt his foot?

Arab.—God grant us not any neighbour with two eyes.

China.—Let every man sweep the snow before his own doors, not busy himself with the frost on his neighbour's tiles.

Kurd.—When your house is of glass do not throw stones at your neighbour's house.

Cingalese.—The man without clothes busying himself in making jackets for dogs.

Telugu.—The tale-bearer is the associate of the villain; a stripling is a fit minister for an inflexible king; and the monkey is the only companion for the baboon.

Hebrew.—Give the water no passage; neither a wicked woman liberty to gad abroad.

The Hypocrite's Words smoother than Butter.—Ps. 55. 21.

These words were applied by David to his son Absalom, who drove him from Jerusalem, 2 Sam. 15, which made the father wish for the wings of a *dove* to fly away and be at rest, as the dove, sent forth from the ark, found no rest for the sole of her foot. Such a hypocrite was Judas, who betrayed Christ by kissing him.

Bengal.—A hypocrite a *makhala* fruit, beautiful outside, bitter within; a tiger in a *tulsi* grove; outside smooth and painted, inside only straw, *i.e.*, like the Hindu idols stuffed with straw inside. The crow and the cuckoo have the same colour, but a very different voice.

Raghuvansa.—They concealed their anger under signs of joy, as a lake with tranquil surface hides an alligator.

Bengal.—The attachment of the insincere a razor's edge.

Afghan.—Under his arms a Koran, he casts his eyes on a bullock.

Malay.—He sits like a tiger withdrawing his claws.

Telugu.—A bear's hug.

Telugu.—At home a spider (demure), abroad a tiger.

Russian.—He kicks with his hind feet, licks with his tongue.

Malay.—To plant sugar-cane on the lips, *i.e.*, a pleasing manner, a false heart.

Modern Greek.—The mien of a bishop with the heart of a miller.

Sanskrit.—A face shaped like the petals of the lotus; a voice as cool (pleasing) as sandal; a heart like a pair of scissors and excessive humility—these are the signs of a rogue.

Strife from Wrath as Butter from Milk.—Prov. 30. 33.

In Arabia and Palestine butter is made from milk, put into a goat's skin, turned inside out, pressed to and fro in one uniform direction, till the unctuous parts are separated, Job 29. 6. An angry man is compared to a city whose walls are broken down: such were Samson, Judg. 16;

Saul, 1 Sam. 20. 30–33; the mob at Ephesus, Acts 16. 28–34; Christ was different, Mat. 27. 14. The fool's wrath is heavier than a stone, Prov. 27. 3.

Shánti Shatak.—The soul excited by anger is like furious elephants breaking the cords with which they are bound.

Turk.—Anger is suppressed by sweetness, as a great wind by a little rain.

Malabar.—Anger is as a stone cast into a wasp's nest.

Cingalese.—Provocation is a stone cast at a cobra.

Japan.—The cracked will break, *i.e.*, people at variance waiting for an opportunity to split.

Arab.—The highest government is governing anger.

Talmud.—Passions are like iron thrown into the furnace, as long as it is in the fire you can make no vessel out of it.

Malay.—Smouldering like burning chaff, *i.e.*, nourishing resentment.

Modern Greek.—The rancour of a camel is unforgiving.

Caste. Honour all Men.—1 Pet. 2. 17.

Telugu.—The elephant is an elephant whether on high ground or low.

Canara.—Does a light in the house of a low caste man not burn?

Turk.—White or black, a dog remains a dog.

Veman.—Why should we constantly revile the Pariah? Are not his flesh and blood the same as our own? And of what caste is He who pervades the Pariah as well as all other men? Acts 17. 26.

Persian.—Contemn no one. Regard him who is above thee as thy father; him who is thine equal as thy brother; and him who is below thee as thy son.

Bengal.—Why not a squirrel instead of a cat, if it catch mice?

Ceremonialism.—Mat. 15. 20.

China.—He sought his own ass, though he was sitting on it.

Prabodly Chandroday.—If funeral oblations nourish the

deceased, why is not the flame of an extinguished taper renovated by pouring on oil? 1 Kings 18. 26.

Veman.—Those who mortify their bodies, calling themselves saints, are yet unable to cure the impurity of their hearts. If you merely destroy the outside of a white-ant hill, will the serpent that dwells therein perish?

Veman.—A thief if he goes to a holy place will only pick the pockets of the comers; he has no leisure to draw near and bow to the God. If a dog enters a house will he tend the hearth? 2 Pet. 2. 22.

Veman.—Religion that consists in contriving various postures and twisting the limbs, is just one straw inferior to the exercises of the wrestler. Is. 58. 5.

Telugu.—Though a man may remove the distance of fifty miles his sin is still with him. Gen. 42. 21.

Veman.—Will the application of white ashes do away the smell of a wine-pot? Will a cord cast over your neck make you twice born?

Canara.—Is a serpent killed by beating its hole? Is salvation obtained by castigating the body? Is. 58. 6.

Cingalese.—Charcoal cannot be made white even though you wash it with milk.

Cingalese.—Your hands and your feet are the same even though you go to Tutocorin.

Telugu.—Those who roam to other lands in pilgrimage to find the God that dwells within them, are like a shepherd who searches in his flock for the sheep he has under his arm. John 4. 20–24.

Telugu.—Even a goat can attain to such "corporeal perfection" as consists in living on leaves: how apt men are to fall into foolish whims!

Tamul.—Will a crow become a swan by bathing in the Ganges?

Urdu.—Filth is got rid of by washing, but not bad habits.

Tamul.—Though one carries a thousand shells to Benares his sin sticks to him.

The Wicked are Chaff.—MAT. 3. 12.

Chaff is *light* and easily carried away by the wind; such are sinners, light in their behaviour, and easily carried away by the wind of temptation and persecution. It is of *little value,* and therefore given over to the fire, Mat. 3. 12. A pound of wheat is worth a hundredweight of chaff; the husk, or chaff, however, is of use to the corn in protecting the grain, so the world sometimes protects the good. Grown together with the wheat for a time, the flail in threshing separates it, so the Judgment Day will for ever divide the sheep from the goats, Mat. 25. The wicked are also compared to *bad money,* Jer. 6. 30; to *bad fish,* Mat. 13. 48; to *moth-eaten clothes,* Is. 50. 9; to *wells without water,* 2 Pet. 2.

Bengal.—The white ant, the cat, and the wicked spoil good things.

Veman.—Profitless are some men, and what though they be born in the world, and what though they die? Are not the white ants of the hillock born also, and do they not die also?

Bengal.—'Tis but threshing the chaff, *i.e.*, labour in vain.

Tamul.—Though a kalam of chaff be pounded, it will not become rice.

Veman.—Even the poison-nut and the bitter margosa are useful as drugs; but the unfeeling vile wretch is utterly unprofitable.

Sanskrit.—To address a judicious remark to a thoughtless man is a mere threshing of chaff.

Cheerfulness.—PROV. 17. 13.

China.—A hut of reeds with mirth therein is better than a palace with grief therein.

Modern Greek.—A hungry belly has no ears.

Tamul.—Food without hospitality is a medicine. 2 Cor. 9. 7.

Turk.—Vinegar given is sweeter than honey.

The Body a Clay House crushed before the Moth.

Job 4. 19.

These words were spoken by a spirit from the other world, who addressed Job at midnight.

The grave is called the *house* appointed for all living, Job 30. 23. The body is compared to a house of *clay* which is *easily swept away* by torrents, the walls of which, owing to rents, are the abodes of snakes. Swallows make their houses of clay.

Manu calls the body "a mansion with bones for its rafters and beams; such a mansion let the soul cheerfully quit, as a tree leaves the bank of the river, or as a bird leaves the branch of a tree; thus he has his body delivered soon from the ravening shark the world."

In Arabia the houses in general are built of white clay, and covered with reeds. Their foundations are laid in the dust or sand, the country affording no firmer basis on which to build; they are exposed to all the accidents of that climate, such as violent winds, and large moving pillars of sand, called sand-floods, by which they are liable to be blown down, or overwhelmed and crushed to the ground, together with their inhabitants, unless they can effect a timely escape.

These desolating calamities more generally begin about sunrise, and usually continue till towards evening; and thus men perish from the morning to evening, without any one regarding it.

Robbers easily dig through the walls of houses of clay, as is the case very often in Bengal. Job 24. 16.

The moth is a small insect which noiselessly and gradually eats through garments, though very feeble, Job 27. 18. The rich are no more spared than the poor, but it especially attacks things not kept clean, and does its works secretly, spoils by degrees; so God gives cleanness of teeth, the palmer worm, the pestilence,

Amos 4. 8; the moth eats the inside when the outside is good, so *Sampson* said when his locks were gone, I will rise up, Judg. 19, 20; so the Jews, 2 Kings 15.

Small insects are a great plague. In Arabia and parts of India people drink bad water, from which comes an egg that produces a worm in the body, from which often comes palsy, gangrene, death.

The clothes-moth is of a white, shining, silver, or pearl colour. It is clothed with shells, fourteen in number, and these are scaly. This insect eats woollen stuffs; it is produced from a grey speckled moth, that flies by night, creeps among woollens, and there lays her eggs, which, after a little time, are hatched as worms, and in this state they feed on their habitation, till they change into a chrysalis, and thence emerge into moths. The young moth, or moth-worm, upon leaving the egg which a *papilio* had lodged upon a piece of stuff, commodious for her purpose, finds a proper place of residence, grows and feeds upon the nap, and likewise builds with it an apartment, which is fixed to the groundwork of the stuff with several cords and a little glue. From an aperture in this habitation the moth-worm devours and demolishes all about him; and when he has cleared the place, he draws out all the fastenings of his tent; after which he carries it to some little distance, and then fixes it with the slender cords in a new situation. This perishing condition of *a moth-eaten garment,* as also of *the insect itself,* is referred to in Isa. 51. 6, 8: "*The earth shall wax old as doth a garment,* and they that dwell therein *shall die in like manner.*"

He who builds his fortunes by methods of injustice is by Job 27. 18 compared to the *moth,* which, by eating into the garment wherein it makes its habitation, destroys its own dwelling. The structure referred to is that provided by the insect, in its larva or caterpillar state, as temporary residence during its wonderful change from a chrysalis to a winged insect.

Urdu.—The body is a skin filled with wind.
Bengal.—Plastering an old hut.
Tamul.—The body is an inscription on water.

The Wicked are Clouds without Water.—JUDE 12, 13.

Wicked like clouds without water in four points :—

Clouds without water may be of some use in giving shade, but they do *not fertilize* the land, which full clouds, called the bottles of Heaven, Job 38. 37, do; they are *empty,* and *easily carried* away, as is seen in famines in India arising from droughts; they *darken* heaven, hence the day of the Lord is called clouds and darkness, when storms and lightning arise; the clouds are God's chariot, and He holds the winds in His fist, Prov. 30. 4. Christ is the bow in this cloud, as he was the pillar of cloud in the wilderness, the guide of His people, which had a dark side to the enemy and a bright one to friends.

Clouds are sometimes very beautiful, but useless; so a bad person doing well in the world.
Malay.—Flourishing like a weed beside a cesspool.

A Boaster like Clouds without Rain.—PROV. 25. 14.

Such were the builders of Babel, Gen. 11. 4–9.

Bengal.—A pedlar in ginger getting tidings of his ship.
Syriac.—Mount not a horse which does not belong to you—*i.e.*, boast not of an art you are ignorant of.
Tamul.—He is on foot, his words are in a palankin.
Tamul.—If a low-bred man obtain wealth he will carry an umbrella at midnight.
Bengal.—A devotee of yesterday, with matted hair down to his heels.
Tamul.—A gold vessel does not sound, a brass one does.
Bengal.—A truly wealthy man, one plough to seven tailless oxen.
Russian.—Boast of the day in the evening, Jas. 4. 13.
Sanskrit.—The little fish splashes in even a mouthful of water.
Arab.—A learned man without work is a cloud without rain.

The Fickle like the Morning Cloud and Early Dew.—Hos. 6. 4.

The *Lalita Vistara* compares life to an autumnal cloud. The *Shánti Shatak* says: "As the *lightning* by its flashes merely drives away the darkness for an instant, so are those who decide for a while to root out sensual desires from their minds." The *morning* cloud is very beautiful with its golden hues, and colours shifting and changing every minute. Early in the morning every blade is glistening with the early dew, and the light clouds are painted with all those gorgeous colours by which they seem to prepare themselves for the return of their absent king, the sun! Thus beautiful is early piety, as in Samuel's and Timothy's case, though it did not pass away. But how soon do those hues and those jewels of the early morning pass away! Long before the sun has attained his meridian height, the sky has become cloudless, and the parched land seems in vain to thirst for the refreshing dew and the kindly shower.

While in Egypt it rains sometimes only once in two years, were it not for the dews of night and inundations of the river, all vegetation would perish. Peter's resolution not to deny Christ passed away as a morning cloud before the sun of temptation; so did Judas's before the sun of gold.

Telugu.—Like the post fixed in the mud, which swings to and fro.
China.—Who stands still in mud sticks in it.
Tamul.—A pliant thorn will not penetrate.
Bengal.—One foot on land, the other on water
Polish.—The stone often moved gathers no moss.
Malay.—Like a saw with a double edge.
Telugu.—Waking the master, giving the thief a stick.

A Forgiving Spirit as Coals of Fire on an Enemy's Head.—Prov. 25. 21, 22.

Metal is difficult to melt placed on the top of a fire of burning coals; it may be placed at the sides, still no melting; but put the coals on the top or head of the vessel, and the metal soon flows down in a stream. So your enemy's hostility to you may be softened by kindness in every way; as fire to the metal, so kindness to an enemy. The Italians, however, say, revenge of a hundred years old has still its sucking teeth—*i.e.*, never grows old.

> The sandal-tree, most sacred tree of all,
> Perfumes the very axe which bids it fall.

Forgiveness, like fire, consumes the dross of passion, purifies the metal of the soul, melts and makes malleable the hardest metal of envy.

The hardest metals are melted by heaping coals of fire upon them. Such was Saul, 1 Sam. 24. 16–21, whose hard heart was melted by David's spirit of forgiveness. A forgiving spirit, or charity, covers many sins, Prov. 10. 12.

Tamul.—The rock not moved by a lever of iron will be opened by the root of a green tree.

China.—The more we approach an enemy, the more the tigers of the heart become lambs.

Turk.—Provoke the bees, they only sting.

Arab.—Punish your enemy by benefiting him.

Arab.—The generous can be known by his eyes, as the horse's age by its teeth.

Russian.—Love will teach even a priest to dance.

Russian.—Sweet words break the bones.

Russian.—Bread and salt humble even a robber.

Sadi.—The sharp sword will not cut soft silk.

Sadi.—By gentleness you may lead an elephant by a hair.

Tamul.—The tree affords shelter to him who fells it; the earth supports him who digs it.

Welsh.—Faults are thick when love is thin.

Mahalherat.—Conquer a niggard by generosity, a liar by truth, a cruel man by patience, and a bad man by goodness.

Sanskrit.—With fire, fire is kindled, 1 John 4. 19.

Tamul.—A fracture in gold vanishes when exposed to fire; the anger of the good in like manner passes away.

Contentment with Godliness, Great Gain.—1 TIM. 6. 6.

Contrast Paul in prison, Phil. 4. 11, 13, 18, with Ahab in a palace, 1 Kings 21. 4. He is poor that wanteth more.

Chanakyea.—Contentment with little, sound sleep, vigilant watching, gratitude and fortitude, are virtues inherent in the dog, and are to be learnt from it, Job 12. 7.

Arab.—The world is a corpse and those who seek it are dogs.

Afghan.—Like a mad dog, he snaps at himself.

Malay.—Will the dog be ever satisfied, however much rice you might give him.

Tamul.—Wash a dog, place him in the middle of the house; he will wag his tail, go out and eat filth.

Sanskrit.—Who has reached the limit of desire?

Malabar.—Though you dip in the sea, you receive only as much as your vessel will hold, Ph. 4. 11.

Arab.—The ass went seeking for horns, and lost his ears.

Telugu.—If you are content with a girdle, no poverty will distress you, 1 Tim. 6. 8.

Arab.—Food supports life, contentment the soul, 1 Tim. 6. 8.

Persian.—Live contented, you will be a king, 1 Tim. 6. 6.

China.—Tanks may be filled up, but man's heart can never be closed.

Telugu.—When a Jangam (fakir) was told his house was on fire, he said, I have my bag and my bowl with me.

Arab.—To abstain from desires is riches.

Tamul.—A contented mind is a specific for making gold.

Talmud.—Who is the rich? He who has subdued his passions. Who is the wise? He who learns from all. Who is the hero? He who subdues his passions.

Badaga.—He had nothing and was content. He became rich and is discontented, Eccles. 6. 9.

A Threefold Cord of Brotherly Unity.—ECCL. 4. 12.

There is more pleasure in what is shared with another, and help is often necessary—if one man, as Joseph, is in a pit, he requires some one to take him out. God said of Adam in Paradise, "It was not good for man to be alone," Gen. 2. 18. The *Ramsanchis,* a sect of Western India, say regarding society, "A solitary lamp, however brilliant, casteth a shadow beneath it; place another lamp in the apartment, and the darkness of both is dissipated."

Soldiers' union is their strength. A father, on *his death-bed,* represented unity by a bundle of sticks.

Love, like *fire,* streams forth by natural results and unavoidable emanations; like the *vine,* it withers and dies if it has nothing to embrace.

The Apostles were sent forth two by two, Luke 10. 1; in the body all instruments of action are by pairs—hands, feet, eyes, ears, legs. The live *coal* left alone soon loses its vital heat. Iron sharpens iron, Prov. 27. 9, 17; Ex. 18. 7, 9.

Bengal.—With men of one mind even the sea might be dried up.

Bengal.—Love, like a creeper, withers and dies if it has nothing to embrace.

Turk.—The vessel which trusts to a single anchor is soon wrecked.

Badaga.—A single coal does not burn well; a companionless traveller finds the journey tedious, Ecc. 4. 9.

Russian.—With one hand I do not even tie a knot.

Tamul.—Gruel served in the house of a united family is enjoyable.

Afghan.—You cannot clap with one hand alone.

Mahalherat.—Kinsmen resemble firebrands; separate they smoke, united they blaze.

Mahabharat.—Those well united trees which stand together in a clump, resist the fiercest winds, owing to their mutual support.

Sanskrit.—A chariot will not go on one wheel.

Sanskrit.—Stay with five,* walk along with five, eat along with five, with five there is no sorrow.

Worldly Joy is the Crackling of Thorns.—Eccl. 7. 6.

Thorns at first blaze under a pot as if they would give out a mighty heat, but the water in it is cold. Such is

* Referring to the *Pauchayat,* or Indian jury of five persons.

worldly enjoyment: all noise and smoke—no heat; cold as moonbeams. Such is drunkenness—a sweet poison. The wicked are compared to thorns because they are very troublesome and useless, and often cause great pain; while the crackling is quickly over and with little effect, as thorns when blazing, though they make such a noise and fire, give little heat to the water. Similar is the Bengali proverb, *a fire of rags;* or the Basque, *a fire of straw.*

All earthly things are like the *earth,* founded on nothing; they are like *Absalom's mule,* they will most fail us when we have most need of them, 2 Sam. 18. 9; a velvet slipper cannot cure the gout.

Dried cow-dung was the fuel commonly used for firing, but this was remarkably slow in burning; a very striking contrast to thorns and furze, speedily consumed with crackling noise. On this account the Arabs would frequently threaten to burn a person with cow-dung, as a lingering death.

Worldly joys are short, like a fly buzzing about a candle. *Herod* the king was gorgeously arrayed, so that the people worshipped him, but he was soon after devoured by worms, Acts 12. 23. Queen *Jezebel,* a handsome woman, enjoyed her grandour but a short time, and was eaten up by dogs, 2 Kings 9. 10, 35. *Belshazzar* in his grand banquet at Babylon, a city larger and mightier than Delhi, had his empire taken away at once, as foreshewn by a handwriting on the wall, Dan. 5. 5, 6.

Syrian.—Girl, do not exult in thy wedding dress, see how much trouble lurks behind it.

China.—Look not at the thieves eating flesh, but look at them suffering punishment

Cingalese.—Like getting on the shoulder of a man sinking in the mud.

Talmud.—The world is like a wheel with buckets attached —the empty become full, the full become empty.

Bengal.—The actor's promotion is nothing, only lasting two hours.

Arab.—The worst day for a cock is when his feet are washed—*i.e.*, previous to being killed, Jas. 5. 5.

Persian.—No honey without a sting, no rose without a thorn.

China.—Dragging for the moon reflected in the water.

Badaga.—For the nourishment of a day he sacrificed the food of a year.

Badaga.—In trying to save a drop of ghi (butter) he upset the ghi-pot.

China.—To gain a cat but lose a cow.

Telugu.—Like going to Benares and bringing back dog's hair.

Telugu.—Like a bag of money in a looking-glass, Ps. 73. 20.

China.—To fell a tree to catch a blackbird.

Talmud.—The thorns make a loud noise in burning; not so wood.

Shánti Shatak.—The stomach is satisfied with little food, even with vegetables; but the heart, although gratified with the fulfilment of more than an hundred *desires*, is incessant in pursuing after more, Eccl. 6. 9.

Courteousness.—1 Pet. 3. 8.

Afghan.—Be it but an onion, let it be given graciously.

Sanskrit.—Complaisance empties the purse.

A Cruel Man troubles his own Flesh.—Prov. 11. 17; 12. 10.

The tender mercies of the wicked are cruel. So Pilate, Luke 23. 16. *Joseph's brethren* illustrated it in their treatment of their brother, whom they cast into a pit, Gen. 37. 24. *Adonizebek* had his barbarity in cutting off men's toes visited on himself, Judg. 1. 6, 7. *Haman's* cruelty involved his own sons, Esth. 9. 25; on the other hand, *David* showed his kindness by rescuing a lamb, even endangering his own life for it, 1 Sam. 17. 34.

Afghan.—The kid's bleating is the wolf's laughter.

Urdu.—Boy's play is death to the birds.

The Cursing of the Wicked Vain.—PROV. 26. 2.

Balaam's curse came not on Israel, Neh. 13. 2; nor Goliath's, 1 Sam. 17. 43.

Badaga.—The jackal howls—will my old buffalo die?
Turk.—The dog barks—still the caravan passes.
Cingalese.—Will the barking of the dog reach the skies?
Bengal.—A dog's bite is below the knees.
Tamul.—If a dog bark at the mountain, will the mountain be injured, or the dog?
Badaga.—If the cock crow, daylight will appear; will it be so if the dog barks? Therefore do not listen to a fool.

Bad Company the Unfruitful Works of Darkness.—EPH. 5. 11.

Shánti Shatak states: "Oh! ye mind like fish, swim not in the waters of woman's beauty, for women are like nets." The *Telugus* say: "Unless you had touched garlic, your fingers would not have smelt;" "among a hundred crows what could one cuckoo do?" "what does a weaver want with a young monkey?" "bad company is friendship with a snake fencing with a sword." *Veman* compares "entertaining a bad man in your house to a fly entering the stomach; will it not torment you? How should the saint mingle with men? When a drop of water is converted into a pearl, will it again unite with its former wave?"

Bad company is called the unfruitful works of darkness; they turn God's grace into lasciviousness, Jude 4, like the soldiers who said, "Hail, king!" yet spat in Christ's face. Fellowship with the wicked is necessary in business, 1 Cor. 5. 10; the tares and the wheat are together in the Church; Christ went, however, as a physician, not as an associate; such as Joseph in Egypt, Nehemiah in Persia, Lot in Sodom, Daniel in Babylon.

Raghuvansa.—A good woman, beset by evil women, is like the chaste mimosa surrounded by poisonous herbs.

Bengal.—He who goes to Ceylon becomes a demon.

Arab.—When the crow is your guide he will lead you to the corpses of dogs, Mat. 23. 16.

Malabar.—When we strike mud we get smeared over, 1 Cor. 15. 33.

China.—The stag and the tiger do not stroll together.

Arab.—A torrent mixed with mud flowing on in darkness, Ps. 5. 9.

Arab.—Follow the owl; he will lead you into a ruined place.

Talmud.—No man can remain with a snake in a cage.

Persian.—Friendship with a fool is like a bear's embrace.

Chanak.—Shun a wicked person, though endowed with knowledge. A serpent, though adorned with gems, inspires terror.

China.—The stag and the tiger do not tread the same path. A friendship between coal and ice.

Talmud.—To the wasp we must say, Neither thy honey nor thy sting—*i.e.*, with some people have nothing to do.

Arab.—Converse with the bad is going to sea.

Persian.—Yoke not a camel and a cat together.

Afghan.—A bear's friendship is to scratch and tear.

Turk.—Yoke not to the same carriage a camel and an ox.

Afghan.—Who lives with a blacksmith will at last go away with burnt clothes.

Bengal.—You only stink your hand by killing a musk rat.

Modern Greek.—If you sit down with a lame man, you will learn to halt.

Bengal.—The ram has entered the horse's stable—*i.e.*, a fool among the intelligent.

Tamul.—The fowl brought up with the pig will eat dirt.

Polish.—Inquire after a neighbour before you purchase a house; inquire after a companion before you make a journey.

Bengal.—Blackness leaves the coal when the fire enters—*i.e.*, the improving effect of good company.

Talmud.—Near to the perfumer is fragrance.

Persian.—One scabby goat infects the flock.

Urdu.—No twisting a rope of sand. Is the bullock's sore tender to the crow?

Telugu.—Among a hundred crows what can one cuckoo do?

Telugu.—The bullock pulled towards the sun and the buffalo towards the shade.

Malay.—Will oil mix with water?

Kurd.—Who talks with the smith receives sparks.

China.—Near putrid fish you will stink. Though conversing face to face, their hearts have a thousand hills between them.

Telugu.—If you drink milk under a date-tree, they will say it is toddy.

Modern Greek.—If you sit down with one who is squint-eyed in the evening, you will become squint-eyed or cat-eyed.

Sanskrit.—A bad man, though adorned with learning, is to be shunned. Is a snake adorned with a gem not to be feared?

Owe no Debt but Love.—Rom. 13. 8.

See Parable of Debtor, Matt. 18. 28.

Bengal.—The goat tied up is at the will even of a child—*i.e.*, the debtor, Matt. 18. 30.

Turk.—Rather hungry on going to bed than debts on rising.

Telugu.—Rice, water, and salt without debt are good.

Japan.—An angel in borrowing, a devil's face in returning.

Basque.—He shuts one hole by opening another—*i.e.*, he pays his debts in opening new loans.

Decision.—No Serving Two Masters.—1 Kings 18. 21.

Malay.—We don't feel cold on going into the deep water.

Arab.—It is hard to chase and catch two hares.

Afghan.—Do not take hold of sword-grass; but if you do, grasp it tight.

Modern Greek.—Two water-melons cannot be carried under one arm.

Russian.—Better not to fire on the tiger than to wound her.

Syriac.—Be not water, taking the tint of all colours.

Galic.—Strike at every tree, yet none is felled.

Malay.—To be out of temper with water in the hold—*i.e.*, to be sulky and do nothing when the boat has sprung a leak.

Talmud.—To the wasp we must say, Neither thy honey nor thy sting—*i.e.*, with some people have nothing to do.

Basque.—Who goes quickly goes twice.

Telugu.—Before cutting down the forest, is it necessary to consult the axe?

Deeds, not Words.—Jas. 2. 6.

Afghan.—Who loves, labours.

Telugu.—Sweet words, empty hands.

Telugu.—Your mouth a sweet plum, your hand a thorn bush.

Urdu.—A lofty shop, but tasteless sweetmeats.

Urdu.—Kindness, but no milk.

Turk.—Though they are brothers, their pockets are not sisters.

Turk.—To speak of honey will not make the mouth sweet.

Turk.—It is not by saying Honey, honey, that sweetness comes into the mouth.

Bengal.—By words he softens the minds, but words will not soften the rice.

Galic.—The nodding of the head does not make the boat to row.

Telugu.—His words leap over forts, his feet do not cross the threshold.

Telugu.—Great words, but small measure.

Russian.—A tale is soon told; a deed is not soon done.

Italian.—Words are women, deeds are men.

Telugu.—It is easy to talk, but hard to stay the mind; we may teach others, but cannot ourselves understand; it is easy to lay hold on the sword, but hard to become valiant, Matt. 7. 26.

Russian.—Many counsellors, few helpers.

Telugu.—If you do not ask me for food and raiment, I will care for you as my own child.

Canara.—Knowledge consisting of words is an earthen vessel with holes.

China.—We do not cook rice by babbling.

The Double-Minded.—Unstable as a Wave.—Jas. 1. 8.

There are *double-tongued*, 1 Tim. 3. 8; the double-minded, *as tepid water*, to be spued out, Rev. 3. 16.

Malay.—Do not embark in two boats, for you will be split and thrown on your back, Luke 16. 13.

Arab.—Riding two horses at the same time.

Turk.—Who stands hesitating between two mosques returns without prayer, Matt. 6. 24.

Russian.—He hunting two hares does not catch even one.

Arab.—Doubt destroys faith as salt does honey, Rom. 14. 23.

Bengal.—He sees Jagannath's car, and sells plantains at the same time.

Modern Greek.—A rolling stone gathers no moss.

Telugu.—A double-minded man is a post in the mud swinging to and fro—*i.e.*, one who wakes the master, and gives the thief a stick.

Cast not Holy Things to Dogs.—MATT. 7. 6.

Sacrificial remains were not to be given to dogs, as they were counted so unclean.

The wicked resemble dogs in ten points :—

1. *Differ in disposition and size*, yet all are dogs. The young man that Jesus loved was a sinner as well as Judas; the Pharisee as well as the publican, Mark 10. 21.

2. Some are *vile, beastly*, eat dead bodies in the river, licked Lazarus's sores, Luke 16. 21; Ahab's blood, 1 Kings 22. 38. Such are men enslaved to diverse lusts.

3. *Churlish, snappish ;* bay at the moon; so the Jews gnashed on Stephen with their teeth, Acts 7. 54.

4. *Bite and tear men ;* so do bloodhounds, bulldogs, Jer. 15. 3; such was Paul before his conversion. Some bark and bite not; others bite, but bark not; so some injure secretly, while chains are necessary for very fierce ones.

5. Some used as *hunters*; so the devil used persecutors, Ps. 22. 16.

6. *Bite each other ;* so the Egyptians destroyed each other as well as the Jews; so in the case of Babylon and the Jews

7. *Greedy*, Is. 56. 11; never satisfied.

8. *Become sometimes mad,* then great mischief arises, Phil. 3. 2.

9. *Lazy;* hence the proverb, "A dog's life, hunger and ease;" the prodigal son fed on husks, Luke 15. 16.

10. *Shut out* of doors. Without are dogs, Rev. 22. 15.

Some dogs watchful, loving, and protecting; yet all dogs throw up when sick a loathesome vomit and swallow it again; so those who turn back to sin, Prov. 26. 11; applied to the Gentiles by Jews, Matt. 15. 27.

Beware of dogs, Phil. 3. 2; unfaithful ministers dumb dogs, Is. 56. 10. A false teacher, so called, 1 Sam. 24. 14; so the Sodomites; Pharaoh.

Chanak.—What use of science to a man without sense, or a looking-glass to a blind man?

Telugu.—What does a bullock know of the taste of parched grain? What does an ass know of the smell of perfume?

Bengal.—Krishna's name in a crow's mouth. Feeding a dog with pulse.

Arab.—The world is a carcase, and they who seek it are dogs.

Telugu.—Will a dog recognize the priest; it will only snap at him, seize and tear the calf of his leg, Mat. 7. 6.

Telugu.—If authority be given to a low-minded man, he will chase away all the honourable: can a dog that gnaws shoes taste the sweetness of the sugar-cane?

Bengal.—The thief and hog have one road—*i.e.*, impurity.

Meek as a Dove.—Matt. 10. 16.

A soft tongue breaketh the bone, Prov. 25. 15. David, suffering from the wicked, wished to have the wings of a dove, which flies very rapidly, and loves freedom like the dove imprisoned in the ark, Ps. 55. 6.

The meek resemble a dove in four points:—

1. *Harmless* in the midst of a crooked generation, Phil. 2. 15; yet he is to be wise as a serpent, Matt. 10. 16.

2. Hates *impure* things, not like the crow or jackal; the Holy Spirit in the form of a dove descended on John at his baptism, Matt. 3. 16.

3. *Shuns* birds of prey; its mild eye very different from the hawks; it is mild, but sharp, enabling it to flee from danger.

4. Loves its *home:* if taken hundreds of miles away, it will find its way back; hence it is used to carry letters tied to its legs. The believer's home is with dove-like men in the clefts of the Rock of Ages.

Abraham, though the elder, waived his right of choice for the sake of peace, and promptly removed all occasion of strife, Gen. 13. 7–9; and God put honour upon him after his disinterestedness, Gen. 13. 16. It is called sheepishness to be meek, but it is a likeness to Him that was as a sheep before the shearers, not opening his mouth, Isa. 53. 7; it is a portion of His spirit. The meek shall inherit the earth, Matt. 5. 5.

Hebrew.—Kindle not the coals of a sinner, lest thou be burnt with the flame of his fire.

Persian.—A pleasant voice brings a snake out of his hole.

Turk.—One drop of honey catches more bees than a ton of vinegar.

Turk.—Tread not on a sleeping snake.

Turk.—Have in life the force of a lion, the sagacity of an elephant, and the sweetness of the lamb.

China.—Rousing a sleeping tiger exposes to harm.

China.—Stir not the fire with a sword—*i.e.*, provoke not by anger.

Russian.—Good greeting softens a cat.

Telugu.—The Ganges flows with a tranquil course, but a foul *stream* rushes with a roar. Thus the base can never be mild as the noble, Luke 21. 19.

The Wicked are Dross.—Ps. 119. 119.

The wicked are made of the earth, and return to it; they prosper in the earth; not so the righteous. Nettles grow in any soil, Ps. 37. 1, 2; not so flowers.

The wicked like dross in six points:—

1. Resemble the metal, but only in *appearance*; so the wicked, Ps. 66. 10, have a name to live, Rev. 3. 1.

2. To be *burnt* and consumed in the fire; not so silver, which is only refined; wicked like a house on the sand, Matt. 7. 27; Ezek. 22. 20.

3. Mixed with pure metal only *temporary;* so the wheat and chaff, Matt. 13. 30; the sheep and goats are only together for a time.

4. *Unprofitable;* the good are gold or diamonds, though esteemed in the world the offscouring, 1 Cor. 4. 13.

5. God takes away the dross by judgment, Matt. 3. 12; by church censures, 1 Cor. 5. 5. Dross more *abundant,* Luke 13. 23, 24.

6. Not *improved* by fire as silver or gold is; Jerusalem was thus compared to a pot, Ezek. 24. 6.

Tamul.—What avail heights in the dunghill? is the town disparaged by being low?

Modern Greek.—This fig-tree is for the fire—*i.e.*, a useless person.

Tamul.—Of what use is the ripening of a poisonous tree in the middle of a village?

Man's Corruption like the Ethiopian's Skin.—JER. 13. 23.

Man is said, Job 15. 16, to *drink* in iniquity like water—*i.e.*, allusion to the prodigious quantity of water swallowed by a camel on setting out on a journey. Though the corruption from Adam cannot be changed by nature, yet God's Spirit can do it by supernatural power: thus Paul, from being a persecutor of the Christians, in three days so changed as afterwards to become a preacher of Christianity.

Russian.—The wolf changes his hair, but yet remains the wolf. However you bind a tree, it will always grow upward. Though you put oil on a dog's tail, it will never become straight.

Urdu.—If you put a crow in a cage, will it talk like a parrot?

Sanskrit.—The nim tree will not be sweetened though you water it with milk.

Niti Sar.—Though the crow's beak be gold, and his feet diamonds, yet the crow cannot become a swan.

Persian.—A black cat will not be washed white by soap.

Kurd.—Out of a dog's tail you cannot get fat.

Veman.—If you take a bear-skin and wash it ever so long, will it, instead of its native blackness, ever become white? If you beat a wooden image, will it hence acquire any good quality?

Turk.—In washing a negro we lose our soap.

Urdu.—Will the gall-nut become as sweet as the cocoanut, though watered with honey?

Bengal.—The nightingale lays its young in the crow's nest, but the young do not behave as crows.

Tamul.—Are young fish taught to swim?

Tamul.—Though we feed a snake with milk, it will yield poison.

Sanskrit.—By slitting the ear and cutting the tail, a dog is but a dog, not a horse or ass.

The Eye of Faith.—HEB. 11. 27.

The eye of faith differs from the eye of sense in two points. The eye of sense grows dim with age, 1 Sam. 3. 2; the eye of faith brightens; the eye of sense sees not far; the eye of faith sees beyond the stars, like Stephen, Acts 7. 55; or Jacob, who lay at night on the desert, with a stone for his pillow, yet saw a vision of angels, Gen. 28. 12. There are eyes full of uncleanness, 2 Pet. 2. 14; the eyes of the fool are in the ends of the earth, Prov. 17. 24; the proud eye is a lofty one, Psa. 131. 1. Eve was deceived by the eye, Gen. 3. 6; so Achan's eye by the garment, Jos. 7. 21; so Samson's eye by Delilah, Judg. 16. 1; so Ahab, 1 Kings 21. 2; so Nebuchadnezzar, Dan. 4. 27–33. There are three eyes—the eye of sense, common to the brute; the eye of reason, peculiar to man, Mark 8. 18; and the eye of faith, peculiar to the righteous, which can see beyond this world, can see the future, John 8. 56, can see minute things. Bartimeus was blind, yet he had the eye of faith, Mark 10. 46.

Telugu.—The God who destroyed the eyes gave understanding as a compensation.

Turk.—Invisible things are more numerous than visible.

Modern Greek.—The eyes of the hare are one thing, those of the owl another.

Veman.—Large is the eyeball, minute the pupil; yet in the pupil alone exists the source of vision; such are the media through which we see the Deity.

Afghan.—Though the eyes be large, they act through small pupils.

Bengal.—The lame can leap over mountains by God's aid. 2 Cor. 12. 9.

Sanskrit.—Who are destitute of *sight?* Those who do not perceive the future world.

Kurd.—All those who know have eyes and see; all those who know not have only two holes in the forehead.

Badaga.—The son of a king sees more with half an eye than the son of a fool with two.

Arab.—Dim eyes do not ensue when the mind's eyes are bright.

Veman.—Like as the fish in the waters, through desire of the delicious bait, is fixed on the hook and perishes; so a man, if seized with desire, is also ruined, Jas. 1. 15.

Veman.—A good work performed with a pure heart, though small, is not trifling. How large is the seed of the banyan and the mustard tree? Luke 21. 2.

Arab.—The eyes are of little use if the mind be blind. Mark 8. 18.

The Fire of the Tongue.—Jas. 3. 6.

The tongue like a fire in three points:—

Solomon writes: "A soft tongue breaketh the bone," Prov. 25. 15; so Jacob found, Gen. 32. 4, that a gentle answer softens the heart. The Bengalis say, "Quiet water splits a stone;" the Germans, "Patience breaks iron," Gen. 32. 11–20; 1 Sam. 25. 35.

1. *Fire* gives heat which makes (passion) boil over, while a man of understanding is of a cool spirit, Prov. 17. 27; so Christ, Matt. 27. 12–14.

2. Kindles *great* things, Matt. 12. 36; hence fire called a good servant, but a bad master, Prov. 26. 18–20.

3. *Scorches* and gives pain; so the wicked compared to coals of juniper, Ps. 120. 4, which burn hot and long.

The fire of the evil tongue is kindled from hell; not so the zeal of the righteous, compared to a live coal, Isa. 6. 6; the cloven tongues of fire were harmless, Acts 2. 3.

Tamul.—The words of a babbler are fine dust.
Afghan.—A great spear-wound is well to heal quickly; a severe tongue-wound becomes a sore in the heart, healeth not.
China.—A man's conversation is the mirror of the heart.
Turk.—Who masters his tongue saves his head.

Little Sins like Dead Flies in Ointment.—Eccl. 10. 1.

Telugu—"The remains of a debt, a sore, or a fire should not be left, as they may increase."

Veman—A stone in the shoe, a gadfly in the ear, a mote in the eye, a thorn in the foot, and a quarrel in a family, however small in themselves, are unspeakably tormenting, 2 Cor. 12. 7.

The text refers to the acid salts in insects which dispose syrups to fermentation, and then to putrescence, causing a bad smell and sour taste, and so the whole ointment is spoiled, as a little *leaven* leavens the whole lump, 1 Cor. 5. 6; the *tongue* is a little fire, and kindles great things, as the little *helm* of a ship turns a big vessel, Jas. 3. 4. A small leak will sink a great ship: break one link in the chain, the whole goes.

China.—It is with law as with dykes—in whatever part they are broken, the rest becomes useless. No ease for the mouth when one tooth is aching.

Malabar.—A coir improperly twisted will break the whole mass.

Russian.—A spoonful of tar in a barrel of honey, and all is spoiled.

Oriental.—Good qualities efface not bad, as sugar mixed with poison does not prevent the poison being mortal.

Kurd.—A vessel of honey with a drop of poison in it.

Cingalese.—The tree which (when young) you could have nipped off with your nail you cannot afterwards cut with your axe.

Modern Greek.—A little bait catches a large fish.

Urdu.—It is a sin whether you steal *sesamum* or sugar.

Tamul.—Though the thorn in the foot be small, yet stay and extract it.

China.—To spare a swelling till it becomes an ulcer, Jas. 2. 10.

Malay.—One piece of arsenic suffices to kill a thousand crows.

Telugu.—To look at it, it is like a musk rat; but to dig into walls, it is a bandicoot.

Japan.—Poking out the eye with an insignificant twig.

Hebrew.—Of a spark of fire a heap of coals is kindled.*

Life a Flood.—Ps. 90. 5.

This Psalm was composed by Moses towards the close of his wandering in the desert, when human life had been shortened, and when out of 3,000,000 Jews that came into the wilderness only two adults were allowed to enter Canaan.

There are more than 1,000,000,000 of people in the world, composed, like the Ganges and Brahmaputra, of streams of many nations; they make a great noise; like a flood, rise suddenly, and as suddenly go down to the

* There is the well-known homely French and English proverb, "For want of a nail the horseshoe was lost; for want of a shoe the horse was lost; for want of a horse, the rider was lost.

ocean of Eternity. Some of these floods fertilize the soil, while others sweep away cattle and villages; so some men lead the lives of sheep, others of goats.

China.—The waves flowing away chase those that precede; in the world the new-born chase away the old, and they also pass away; no feast lasts for ever.

Russian.—There are not two summers in one year, Jer. 8. 20.

Japan.—As the stars, so man appears little at a distance.

Persian.—The world is like an old building on the banks of a stream—it carries away piece by piece; in vain you stop it with a handful of earth.

Telugu.—If the priest does not come, will the new moon wait for him?

Tamul.—Does any one desire to chew his betel over again? Gen. 47. 9.

Life passes as a Flower.—1 PET. 1. 24.

Though the flowers are clad with a raiment superior in beauty to Solomon's, yet the scythe of death, sunshine, storm, rain, or worms sweep them away. The *Prabodh Chandrodaya* says the society even of friends is a flash of lightning which is dazzling, but momentary. The righteous, like a plant, may lose his flower on earth, but he will he transplanted to the gardens of Paradise.

China.—The swallow plastering its nest is labour lost—*i.e.*, it soon migrates.

China.—We find trees in the mountains 1,000 years old; we rarely find a man 100 years old.

Turk.—Have you ever seen a day which ends not in evening?

Turk.—Happiness is like crystal—when it shines the most it soon cracks.

Arab.—Every day in thy life is a leaf in thy history.

Modern Greek.—Many dead are sitting at the head of the sick man—*i.e.*, many of those who visit a sick man die before him.

Afghan.—Life is not such a mouthful that a man should gulp it down whole; life is not so short that a man should live heedless.

Arab.—Life like a fire begins in smoke, ends in ashes.
China.—The moon is not always round; the clouds sometimes disappear.
Japan.—Life is a light before the wind, Job 7. 7.
Arab.—Like a moth falling on a lighted candle.

God-fearing the Fountain of Life.—Prov. 14. 27.

Fear of God differs from the wicked's fear in five points:—

One kind of fear has torment, 1 John 4. 18; such was Adam's, Gen. 3. 8–10, the devil's, Jas. 2. 19. The other is reverential, and leading to watchfulness; as Joseph, Gen. 39. 9, Noah, Heb. 11. 7. This is the beginning of knowledge, Prov. 1. 7.

Arab.—The fear of God makes the heart shine.
Afghan.—The shelter of a tamarisk is equal to that of a mountain for a man who fears not God—*i.e.*, no restraint in wickedness for those not fearing God.
Arab.—There are four things God cannot do: He cannot lie; He cannot die; He cannot deny Himself; and He cannot look favourably on sin.

The Heart the Fountain of Action.—Mat. 15. 19.

Sanskrit.—If the heart be impure, all actions will be wrong.
Turk.—The eyes are a balance of which the heart forms the weight.
Telugu.—A good work performed with a pure heart, though small, is not trifling. How large is the seed of the banyan and the mustard tree? Luke 21. 2.
Sanskrit.—The poison of a scorpion is in his tail, of a fly in his head, of a snake in his fang; but of a bad man in his whole body, Isa. 1. 5.

The Wicked are Foxes.—Luke 13. 32.

Herod the king was called a fox, because he tried to catch Christ by cunning, Luke 13. 32, Mat. 2. 8; *false teachers* are also so called, Ezek. 13. 4; they used rough garments to deceive, Zech. 13. 14, in imitation of the true teachers, who wore sackcloth and hairy garments.

The wicked are like foxes in five points :—

1. *Craftiness.* The fox when pursued and caught pretends to be dead; he uses his tail to catch crabs; he has many entrances to his den; he moves crookedly and steals up lightly, Neh. 4. 3, yet he does not escape.

2. *Cruel* and *destructive.* He destroys more than he kills; makes havoc among grapes.

3. Attacks *at night;* the wicked called children of darkness, 1 Thess. 5. 5.

4. *Greedy.* The fox eats all kind of filthy putrid things, lives on filth, digs up dead bodies.

5. Moves *in packs* to destroy; so Samson used three hundred of them with lighted brands to their tails to fire the corn, Judg. 15. 4; the wicked combine to do evil.

Christ said even the foxes had holes, but he had not where to lay his head, Luke 9. 58.

Turk.—The fox goes at last to the shop of the furrier.

Friendship like Perfume, rejoicing the Heart.—Ps. 27. 9.

Abraham was the friend of God, Jas. 2. 23; Jonathan and David had close friendship, 1 Sam. 18. 1.

Urdu.—The friendship of the base is a wall of sand.
Arab.—A bad friend is like a smith, who, if he does not burn you with fire, will injure you with smoke.
Arab.—A fool or unlearned is an enemy to himself: how is he a friend to others?
Arab.—Three things are not known except in three points: courage except in war, the wise except in anger, a friend except in adversity.
Afghan.—God will remain, friends will not, Prov. 18. 24.
Turk.—Friends are one soul in two bodies.
Gujerat.—A rat and cat's friendship.
Persian.—Friendship with a fool is the embrace of a bear.
Talmud.—A man without a friend is a left hand without the right.

China.—It is only with the eye of others we see our own defects.

China.—Without a clear mirror a woman cannot know the state of her face; without a true friend a man cannot discern the nature of his actions.

Afghan.—The ass's friendship is kicking.

Telugu.—The friendship between fire and water.

Japan.—A friend at hand is better than relations at a distance.

Kirat Arjun.—The friendship of the bad is like the shade of some precipitous bank with crumbling sides, which, falling, buries him who sits beneath.

The Wicked like Goats.—MAT. 25. 31, 33.

The devil is worshipped in some countries under the form of a goat.

The goats like the wicked in four points:—

1. *Feed among sheep*; but the Great Shepherd will separate them at the judgment-day; so hypocrites in a church as tares among wheat.

2. *Mischievous*; destroy trees, plants; hence bad princes so called, Zech. 10. 3.

3. *Unclean*; so the wicked, 2 Pet. 2. 7.

4. *Greedy*. A hundred goats will eat as much as a thousand sheep; so *Ahab* coveted *Naboth's* vineyard, though he was so rich himself, 1 Kings 21.

Bengal.—What will not a goat eat or a fool say?

Chanak.—An uneducated man in society is a crane among swans.

All Flesh is Grass.—ISA. 40. 6.

What is more frail than grass? In tropical countries it comes up in the spring, flourishes for a short period, and is then cut down; or, if not severed from its root by the scythe, it soon withers away. In India especially the great heat of the sun quickly withers away the grass, which becomes quite brown, or disappears in the hot weather. So weak are we, and so unable to resist the stroke of death. We come up, and are cut down! The spring-time of life is soon gone, the season of harvest comes, and death strikes the fatal blow. Nothing can make man a solid substantial being, but the being born again of the incorruptible seed, the Word of God, which will transform him into an excellent creature, whose glory will not fade like the flower, but shine like an angel's face.

Gratitude the Memory of the Heart.

Praise, the expression of gratitude, is called the fruit of the lips, Heb. 13. 15; a garment, Isa. 61. 3; see the case of the lame man in the Temple, Acts 3. 8; of the chief butler, Gen. 40. 23; and of the parable of the two debtors, Luke 7. 41–43.

Tamul.—A benefit conferred on the worthy is engraved in stone; on the unkind, written in water.
Malay.—The bean forgets its pod, Isa. 51. 1.
Bengal.—Having eaten his salt, he esteems his virtues.
Cingalese.—A line inscribed in water—*i.e.*, the ungrateful.
Telugu.—Blows with stones to the bearing tree.
Talmud.—Do not throw a stone into the well out of which you have drunk.
Tamul.—The physician who cured the striped tiger of his sickness became his prey.
Tamul.—A benefit conferred on the worthless is an earthen vessel falling on a stone.
Telugu.—A dog instinctively recognizes the kindness shown to it; how base is the man who feels not the good that is done to him, Luke 17. 17.
Tamul.—The scorpion stings him who helps it out of the fire.
Turk.—The dinner ended, we value no more the spoon.
Persian.—He eats the salt, breaks the salt-cellar.
Tamul.—The rogue feels only when he is punished: the farmer feels grateful when the rain falls.

Russian.—The sheep does not remember its father; it bears only grass in mind.

Idleness makes the House drop through.—ECCLES. 10. 18.

The ant makes hay when the sun shines—has no guide: not so the idler, who lets the house leak.

The marks of the sluggard or idler are—(1) Loves not *difficulties;* will not plough by reason of cold, Prov. 20. 4; (2) loves not *disturbance,* though death's handwriting may be on the wall; (3) enjoys not the good *in hand;* roasts not what was taken in hunting, Prov. 12. 27; (4) his way hedged with *thorns,* Prov. 15. 19; such were the ten tribes—too lazy to go up to Jerusalem, 1 Kings 12. 28; so with the servant in the parable of the talents; (5) allows *weeds* on his fields, Prov. 24. 30; (6) *desires only,* but makes no efforts; so Balaam wished the death of the righteous, but led not the life of the righteous, Num. 23. 10; (7) makes no *progress,* turns as a door on the hinges, Prov. 26. 14; (8) makes *excuses;* there is a lion in the way, Prov. 22. 13.

Telugu.—The idle man eats like a bullock, and sleeps like a dog.

Telugu.—In a neglected house devils take up their abode.*

Bengal.—The date fell on his moustaches; he was too lazy to put it into his mouth.

Hebrew.—Idleness is the mother of all vice.

Tamul.—Opening the mouth when one says gram (oats), and shutting it when one says bridle.

Tamul.—Being without work, the barber is said to have shaved his wife's head.

Persian.—Water long stagnant becomes putrid.

Finnish.—By sleeping we do not gain money; by sitting no fortune is to be had.

Arab.—A well is not to be filled with dew; equivalent to the French—"He that will eat the kernel must crack the nut."

* Very similar to the Italian proverb, which has found its way into English, "An idle brain is the devil's workshop."

Tamul.—Plants of learning must be watered with the rain of tears.

The Inner and the Outer Man.—2 Cor. 4. 16.

Also called the old and the new man, Eph. 4. 24; the old and new Adam; the flesh and the spirit, Rom. 8. 1.

The Hindus write of various *koshas* or sheaths enveloping the body. Peter calls the inner man the hidden man, 1 Pet. 3. 3–4.

By the *outer* man is meant the body and senses; by the *inner* man the heart and spirit; both very different—the bodily eye might grow dim while the eye of faith grew brighter. The *Arabs* say, "Dim eyes do not injure when the mind's eye is bright." His youth is renewed like the eagle's, Ps. 103. 5. St. Paul's setting sun was fine; he was, like the swan, said to sing as sweetly in winter as in summer.

Atmabodh.—The wise man during his residence in the body is not affected by its properties, as the firmament is not affected by what floats in it.

Telugu.—The tamarind may be dried, but it loses not its acidity.

Bengal.—A clever woman is not old, though aged, but has the sweet sap of wit in her.

China.—The man grows old, not so his heart.

Persian.—Don't despise pepper because it is so small; eat, and see how pungent it is, 2 Cor. 10. 10.

Russian.—The needle is small, but pierces sharply.

Veman.—Though a vessel be broken, a new one is easily procured. Is it then marvellous that after a man's death he should acquire a new body? 2 Cor. 5. 2.

Sanskrit.—The form is small, the qualities great.

Telugu.—An old tree has a firm core.

Tamul.—Though broken to pieces, a golden pot will still be gold; of what use is an earthen pot when broken?

Cingalese.—A gem is a gem, though found in a dunghill.

Veman.—Worked chasings are various, but all gold is the same; these *earthly* tenements vary, but the soul is one; viands are many, but hunger is always the same.

Telugu.—If you look at a grain of pepper, it is externally black; if you bite it you perceive that internally it is pungent. Thus imperceptible is the worth of the excellent.

The Lamp of the Wicked put out.—PROV. 13. 9.

The wicked are driven away, Prov. 14. 32. Lamps were used by the Jews at weddings and on festive occasions, a man in prosperity is compared to a blazing lamp in adversity, he is ready to slip with his feet, Job 12. 5, or to a lamp extinguished. The lamp of the wicked gradually fails of oil, Mat. 25. 3–8, and in its extinction a stench from the wick arises; so the memory of the wicked.

Canara.—The fly (the poor man) is eaten by the frog (the rich man), and both are eaten by the serpent death, Prov. 30. 23.

Sanskrit.—Time is stronger than all things else.

Man Fades as a Leaf.—ISA. 64. 6.

Life like a leaf in four points:—

The change comes on *gradually;* we scarcely perceive a difference day by day, but after the interval of a week it is distinctly seen; the leaf changes from a green to a pale hue when about to fall, the breeze snaps the link by which the shred was joined to its branch, and wafts it to its resting-place beneath the parent tree, where it rots or serves as fuel or manure. Such is the strength of men: the freshness of youth passes into the maturity of manhood, and thus by gradual steps the feebleness of age comes on: grey hairs are on him, yet he knoweth it not, Hos. 7. 9. "The dust returns to the dust."

The leaves with which the earth is strewn, and which serve to manure it, will know no second spring; not so the body, which will rise in the morning of the resurrection, Dan. 12. 2.

A leaf is light and unsubstantial. A leaf fades in various ways *silently.* The myriad leaves that glitter in the sunshine of spring or flutter in the breeze will be strewn on the ground in autumn; but when one shall fall and how long another shall hang who can tell? One falls withered by a worm at its root in early summer; a second is nipped by the frost, a third is shaken off by a rough wind, and the fourth, soon after it has burst from the bud in spring, is smitten by mildew. All will fall at some time; so with men. The population of the globe, 1,000,000,000, will in a generation be off the tree of life: some drop in childhood's spring, some in ripe manhood, and some hang on till the winter of age arrive. The time is short to all, and the short time is uncertain to each.

The conquerors in the Grecian games were crowned with leaves. These, though beautiful, soon faded away. beauty, like glass, is brittle; trusting in fading beauty is like anchoring in a floating island. The righteous, though his outer man decay, is an evergreen leaf.

China.—Man's life is like a candle in the wind, or hoar-frost on the tiles.

Afghan.—Parents say, Our boy is growing up; they forget his life is shortening.

Turk.—The dust of the tomb fills the eye of man.

Lip Love as Sounding Brass.—1 Cor. 13. 1.

Bengal.—By words only the moistened rice is not made into a confection.

Bengal.—A false friendship is like a bank of sand.

Bengal.—Now, you, as it were, give me the moon, but shortly you will give me a flogging.

Bengal.—In words a tiger, in fighting a lizard.

Bengal.—My house is your own; but if you ask for food, you are my enemy.

Telugu.—A barking dog never bites; does gold ever ring like bell metal?

Use the Means.

Telugu.—God gives food, but does he cook it and put it in the mouth?

Telugu.—Can your house be burnt down with hot water?
Telugu.—By digging and digging the truth is discovered.
Telugu.—When the field was sown without being ploughed, it yielded without being reaped—*i.e.*, it yielded nothing.
China.—Better go home and make a net than go down the river and desire to get fishes.
China.—No one can sew without a needle, no one can row without water.
China.—A dry finger cannot lick up salt.
Afghan.—Though God is almighty, he sends not rain in a clear sky.
Turk.—Don't descend into a well with a rotten rope.
Turk.—What can a stout ox do with a bad plough?
Turk.—Knowledge is not acquired in a feather bed.
Turk.—Who desires the rose must also consent to the thorn.
Turk.—Knowledge is not gained on a bed of roses.
Russian.—God help us, but don't lie on your back.
Russian.—A good head has one hundred hands.
Talmud.—If a man goes not after wisdom it does not come to him.
Telugu.—Scratching one's head with a firebrand—*i.e.*, the remedy worse than the disease.
Telugu.—Swimming over the Godaveri by catching hold of a dog's tail, Luke 14. 31.
Urdu.—He sets up for a druggist with one bit of assafœtida.

Gravel fills the Mouth of Deceit.—Prov. 20. 17.

The *Lalita Vistara* states: "Desires are regarded by the wise as the edge of a sword covered with honey, or as the head of a serpent leading to quarrels, as a corpse among dogs."

Diverse weights are an abomination to the Lord, Hos. 12. 7, Deut. 25. 13–16. A bribe-taking judge is called a briar, Micah 7. 4.

Jacob deceived his father with a kid, Gen. 27. 9–14, &c.; more than forty years after, his children deceive him with a kid, Gen. 37. 31, 32. *David* artfully contrived the murder of Uriah by the sword, 2 Sam. 11. 14, 15; and the providence of God so appointed it that the sword never departed from his house, 2 Sam. 12. 10. So with *Haman*, Esther 7. 10, and the attempt to assassinate Ahasuerus, Esther 2. 21–23.

The Jews put Christ to death that the Romans might not come and take away their place and nation; by that very act they drew down the vengeance of God, which God appointed the Romans to execute, John 11. 48.

Urdu.—A wooden pot cannot be often put on the fire—*i.e.*, deceit cannot be often repeated.

Bengal.—The low fellow's words are like the tortoise's head, which can be drawn out or put in according to circumstances.

Turk.—The liar's house is on fire, but no one believes it.

Telugu.—A trader in the air—*i.e.*, an impostor.

Bengal.—He tells the thief to rob; he bids the householder be on his guard.

The Safe Guide.—Ps. 48. 14.

A guide is necessary in a strange place; such the world is—a wilderness where there are bad roads, few wells, storms of sand arise, and the dread of robbers.

God directs men's steps; so Pharaoh's daughter found Moses when she went to bathe, Ex. 2. 15; Saul, in search of asses, obtained a kingdom, 1 Sam. 9. 3–15; Paul, on his way to Damascus, saw Christ, Acts 9.; David's case, 1 Sam. 17. 53.

Russian.—Man plans, but God fulfils.

China.—Man sees but the present, God all things.

Arab.—Man thinks, God guides.

Urdu.—God is the guardian of a blind man's wife.

China.—A man depends on God as a ship on its rudder.

Urdu.—One door is shut, but a thousand are open.

Mahabharat.—Like a gem strung upon a thread or a bull tied by a nose rope, a man follows the command of the Disposer (God) as the tips of grass are swayed by the blasts of a strong wind.

The Hoary Head of the Righteous a Crown of Glory.

PROV. 16. 31.

The Jews required persons to rise up when at a distance of four cubits from an old man. The Romans punished with death those not rising up before the hoary; and God sent two bears to devour the men who called Elisha bald-headed, 2 Kings 2. 23.

The Germans call grey hairs death's blossoms; the Bible says, *if* found in the way of righteousness, they are a *crown* of life—*i.e.*, unfading, and an ornament, a sign of dominion and victory. Men are like *wine;* age renders the good mellow, but makes the bad sour, or like *chimneys* long foul, which, if not swept, are at length fired. Old sinners are like *vessels* long abroach, in which nothing is left but the lees and dregs of ignorance and sin.

Examples of good old righteous people in *Samuel,* 1 Sam. 25. 1; *Elisha,* 2 Kings, 13. 14; *Jacob,* Gen. 47, 10; *Anna,* Luke 2. 36.

The righteous, though old in body, is a new man in religion, 2 Cor. 5. 17; his youth is renewed like the eagle's, Ps. 103. 5.

Arab.—Hoary hairs are death's messengers, Hos. 7. 9.

Afghan.—Though the mallet be old, it is sufficient to smash the pitcher.

China.—In clothes we admire novelty; in men, old age.

Arab.—The gravity of old age is fairer than the flower of youth, Job 23. 6, 7.

Hebrew.—Wisdom is the grey hair unto men.

The Body of a House.—2 COR. 5. 1.

The *Probodh Chandrodaya* compares the soul to a taper confined in a dwelling which has nine openings. The *Shánti Shatak* says: "It is absurd to lament the loss of youthful joy and a lively countenance, which floated off like the sportive and short-lived billows in the Jumna." *Veman* writes: "When a bubble stands on water, a rapid rush in passing destroys it. Alas! what affection men feel for the frail earthen vessel of the body."

The word "house" sometimes means property, as when referred to the Pharisees who devoured widow's houses, Matt. 23. 14. But "house" more generally means a place to dwell in. The body is the earthly house in which the spirit dwells, and the grave is called "the house appointed for all living," Job 30. 23, because every one now living must at last abide there as in a house. The tabernacle and temple were called "the house of God," as there God dwelt among his people by the signs of His gracious presence, and His glory appeared in the cloud, and shone forth from between the Cherubim over the Ark. And thus Jacob, when he set up the stone which had formed his pillow, called the place Bethel, or the house of God, to signify that the Lord had revealed himself in that place, Gen. 28. 17.

Solomon says, Eccles. 12. 1–7, in old age *the keepers of the house*, the knees, the pillars, tremble with paralysis; the *grinders*, or teeth, are like the women who ground meal; the eyes are the *windows*, the sight becomes dim, Gen. 27. 1; 48. 10; the *lattices* of the windows afford less light to pass through, Judges 5. 28; 2 Sam. 6. 16; the *doors* are shut to enable the old to sleep; the *daughters of music* brought low, are singing or nautch girls; the house tumbles, and its tenant goes to his long home. Who builds stronger than a mason, a shipwright, or a carpenter? The gravedigger: the house that he makes lasts till Doomsday. The believer's sun breaks through the clouds of old age; the golden chain, which binds his heart to heaven, is waxing stronger and stronger, its links are growing more firm; his house is tumbling, but he has a building made without hands, 2 Cor. 6. 1, in a city without foundations.

Hearing, not Doing, as a House on a Sandy Foundation.

MATT. 7. 26.

Tamul.—By pronouncing the word fire, will the mouth be burnt?

Telugu.—Will empty words fill bellies?

Arab.—He who has made a hole in the corn-sack has become a preacher.

Arab.—A learned man without practice is a cloud without water.

Tamul.—Hunger is appeased by eating: will it be so by looking at food?

Moderation—*i.e.*, **Avoiding Extremes.**—PHIL. 4. 5.

Arab.—In shunning the bear he fell into the pit.

Persian.—Be not all sugar, or the world will swallow thee up; be not all wormwood, or the world will spit thee out.

Turk.—To avoid the smoke, do not throw yourself into the fire.

Bengal.—An excessive noise is of no use, Eccles. 7. 16.

Malay.—From fear of the ghost to clasp the corpse.

Talmud.—Eight things difficult to enjoy in abundance, but in moderation good—labour, sleep, riches, journeying, love, warm water, bleeding, and wine.

Malabar.—If you engrave it too much, it will become a hole.

Tamul.—If taken to excess, even nectar is poison.

Malabar.—Even new clothes may be rent if pulled forcibly.

Russian.—He ran from the wolf and fell in with the bear.

Talmud.—Three things in great quantity bad, but a little good—leaven, salt, and liberality.

Malay.—To fall into the jaws of the tiger after escaping from the mouth of the alligator.

Syriac.—Too much tying loosens.

Russian.—Sweet as is honey, two spoonfuls of it cannot be taken at one time.

China.—While keeping a tiger from the front door the wolf enters in at the back.

China.—The excess of joy is sorrow; of wine, drunkenness.

Basque.—The cord of a violin is broken in stretching it too much.

Tamul.—Why eat, seeing you know not how to eat with moderation?

Telugu.—Because the sugar-cane is sweet, are you to chew it with the roots?

China.—To call the tiger to chase away the dog.

Tamul.—It is said the snake, afraid of the charmer, sought the friendship of the rat.

Basque.—By filling it too much the sack burst.

Tamul.—Joy and grief must be regulated by moderation.

Tamul.—Act as one who warms himself; do not burn yourself.

Sanskrit.—Excess is to be avoided in all things.

Galic.—Though the old woman is better of warming, she is not better of being burnt.

The Mote in a Brother's Eye, a Beam in Your Own.

MATT. 7. 3.

Humility teaches us to regard others as better than ourselves. St. Paul, though the chief apostle, called himself the chief of sinners, 1 Tim. 1. 15.

Russian.—A pig came up to a horse and said, Your feet are crooked, and your hair is worth nothing.

Bengal.—The sieve says to the needle, You have a hole in your tail.

Tamul.—The defects in the eyelash are not apparent to the eye.

Japan.—At the foot of the lighthouse it is dark.

Kurd.—No one says my milk is sour.

Cingalese.—The man without clothes busying himself in making jackets for dogs.

China.—Let every one sweep the snow before his own door, and not busy himself with the frost on his neighbour's tiles.

China.—The crow mocked the pig for his blackness.

Kurd.—When your house is of glass, do not throw stones at your neighbour's house.

Bohemian.—The pot punishes the kettle; ye are both black.

Malay.—The mortar's complaint to a drug.

Modern Greek.—The ass said to the cock, Big-headed.

Sanskrit.—They know not their own defects who search for the defects of others.

Stiff-necked.—Ps. 75. 5.

The Jews were called a stiff-necked people, Acts 7. 51. The old world had its neck hardened by resisting the preaching of Noah for 120 years, 1 Pet. 3. 20; its people were swept away by the Flood, altogether unexpectedly to themselves, Luke 17. 26, 27. So were Sodom, Gen. 19, Eli's sons, 1 Sam. 3. 13. Pharaoh's hard neck was reproved by the Ten Plagues; but continuing obstinate in his rebellion against God, Pharaoh was overtaken with sudden destruction at the moment he thought himself sure of his prey, Ex. 14. 28. So Ahab, 1 Kings 17. 1; 18. 18.

Tamul.—A stubborn wife is a mat rolled up—*i.e.*, useless.
Russian.—He bows to the ground, but bites his toes.
Tamul.—A stubborn man and a crocodile are alike, they will not lose hold of what they have seized.

Woman's Ornament the Hidden Man of the Heart.

1 Pet. 3. 3, 4.

The *hidden* man of the heart here means a meek and quiet spirit called the *inner* man, in contrast with the outer man, the body or countenance; thus Paul states, though his outer man perish, his inner man is renewed day by day, 2 Cor. 4. 16. See Solomon's description of a virtuous woman, Prov. 31. 10–31; a contentious woman is compared to a continual dropping, Prov. 27. 15; she is a moth to consume her husband's estate. Women are to adorn themselves with shamefacedness, 1 Tim. 2. 8, 9.

Ornaments in dress are condemned as exciting the *passions*, encouraging *pride*, hindering *alms*, 1 Tim. 2. 9, 10; wasting *time*, Eph. 5. 16, the prophets wore rough garments, as Elijah, 2 Kings 1. 8; Jezebel painted her face; Herod was arrayed gorgeously, and was eaten up of worms, Acts 12; so the rich man clad in purple before going to hell, Luke 16; so Absalom.

Telugu.—The tamarind may be dried, but it loses not its acidity.
Veman.—Look closely at musk; its hue indeed is dark, but

its fragrance perfumes all things; thus hidden are the virtues of men of weight.

China.—We ask four things for a woman—that virtue dwell in her heart, modesty in her forehead, sweetness in her mouth, and labour in her hands.

Chanak.—As the sea defends the earth, a wall the roof, a king the nation; so does modesty a woman.

Chanak.—As the voice forms the beauty of the cuckoo, learning of an ugly man, mercy of an ascetic; so is conjugal fidelity the beauty of a woman.*

Arab.—An immodest woman is food without salt, Luke 14. 34.

China.—Modesty is woman's courage.

Russian.—The man is the head of the woman, but she rules him by her temper.

Russian.—The wife does not beat the husband, but her temper rules him.

Japan.—When the hen crows the house goes to ruin.

China.—

A bustling woman and crowing hen,
Are neither fit for gods nor men.

China.—Silence and blushing are the eloquence of a woman, Tit. 3. 3.

Persian.—If you be a cock, crow; if a hen, lay eggs.

Russian.—It never goes well when the hen crows.

Russian.—The hen is not a cock, nor is a woman a man, Prov. 31. 10–31.

Russian.—A woman's praise is in her household.

Kural.—

Of what avail are prisons barred,
Their chastity is women's guard.

Malay.—

A whole herd of buffaloes might be shut up in a pen,
There is one thing not to be guarded—a woman.

Turk.—Long hair, little brain, 1 Tim. 2. 9.

Patient as the Husbandman.—Jas. 5. 7.

Turk.—The tree falls not at a single stroke.

Turk.—Patience is the key to joy.

Turk.—We mount the ladder step by step.

* The English proverbs are—Beauty is but skin deep; is but dross if honesty be lost.

Turk.—By patience grape juice becomes wine and the mulberry leaf satin.

Turk.—With zeal and patience the mouse pierces a plank.

Turk.—We always make advance, says the tortoise—*i.e.*, slow, but sure.

Arab.—Many locks are opened by patience.

Arab.—The noisy cat catches nothing.

Arab.—It may be a fire, to-morrow it will be ashes.

Persian.—Patience is a tree whose root is bitter, but its fruit very sweet.

Bengal.—Pull the ear, the head follows.

Bengal.—Having a firm hold on all sides, mount the horse.

Russian.—The dog barks, the wind carries it away.

Afghan.—When a stone is stirred in filth the stench increases.

Malabar.—By running in the boat, do we come to land?

Tamul.—Will the barking dog catch game?

Malay.—Hillocks even are filled up by white ants.

Tamul.—If a cloth be spread on a thorn-bush, it must be taken off with great care, Prov. 19. 2.

Arab.—A poor man without patience is a lamp without oil.

Sanskrit.—A jar is gradually filled by the falling of water-drops.

Cast not Pearls before Swine.—MATT. 7. 6.

Tamul.—Like reading a portion of the Veda to a cow about to gore you.

Telugu.—A garland of flowers in a monkey's paw.

Japan.—Gold coins to a cat.

Tamul.—Though religious instruction be whispered into the ear of an ass, nothing will come of it but the accustomed braying.

Arab.—He who brings up the young of a snake will only get stung.

Persian.—It is folly to give comfits to a cow, Luke 7. 32.

Veman.—If an unlucky fool should even find the philosopher's stone, it would never remain in his hands, but vanish; it would melt away like the hail-stones that come with the rain, Prov. 12. 27.

Veman.—Though you anoint an ass all over with perfumes, it feels not your fondness, but will turn again and kick you, Mat. 7. 6; Prov. 27. 22.

Telugu.—What can a pig do with a rose-bottle ?
Sanskrit.—Beneficence shown to the mean is writing on the sand.

Perfection.—Ps. 119. 96.

The more holy a man is, the more sensible he is of his unholiness.

China.—There are two good men: one dead, the other unborn.
Arab.—Only the grave-clothes change the physical nature.
Persian.—Sweetmeats without smoke.
Telugu.—The fire-place takes the crookedness out of the stick—*i.e.,* the funeral pyre alone takes away men's evil qualities.
Tamul.—Even an elephant may slip.
Persian.—Where is the person who has not soiled his garments ?
Breton.—Who wishes a horse without defects ought to go on foot.
Turk.—Who seeks a friend without a fault remains without one.
Arab.—A good horse will stumble, a good knife will be blunted.
Bengal.—Ink spots may be removed by washing; natural disposition only by death.
Japan.—The teeth sometimes bite the tongue—*i.e.*, the best friends will sometimes fall out.
China.—There are straight trees on the mountains; no straight men in the world.

Sin as a Poisonous Serpent.—Ps. 58. 4, 5.

The poison of serpents is like sin in five points:—

1. *Inflames;* so the fire of passion.

2. *Spreads* very quickly; there are Indian cobras whose poison kills in twenty minutes—like lightning the poison goes through the body. Adam's sin has spread through the world.

3. *Small* in the beginning, the wound of the cobra scarcely visible, as the Bengali proverb—" It goes in a

needle, comes out a ploughshare." Eve ate an apple, but it poisoned the whole human race.

4. Bite not *painful*, but the effect deadly, Deut. 32. 33; Job 20. 12; so the pleasures of sin for a season.

5. The serpent has a *beautiful* skin—such was Absalom, beautiful but disobedient to his father David; he raised a rebellion against him. 2 Sam. 15. 6.

Telugu.—A year to a potter and a day to a cudgel, Rom. 5. 13.

Man as Clay; God as the Potter.—Isa. 64. 8.

The nations before God compared to the drop of a bucket, Isa. 40. 15; to the small dust of the balance, Isa. 40. 15. All things made on earth are frail, and easily broken: and though they are finely figured, painted, and gilded like porcelain, they are but earth still, and a fall destroys them.

Man comes from the hands of the Maker, as clay from the hand of the potter; and is called a *vessel*, because he has capacity to hold either good or evil, a vessel of wrath or a vessel of destruction. Paul is called a chosen vessel, and the wife the weaker vessel.

We are as clay in God's hands, and formed of the dust; He had the most absolute right to form us as vessels to honour or to dishonour, and to endue us with powers of mind and body of such extent, capacity, and efficiency, as might seem good unto Him. He had a right to determine the duration and conditions of our being, to appoint the bounds of our habitations, and all the circumstances on which our happiness and welfare in any degree depend. He was pleased to create man in his own image as a vessel unto honour; a little lower indeed than the angels, but still endued with noble faculties, and crowned with dominion over the beasts of the field; when man "marred" this Divine image and beauty by his own sinful folly. God had the most absolute right either at once to "dash him in pieces as a potter's vessel," or to continue his existence, and appoint him a new probation, on such conditions as he might see fit to enjoin, with whatever advantages or disadvantages he might be pleased to assign; man is like the moth which, flying at the candle, only gets burnt.

Persian.—The titmouse holds up its feet that the sky might not fall upon it.
Telugu.—Like a grasshopper jumping into the fire—*i.e.*, to try to extinguish it.
Russian.—The earthen pot cannot contend with the brass one.
China.—On the egg combating with the stone, the yolk came out.
Persian.—The breath of the gnat will not put out the sun.
Gujerat.—Biting a stone breaks the teeth.
Bengal.—Who has made the thorn so sharp?—*i.e.*, a man's abilities are from God.
Bengal.—When one spits at the moon it falls back on one's self.
China.—To run against a nail, Acts 9. 5.
Bengal.—The tailless ox pushing at the elephant.

Prudence.—Matt. 10. 16.

Noah showed foresight in building the ark, Heb. 4. 7; Pharaoh's servants, Exod. 9. 20, 21; so do the stork and ant, Jer. 8. 7.

Arab.—The chameleon does not leave one tree until he has secured the other.
Russian.—Measure your cloth ten times, you can cut but once.
Chanak.—A wise man moves with one foot, stands fast with the other, and does not quit the station he occupies without well considering that which he intends to go.
Arab.—If thou canst not take things by the head, then take them by the tail.
Russian.—A good fox has three holes.
Malabar.—Before you leap, look at the ground, Prov. 22. 3.

African.—No one measures the river with both his feet.

Arab.—The servant, deceived by the cold of the morning, provided no water for the heat of the day.

Sanskrit.—A king perceives by his ears; the learned by their intellect; a beast by scent; and fools by the past.

Afghan.—Though your enemy be a rope of sand, call him a serpent—*i.e.*, do not despise an enemy.

Bengal.—Who sets the weir betimes, eats plenty of fish.

Gujerat.—A straight finger scoops not out clarified butter.

Turk.—Speak not of stones to a fool lest he cast them at thy head.

Tamul.—Ants before rain carry their eggs to a higher place.

Turk.—Approach not bees without having thy head covered.

Sanskrit.—Fools learn only by the past—*i.e.*, experience is a dear school.

Punctuality, or Work while it is Day.—John 9. 4.

See the parable of the *Foolish Virgins*, who found the door shut. The coming of the Bridegroom surprised the wise virgins or bridesmaids with joy, the foolish with terror.

Jeremiah (8. 7) reproves the people for not using their opportunities; he recommends them to be like the swallow and stork, who prepare at a suitable moment to leave a wintry climate for sunlit lands; not like the ostrich, who when pursued hides its head between its legs, fancying because he does not see the danger there will be none. Time and tide wait for no man. Mat. 25. 10.

Persian.—A poor man waited 1,000 years before the gate of Paradise; then, while he snatched one little nap, it opened and shut.

Persian.—The stream which has passed down does not come back to its former channel.

Arab.—Four things cannot be brought back—a word spoken, an arrow discharged, the Divine decree, and past time.

Arab.—Occasions, like clouds, pass away.

Arab.—It is little use to hammer cold iron.

Bengal.—Having drunk the water, he asks the caste of the giver.

China.—It is little use to light a fire when the breeze is blowing.

Talmud.—The owl and the hen waited together for the morning: "The light is of use to me," said the hen; "but of what use is it to you?" 1 Thess. 5. 5.

God's Influence as Rain on the Mown Grass.—Ps. 72. 6.

The heart of man is often compared to the *hard ground*, which must be ploughed or softened before it can either receive the good seed, or can bring forth such crops as the sower looks for in their season; it is sometimes called a "*stony* heart;" and the doctrine is then spoken of as "a *hammer* that breaks the rock in pieces;" or "a *two-edged sword*, piercing even to the dividing asunder of soul and spirit, and of the joints and marrow." God's gentler influence is alluded to when it is likened to rain or dew; more gentle, but not less powerful, than when it acts as a *sword*, or "as a *fire*," or as a *hammer*, or as the rain of God's fury on the wicked, Job, 20. 23.

The ground is sometimes so hard and parched in summer in tropical countries that it might almost be taken for rock, and can be broken only by the most violent effort; yet, when "a gracious rain" is sent upon it, by degrees the hardness gives way, and it is again such as to receive into its bosom the seeds which shall bear fruit in due season. And thus has many and many a heart, which seemed "as hard as a piece of the nether millstone," been softened and penetrated by the heavenly doctrine in due time. Job 23. 16.

Rain deserves to be called a present from heaven. As the consequences of a continued drought would be fatal to us, as seen in India, so the advantages which the refreshing showers afford are equally precious. The heat of the sun acts without interruption on the different bodies on earth, and continually draws thin particles from them, which fill the atmosphere in the form of vapours. We should breathe those dangerous exhalations with the air, if now and then they were not carried off by the rain, which precipitates them upon the earth, and thus clears and *purifies* the air. The rain is not less useful in *moderating* the burning heat of the atmosphere, as we see in the rainy season in India, Isa. 44. 3, when the rain falls from a higher region, and brings to the lower a refreshing *coolness*, of which we always feel the agreeable effects when it has rained. It is also to the rain we must partly attribute the *origin* of fountains, wells, lakes, brooks, and consequently rivers such as the Amazon of America, 180 miles wide at its mouth. We are supplied in abundance with those sources of water in the wet and rainy seasons, whereas they evaporate during a long drought. The earth and vegetables languish for want of these fruitful showers, without which everything would perish, for rain is in many respects the *food* of vegetables; it circulates in their finer veins, and in the vessels of plants and trees, and conveys to them those beneficial juices which preserve their life and give them growth. When it pours on mountains, it sweeps from them a soft, rich, and fruitful earth, which it deposits in the valleys where it falls, and which it fertilizes. The valleys of the Ganges and Nile have been thus formed.

Among the Egyptians the prophet carried in his hand a pitcher, as a symbol of his dispensing the water of learning. In the *Lalita Vistara* it is said that Sakhya Muni "will render calm and cool by the rain of the law those who are devoured by the fire of envy and passion."

God's influence like rain in four points:—

1. Sometimes comes *irresistibly*, Isa. 60. 10, 11.

2. *Varies*—sometimes in torrents, at other times in showers. The feast of Pentecost, when 3,000 were converted, was a torrent. Lydia's case was the gentle shower, Acts 16. 14; so was Timothy's case.

3. Falls in drops in *succession;* so line upon line, Isa.

28. 10. Men, like narrow-mouthed vessels, cannot receive much at a time.

4. At God's *pleasure*. In some countries the rain falls in torrents; in Egypt scarcely any falls.

Redeeming the Time.—EPH. 5. 16.

The text treats of laying up time as a thing of value, such as the dying, who know the preciousness of time; there is only one building eternal, 2 Cor. 5. 1. Solomon says, Eccles. 3. 3–7, there is a time to break down, such as happened to the walls of Jerusalem, 2 Kings 25. 4–15; there is a time to cast away stones, as in building memorials, Gen. 30., Jos. 4. 1–9; so Paul threw things overboard in the shipwreck, Acts 27. 38.

The English say, "Time and tide wait for no man;" the Bengalis say, "When the rice rises in the pot, quick, quick, quick;" in hell they know the worth of time; the sinner's to-morrow will never come; Jerusalem had its time, but it knew it not, Luke 19. 42; a Jewish rabbi, asked when a man should repent, said one day before his death. Christ came in the fulness of time, Gal. 4. 4; and our times are in God's hands, Ps. 31. 15.

Time brings changes; thus one man who in the morning was worshipped, in the evening was hung up as food for crows, Esth. 7. 1–10; one great king became mad, Dan. 4. 32; see the fate of a king in the midst of a feast, Dan. 5. 30.

Arab.—Opportunities pass away like clouds.
Persian.—The arrow, once shot, never returns to the bow, Eccles. 11. 3.
Russian.—Summer never comes twice in a year.
Arab.—The best teacher is time.
Sanskrit.—Repairing the tank after the water had escaped.

Sparing the Rod, hating his Son.—PROV. 13. 24.

Sweet honey is sucked out of the bitterest herbs;

scouring makes a vessel shine the brightest; so with punishment. Eli neglected to restrain his sons, 1 Sam. 3. 13; this proved their ruin, 1 Sam. 4. 11. Such apparent kindness was cruelty. David did not restrain Absalom, 2 Sam. 14. 25, and it led to his ruin, 1 Kings 12. The best horse needs breaking, so the best child restraining.

Bengal.—Sand sharpens a knife, a stone an axe, good words a good man; so a thrashing does a rogue.

Talmud.—A word is enough for a wise man, a stick for a fool.—So in Arabic.

Telugu.—An iron ladle for a stone pot.

Afghan.—

The porcupine says, O my soft little son, softer than butter.
The crow says, O my son, whiter than muslin.

Afghan.—

The ungrateful son is a wart on his father's face.
To leave it is a blemish: to cut it a pain.

Illustrate Eli's sparing the rod by an Afghan proverb?

The Root of all Evil is the Love of Money.—1 TIM. 6. 10.

St. Paul calls covetousness idolatry, Eph. 5. 5; covetousness implies distrust of God, Luke 12. 29; we are to ask only for our *daily* bread, Mat. 6. 34; hasting to be rich leads to wrong means, as with Judas, Balaam, Ahab, Ananias, Simon Magus; their root of money-love spreads like the banyan, its branches very wide in discontent and carelessness of the poor. (See the parable of the Unjust Steward and Rich Worldling, Luke 12. 15–21.) Christ said, "Ye cannot serve God and Mammon;" or, as the Bengalis have it—"One foot on land, the other on water." The ostrich cannot fly high because of its wings; and Jacob with his flock had to travel slowly, Gen. 33. 13. He is not rich who possesses much, but who desires little; the evil lies not in the mere acquisition of money—thus Abraham, the father of the faithful, was wealthy, Gen. 13. 2; so was David, the man after God's own heart,

1 Chron. 28. 10; 29. 1–16. Theirs was not filthy lucre, Tit. 1. 7.

Turk.—The stomach of the covetous is satisfied; his eye never.

Malabar.—Money is the hatchet to separate pleasant friends.

Arab.—The gaping mouth of covetousness is not filled except by the earth of the grave, Ps. 146. 4.

Arab.—Covetousness is the punishment of the rich; a rich miser is poorer than a poor man.

Arab.—Riches are the fomenters of desire; the thirst after wealth is more vehement than after water.

Arab.—Covetousness has for its mother unlawful desires, for its daughter injustice, for its companion vileness.

Turk.—To ask bounty from a covetous man is to dig a trench in the sea.

Syrian.—Like the monkey's fat, which does not melt or soften.

Kurd.—The camel carries sugar, yet eats thorns.

Telugu.—Avarice knows not shame; sleep (of the covetous) knows not comfort.

Persian.—The miser has locked up the gate of heaven.

Mahabharat.—The bolt of the door of heaven is made by covetousness.

Persian.—Fat does not come from a stone—*i.e.*, the miser is stony-hearted.

Bengal.—An ox carrying sugar—*i.e.*, a miser enjoying not what he has.

Bengal.—Even iron swims for gain; from covetousness came sin, from sin death.

Persian.—A man attempted to swim with a load of iron on his back, Hab. 2. 6.

Afghan.—Though the river be large, it is on the dog's tongue—*i.e.*, misers have much, but can spend little on themselves.

Afghan.—Wealth is his who eats it (enjoys), not his who keeps it.

Tamul.—Patient endurance is the root of religious merit; avarice the root of sin.

Arab.—The thirst after gold is worse than tho thirst after water.

Sanskrit.—Man is the slave of money.

Rottenness of the Bones in Envy.—PROV. 14. 30.

If the bones, the mainstay of the system, be rotten, the whole body becomes sick—a slow and torturing death takes place ; so envy is the soul's rottenness.

Envy converts the happiness of which it is the witness into wormwood and gall for its own cup, and transforms the honey of another man's comfort into the poison of asps for its own bosom : it is an instrument of self-torment —a burning ulceration of the soul—a crime which, partaking of the guilt, partakes as largely of the misery of hell. *Cain*, the first murderer, slew his brother at the instigation of this vice, Gen. 4. 4 ; *Saul*, under the influence of envy, plotted for years the slaughter of David, 1 Sam. 18. *Ahab*, the king of Israel, pined for the vineyard of Naboth, and shed his blood to gain it, 1 Kings 21.; it was envy that perpetrated that most atrocious crime on which the sun refused to look, and at which Nature gave signs of abhorrence by the rending of the rocks—the crucifixion of Christ, Mat. 27. 18.

The envious man is a man of the worst diet, for he consumes himself, and delights in pining : a thorn-hedge covered with nettles ; a peevish interpreter of good things ; and no other than a lean and pale carcase, quickened with a fiend. Envy is painful to ourselves, and injurious as rust is to iron or the moth to cloth ; therefore called " the rottenness of the bones." It arises from pride, and is carried out in covetousness and evil desire, ending in discontent. Envy is discontentedness at another man's good and prosperous estate, holiness, esteem, renown, and ability. In carnal things it is sordid, in higher things it is devilish. In the one we partake with the beasts, who ravenously seek to take the prey from one another ; in the other with the devils and evil angels, who, being fallen from happiness, now malign and envy those that enjoy it. St. James 3. 14, calls it " *bitter* envying," to distinguish it from that holy emulation which makes us strive who shall excel each other in the ways of godliness; as also from true zeal for God's glory. It proceeds from the overflow of gall and choler, that root of bitterness that is in the heart; it is bitter to ourselves and others, it makes us unpleasant to those with whom we converse; and though it be sweet for the present, yet, when conscience is opened, and we taste the fruits of it, it proves bitterness in the issue. Envy is but a cockatrice egg, that soon brings forth strife. The world had an early experience of it. Satan envied Adam and Eve. Pride the first sin in Adam; envy the second in Cain. There was envy between *Abraham* and *Lot's* herdsmen, Gen. 13. 7, then *Joseph's* brethren envied him, and conspired to slay him, Gen. 37. 4. So in *Saul* and David's case, 1 Sam. 18. 9.

Bengal.—In seeing another's wealth, it is not good to have the eyes smart.

Gulistan.—I can avoid injuring the mind of any one, but what shall I do to the envious man who carrieth the injury in his own breast? Die, thou envious wretch, since thou canst not be cured of the disease under which thou labourest, but by death.

Arab.—Envy is a raging fever; envy has no rest; the wise no poverty.

Turk.—No mountain without mist; no man of merit without detractors.

Oriental.—Virtue is always exposed to envy; we cast not stones at a barren tree.

Afghan.—The horses were shoeing themselves, the frogs held up their feet—*i.e.*, to be shoed also.

Tamul.—An enemy's envy is his own punishment.

Tamul.—Envy thou not the glory of a sinner.

Tamul.—Thou knowest not what shall be his end, Prov. 24. 20.

Japan.—Lepers envious of those with sores.

Hebrew.—The ear of jealousy heareth all things.

Hebrew.—Envy and wrath shorten the life.

Hebrew.—Carefulness brings age before the time.

Hebrew.—The envious man has a wicked eye.

Hypocrites' Hope a Rush in the Mire.—JOB 8. 11–15.

The *Telugus* compare visionary hopes to a bag of money seen in a looking-glass. The rush springs out of the mire, and its growth is as rapid as its greenness is bright "before the sun;" while the bed in which it grows is filled with the season rains, it flaunts itself as if in scorn of the more valuable blade in the neighbouring furrow, and gains more notice from the uninstructed eye, yet it is always a worthless plant, and as soon as the torrent is dried up by the heat of summer, it withers in a day; so the rich fool's hopes of long life, Luke 12. 16–20. So Goliath's head was cut off with the very sword he hoped to kill David with, 1 Sam. 17. 44–51.

Hypocrites are Whited Sepulchres.—MAT. 23. 27.

Sepulchres were beautiful without, loathsome within; hence they were away from cities, as those who touched the dead were accounted polluted.

Hypocrites likened, Luke 11. 44, to *graves* that appear not, because covered with grass and weeds—their throat an open sepulchre, Ps. 5. 9.

Paul called Ananias a *whited wall*, Acts 23. 3.

These hypocrites worshipped God with their lips, while their hearts were far from him, Mat. 15. 8, and by their extortions they devoured widows' houses, Mat. 23. 14.

Cain was a hypocrite in worshipping God without sacrifice and pretending not to know where his brother was when he had killed him, Gen. 4. 9; so *Judas* when he kissed Christ after he had betrayed him for 30 pieces of silver, Mat. 26. 49.

Chanak.—A friend who injures your business in your absence, but speaks smoothly when you are present, should be shamed as a bowl of poison with milk on its surface.

Bengal.—The heron is (in appearance) a saint as long as the fish is not in sight.

Bengal.—The female devotee pretends not to eat fish, but there are three on her leaf.

The Righteous the Salt of the Earth.—MAT. 5. 13.

The righteous like salt in three points :—

Salt is remarkable for its own peculiar *savour*, by which its presence in any substance with which it can unite itself is at once detected; spreading itself through any thing with which it is thus mixed, it imparts its own quality of saltness to the previous taste or savour. It has also the quality of *preserving from corruption*, even for a number of years, many substances that would otherwise perish; hence it is an emblem of what is enduring or perpetual.

God appointed that salt should be used in all the sacrifices offered to him: salt was the opposite to *leaven*, for it preserved from putrefaction and corruption, and signified the *purity* and *persevering fidelity* that are necessary in the worship of God. Every thing was seasoned with it to signify the purity and perfection that should be extended through every part of the divine service, and through the hearts and lives of God's worshippers. It was called "the salt of the covenant of God," because, as salt is incorruptible, so were the covenant and promise of Jehovah. Among the heathens *salt* was a common ingredient in all their sacrificial offerings; and as it was considered essential to the comfort and preservation of life, and an emblem of the most perfect corporeal and mental endowments, so it was supposed to be one of the most acceptable presents they could make unto their gods, from whose sacrifices it was never absent.

Salt is the symbol of *wisdom*, Col. 4. 6; of *perpetuity*

and *incorruption*, Numb. 18. 19; 2 Chron. 13. 5, 4; of *hospitality*, and of that *fidelity* which is due from servants, friends, guests, and domestics, to those that entertain them, and receive them at their tables: it is used in this sense, Ezra 4. 14, where *maintenance from the king's table* means *salted with the salt of the palace.* In Russia at the present day when the Emperor visits any of his subjects, bread and salt are presented to him as an emblem of hospitality.

A little salt seasons much meat, and prevents its perishing; so *Lot* was the salt of Sodom, and had there been ten righteous persons in it, the city would have been preserved, Gen. 18. 32. Salt preserves the human body from worms, so the righteous save society from corruption.

Hebrew.—Alms are the salt of riches.
Badaga.—If the curry is without savour, you can put salt into it; but if the salt has lost its savour, with what can it be seasoned? Mat. 5. 13.

Our Days on Earth a Shadow.—Job 8. 9.

Gotthold compares time to an image in the water easily broken; yet the shadow gives shelter for a time, as Jonah found at Nineveh under the gourd, 4. 6. Life like a shadow has *little substance*, is *fleeting;* it is compared in Job 8. 11, to a *rush* springing up in the mud, and drying up before the influence of the sun.

Afghan.—As the sun's shadow shifts, so there is no permanence on earth.
Bengal.—A service fleeting as the palm tree's shade or the cloud's shadow.
Bengal.—There is no hand to catch time.
Sanskrit.—Time is stronger than all things else.

God a Shepherd.—Ps. 23. 1.

God a shepherd in seven points:—

The shepherd *knows* his sheep, so as to be able to distinguish them individually, John 10. 14. Their number, names, place, character, and condition. "I am the good shepherd, and know my sheep." He *provides* for them. The shepherd *protects* them, and for this purpose he is usually provided with a staff or rod, a sling, and if need be with a sword or spear; so David, 1 Sam. 17. 40. He *leads* them often in a barren wilderness with no paths or water, surrounded by wild beasts; so God guides his people by his Providence, Word, and Spirit. "I will go before thee, and make the crooked places straight." "He leadeth me," says the Psalmist, "in the paths of righteousness" in an even and quiet path, in opposition to a path among thorns and stones and cliffs. When exposed to the scorching heat of the sun, or when weary and exhausted, he conducts them to some shady place where he "causes them to rest at noon." By "noon is meant" "fiery trial," whether arising from temptation, affliction, or persecution, or all together. The *lambs* are the objects of his special care and affection, when they become tired, or come to some difficult part in the track, which they cannot get over, the shepherd may be seen "gathering them in his arms," and even "carrying them in his bosom." Christ said, "Suffer the little children to come unto me, and forbid them not, for of such is the kingdom of heaven. And he *took them up in his arms,* put his hands on them, and blessed them," Mark 10. 14–16. Hence also his charge to Peter, "Feed my lambs," John 21. 15. He *numbers* them when they return to the fold to see that none be missing, and if there be an under-shepherd, that he may account to the owner for the sheep committed to his trust and care. When the flocks are large and numerous, and several shepherds are required, *one* is appointed over the rest as the *chief* shepherd. He *restores* the sheep that has strayed, and goes after that which is lost until he finds it. God, as a shepherd, has an immense flock all over the world; gives them peculiar food; always abides. Believers are sheep, easily scattered when away from the shepherd, as were the Jews by the Babylonians.

Mahratta.—An herdsman, with his staff in his hand, guides and protects his cattle. Will not God, with the staff of correction, guide and protect man?

China.—When heaven rears a man, he grows very fat. When men rear one, he is but skin and bone.

Telugu.—Will he who plants the tree not water it?

Modern Greek.—Appointing the wolf a shepherd.

Persian.—The sheep are not designed for the shepherd, but the shepherd for the service of the sheep.

Urdu.—Put ants and dogs to guard sweetmeats.

Russian.—The shepherd shears the sheep but does not flay them.

Sowing to the Flesh Reaping Corruption.—Gal. 6. 8.

The principles of ruin are in ourselves, like the iron which breeds rust, or like filthy garments which produce moths, or ill-humours in the body causing a fever.

The husbandman's labours are often blasted, not so those of the righteous; God will not forget the labour of love, Heb. 6. 10. Husbandmen have to reap every year, the righteous all at once.

Adonizebek was paid in his own coin, Judg. 1. 7; *Ahab's* blood was licked up by the dogs; and *Haman* was hung on his own gallows, Esth. 7. 10. *David* sowed adultery, reaped the sword, 2 Sam. 12. 9, 11; *Joseph's* brethren sowed envy, Gen. 42. 21; *Judas* sowed coveteousness, reaped a halter, Matt. 27. 5.

The Buddhists of Ceylon say—"If any one speak or act from a corrupt mind, suffering will follow the action, as the wheel follows the lifted foot of the ox." An English proverb—"He has made his bed, and he must lie in it," Job 4. 8; they that plough iniquity reap the same, they sowing the wind reap the whirlwind, Hos. 8. 7. The Persians say, "He that plants thorns shall he not gather roses; the field of wrong brings forth death as its fruits,

Prov. 5. 22; he is holden with the cords of his own sin so fire in his lips, Prov. 16. 27; Job 5. 2.

Burma.—Suffering is the necessary consequence of sin, just as when you eat a sour fruit a stomach complaint ensues.

Bengal.—Put your hand in the fire, whether willingly or no, you will get burnt.

Shanti Shatak.—To wherever you roam in sky or ocean, yet your actions from birth up will follow you before the Judge as the shadow the substance.

Telugu.—A man's shadow remains near himself.

Telugu.—If you expect much fruit from few offerings, will it be obtained?

Bengal.—From the jack do you get the mango juice?

Bengal.—"As the sin, so the atonement."

Bengal.—"The ant's wings produce its own death."

Dane.—Whoever will eat the kernel must crack the nut.

Malabar.—When any one has learnt to steal, he must also learn hanging.

Talmud.—The crow brought fire into the nest; it warmed him, but it burnt the nest.

Turk.—Those who sow thorns can only reap prickles.

Persian.—He that plants thorns shall not gather roses.

China.—Ivory does not come out of the rat's mouth.

Russian.—It is not necessary to sow fools, they grow of themselves. God is not in haste, but His aim is sure.

The Hypocrites' Hope a Spider's Web.—JOB 8. 14.

The Italians, to express the community of goods between true friends, say they tie their purses with a spider's web —*i.e.*, easily broken.

The spider weaves its web out of its own bowels, and with wonderful skill prepares a network which far surpasses the most curious product of human workmanship, even the Kashmir shawl in the regularity and fineness of its texture. The spider succeeds in fixing himself even in the mansions of the great, and clings tenaciously to the haunt or home which she has chosen. Prov. 30. 28. Her web is admirably woven for the purpose which she has in view; and such insects, as are incautiously entangled in it, become an easy prey. Yet is it also so frail and slight that a breath might rend it; and at last it is brushed away in a moment by the meanest servant of the house, the sweeper. So the hypocrite's hope is spun out of his own fancies, as the spider's web out of her own bowels; and it consists either in a groundless conceit of his own merits, or in an equally erroneous notion of God's character. The spider when he suspects his web—here called his house—to be frail or unsure, leans upon it in different parts, propping himself on his hinder legs, and pulling with his fore-claws, to see if all be safe. If he find any part of it injured, he immediately adds new cordage to that part, and attaches it strongly to the wall. When he finds all safe and strong, he retires into his hole at one corner, and supposes himself to be in a state of complete security; the web looks very beautiful in sunshine, in a moment, however, any accident, to say nothing of a dirty broom, sweeps away himself and his house.

Bengal.—Trust to the cat, and the buttermilk on the shelf.
Arab.—More faithful than the earth—*i.e.*, which renders all things deposited in it.
Tamul.—Will they let a bug escape because it did not bite?
Japan —A key to a thief.
Welsh.—To pawn a piece of flesh with a cat.
Bengal.—Dancing on an unbaked water vessel.
Talmud.—Be very humble; the hopes of men are worms.
Oriental.—More disappointing than the fire of a glow-worm.

The Lord the Stay of the Righteous.—2 Sam. 22. 19.

A house or wall is tottering, a beam of wind stays it up, such are the ropes to a ship, so creeping plants, unable to stand upright, cling by their tendrils to some stick which becomes their stay; similarly the soul clings to God by the tendrils of faith.

The Nick of Time Taught by the Stork.—JER. 8. 7.

In many countries the storks and many birds are not able to stand the winter; on its approach they congregate and depart in a body for the sunlit lands, returning in the spring, so do the *crane* and *swallow*. Men know the signs of the weather, and when it is time to start on a journey; but when the shadows of life's evening are coming, people do not see the signs of death's approach, Hos. 7. 9. The Italians say, "time is an inaudible file," which destroys gradually without its being noticed. Christ reproached the people, that though knowing the signs of bad weather, they did not know the drift of spiritual things, Mat. 16. 3; so God in Jeremiah reproaches the people for not, like the birds, looking into the future; the wicked are like the ostrich, which, when pursued, hides its head between its legs, fancying because it does not see the coming danger that it will not ensue.

The Sting of Death is Sin.—1 COR. 15. 56.

There are various stings—those of an asp, a bee, a nettle, a wasp; all, however, infuse poison quietly and sharply, and give pain. The devil is the old serpent, who injects the poison of his sting into afflictions and death, while Christ is the brazen serpent, by looking to Whom the wounds are healed. No sting of death was felt by David, 2 Sam. 23. 5; by Joseph, Gen. 50; by Jacob, Gen. 49. 18. There is, however, a love stronger than death, and death may buzz about our ears, but it has lost its sting, Is. 25. 8.

Bengal.—The commision of sin produces the fear of death.

The Sinner's Heart Stony.—EZEK. 36. 26.

The heart of the wicked is like a stone in four points :—

1. *Hard*, yields not to a blow, hence Job 41. 1–34, refers to the heart of the crocodile, hard as the nether millstone; arrows and spears are as stubble to him, they will not enter—such were *Stephen's* murderers, Acts 7. 57. There are stones in India on which the rains and winds have been beating for many thousand years, yet they are not worn, while the instruments used to break these stones are often broken themselves, Luke 4. 29. The seed that falls on stony soil springs not up, as there is no moisture in a stone.

2. *Senseless*, no feeling, Eph. 4. 19; the wicked go as an ox to the slaughter, feeling no danger of their lives; they have no shame, but a brow of brass, Is. 48. 4.

3. *Heavy.*—The thoughts of the wicked are not up to heavenly things, but down to the earthly; their God is their belly; they are of the earth, earthy, 1 Cor. 15. 47.

3. *No motion*, therefore no life.

4. *Cold*, as being without life.

But God's hammer, his word, Jer. 23. 29, breaks the rock in pieces, and gives a heart of flesh, such as *Paul* had, who from a persecutor became a preacher of Christianity; so the hardened *jailor* when he became softened, he began to cry out, Acts 16. 30. This hammer fastens conviction as a nail in a sure place, Is. 22. 23. It softens and smashes the hardest rock.

Persian.—A drop of rain makes no impression on a hard stone.

Kurd.—Grass grows not under a stone.

China.—The heart of the worthless is as unfixed and changeless as a mountain stream.

Persian.—He tries to extract oil from the sand.

Tamul.—The solemn thoughts of the funeral pyre last till each one returns home.

Tamul.—Even stones may be dissolved, the heart of a fool not.

He, Hastening with his Feet, Stumbles.—PROV. 19. 2.

Turk.—Step by step we mount the ladder.

Arab.—Patience is the key of joy, but haste is the key of sorrow.

Telugu.—Why do you cry before you are beaten, he asked; you are going to beat me in future, replied the boy.

Afghan.—The Patan boy and his brother taking a short cut fell over the cliffs.

Afghan.—He takes off his clothes before he reaches the water.

China.—Silly birds fly first.

Russian.—Hurry is good only for catching flies.

Sanskrit.—A small beginning is good.

Sanskrit.—Debt, a sore, and a stain, will be effaced by time.

Sanskrit.—Slowly, slowly place the foot.

The Swallow knows her Time, not so the Ignorant.—JER. 7. 8.

The swallow, like various other birds, is a bird of passage. What was it that skimmed over the stream, where the ripples are so bright in the morning sunshine? It was the first swallow of the returning spring. It has come back in its season—the spring and summer—nor will it leave again till the leaves, which in spring burst from their buds, are withered and falling. When cold and winter are coming, the swallows often remain in a torpid state in the holes of walls or the banks of rivers. The swallow, like the Indian adjutant, is true to the divine law which concerns its return and its departure. It knows the time to come and the time to go, and neither loses the summer pleasantness by delaying its return, nor runs the risk of suffering from the winter frost by prolonging its stay too late. How many do not begin the work of salvation till summer is over, and the winter of life is well-nigh at hand; when, if they work at all, they work with every disadvantage!

Kural.—The learned have eyes, the ignorant have merely two spots on the face.

Slander is a Mall, a Sword, and a Sharp Arrow.
PROV. 25. 18.

The slanderer wounds three at once—himself, him he speaks of, and him that hears. If we cannot stop other's mouths, let us stop our own ears. As soon as a person takes pleasure in hearing slander, he is to be ranked in the number of slanderers. By the approbation of evil we become guilty of it. The witnesses against Naboth showed that a false witness is, in some respects, as bad as a murderer, 1 Kings 21. 13.

In the case of the two false witnesses against Christ the words were true, the evidence false; while they reported the words, they misreported the sense, and thus swore a true falsehood, and were truly foresworn, Mat. 26. 60, 61. So the witnesses against Stephen, Acts 6. 13, 14; Prov. 12. 17. In these last two instances it was not by direct falsehood, but by a partial statement of truth, that they involved themselves in the murder of the innocent; such were the masters of the damsel possessed with a spirit of divination, Acts 16. 21.

China.—Sitting alone, meditate on your own faults—*i.e.*, in conversation talk not of others.

China.—The world's unfavourable view of your character and conduct is like the fleeting clouds from which the brightest day is not free.

Bengal.—The mud sticks not to the back of a pankhal fish; (which is smooth); so calumny with respect to an innocent person.

False Sympathy.—ROM. 12. 15.

Urdu.—One man's house is on fire, another warms himself by it.

Arab.—He roasted his fish in the conflagration.

Telugu.—When the sheep cries will the wolf be grieved?

Telugu.—When one man cried that his beard was on fire, another followed him asking him for a light for his cigar.

Telugu.—Is the bullock's sore tender to the cow?

China.—He may sit in a tub of cold water, but it will not steam.

Bengal.—Sprinkling salt on a new cut wound—*sic* Job's comforters, Job 16. 2.

Polish.—The ox bores with his horns the wounds; the woman with the tongue in her mouth.

Tamul.—A word that lacks sympathy and a rafter that lacks a nail, are useless.

Tamul.—It is said that the wolf wept because the sheep were wet.

Turk.—If my beard is burnt, others try to light their pipe at it, Luke 10. 32.

Temperance, or Self-Control.—Prov. 13. 28.

Russian.—It is not the sword that kills nor the wine that makes drunk.

Turk.—The knife does not make the cook.

China.—Who can govern himself is fit to govern the world.

Kural.—As the hook guides the elephant, we should with the hook of firmness restrain our passions.

Turk.—The chimney never takes fire except from within.

Russian.—The nail is not guilty that the hammer beats it into the beam.

Mahratta.—Man has five senses; if any is not under control his reason will ooze out there as water out of a skin that is rent.

Russian.—Shut the door on the devil, but he will enter by the window.

Afghan.—Though the food was another's, the stomach was your own—*i.e.*, over-eating not the fault of the food.

Tamul.—Why blame the arrow, the archer going free?

Tamul.—No one cuts off the hand because it has struck the eye.

Mahábhárat.—The gods do not, like cattle herds, guard men by carrying clubs; but they endow with understanding him they wish to preserve.

Mahratta.—Man's body is a chariot, the charioteer is himself, and his passions are the horses; if the latter are well managed all goes well.

Temptation.—1 Cor. 5. 9, 10.

Temptations to sin are represented in the *Bible* as stumbling-blocks to trip up the unwary; as the wiles of the devil; as thorns in the flesh; as fiery darts; as sent for sifting; while we are to flee from sin as from the face of a serpent.

Afghan.—Shoes are tested on the feet; a man on trial.

Turk.—If you wish to keep company with a wolf have the dog near.

Bhagavatgita.—

He who, as the tortoise does with its limbs,
Withdraws the senses from the sensual objects everywhere,
His wisdom is confirmed.

China.—One dressed in clothes made of leaves going to put out a fire is in danger.

China.—It is not beauty that beguiles men; men beguile themselves.

China.—Leisure breeds lasciviousness.

Russian.—

The priest comes to us by the trodden path;
The devil comes to us by crossing the fields—
i.e., temptation comes from unexpected quarters.

Guilty is the wolf that has eaten the sheep;
Not guiltless is the sheep that strays into the woods—
i.e., we must be on our guard, however, not to go into his path.

Turk.—The heart is a child, it desires what it sees.

Turk.—The devil tempts man, but the idle man tempts the devil.

Arab.—Where the eye does not see the heart does not grieve.

Telugu.—By experience we learn our weakness.

Telugu.—A man will not build a hut until he has been drenched, nor stoop until he has hit his head.

Veman.—

The crocodile in water can destroy an elephant;
The crocodile out of water is destroyed by a dog—
i.e., go not on the devil's ground.

Avoid Temptation.—Col. 2. 21.

Arab.—Follow the voice of a dog, not of a jackal; the one leads to the village, the other to the desert. If you do not want a fool's medicine, keep away from him.

Afghan.—Who lives with a blacksmith will at last carry away burnt clothes.

Afghan.—Have your ass tethered if you have a thief as your friend.

Afghan.—A low friendship lights a fire on the forehead.

Russian.—Do not tread, doggie, in a wolf's footsteps; he will turn round and eat you.

Russian.—Our eyes are our enemies.

China.—Throwing on stubble to put out the fire.

Tamul.—To roast a crab and set a fox to guard it.

Telugu.—Without eating, you can't tell the taste; without going down into the water, you cannot tell the depth.

China.—What the eye sees not, the heart is not vexed over. The well fed and well warmed indulge impure thoughts; the pined and starved encourage thoughts of stealing.

Afghan.—The bird sees the grain but not the snare.

Japan.—The bird flying in the air troubles not the water.

Telugu.—The fox offered his services for nothing—to guard the sheep.

Urdu.—Can fish remain in a kite's nest?

Telugu.—Like ghi (melted butter) poured on fire.

Veman Telugu.—A crocodile while swimming in water can destroy an elephant; out of the stream it is discomfited easily by a dog. In the water a ship will float smoothly; out of it it cannot crawl even a cubit.

Malabar.—If you sit close to the mortar you will be struck by the pestle.

Tamul.—Play not with snakes; *sic* English "Play not with edged tools."

Afghan.—When edged tools are used, blood flows.

Persian.—Where there is much fire the elephant's foot slips.

China.—Throw on stubble to put out the fire.

Turk.—He who fears the fire shuns smoke.

Arab.—It is only a wise man who despises himself. It is only a fool that trusts his own judgment.

Syriac.—If you wish to be a king become a wild ass—*i.e.*, if you wish to be master of yourself withdraw from society as the wild asses do.

The Body a Tent. 2 Cor. 5. 1–4.

All men are but passengers and pilgrims through this world; not real possessors of anything, but only tenants and occupiers in this transitory life. Some dwell in stately palaces; and many more in poor cottages; but all are born to the same mortality. If the poor man's hut drops into decay, he dies never the sooner; and if the house of the rich is founded upon a rock, he lives never the longer.

The holy patriarchs, *Abraham, Isaac,* and *Jacob,* inhabited no lofty cities, built no strongholds, but lived in tents or tabernacles, with which they removed from place to place, as God was pleased to order them, Heb. 11. 9; very remarkable in their case, in the land which God had promised to them for an inheritance: thereby signifying that they did not accept of the earthly land, but looked for a *better country, that is, an heavenly.* The *children of Israel,* journeying to Canaan, lived by encampments in a wilderness, removing their tents from place to place for forty years, and ending their days in that unsettled way of life. Even when the people were fixed in Canaan, good men still devoted themselves to live as sojourners and pilgrims; thus the *Rechabites,* who renounced the pleasures and possessions of the world, dwelt in tents as their holy fathers had done before, Jer. 35. 7. Even God himself was pleased to partake of the condition of his people; making himself even under the law, that stranger upon earth· which he was to be afterwards under the Gospel as the place of his worship in the wilderness, and long afterwards, was not fixed as a house, but movable as a tent and a *tabernacle;* and when Christ the Word was made flesh he is said to have *tabernacled* amongst us; living as one who renounced this world and all its possessions; more unprovided with house and land than the foxes of the earth or the birds of the air. The passage from this world to the other is much more easy to those who live in this manner. The man of the world, who fixes his abode here, is violently torn away at his death, like the banyan tree pulled up by the roots, and has no prospect after it: but he who lives in a tent can easily remove.

It was an act of faith in *Abraham* to dwell in tabernacles in the land of promise as in a strange country. His practice in this respect was a perpetual confession that he regarded himself only as a stranger and traveller on the earth, and that "he looked for a city which hath foundations, whose builder and maker is God." The *feast of tabernacles* was appointed to remind the children of Israel of the wanderings of their forefathers in the wilderness (when they dwelt in tents), and thus to suggest to them continually the same thought, that this life is only a pilgrimage, and that our true home is elsewhere, that we have here no continuing city, but seek one to come. The Jews even now live in tents or booths made of trees when this feast comes round. Tents were sometimes placed on the house-tops, 2 Sam. 16. 22; sometimes under trees, Gen. 18. 8.

The Moguls lived often in tents, miles in circumference, which cost many lacs of rupees, being decorated with silk and gold; still they were but tents, and exposed to being blown down by storm or consumed by fire.

By faith the righteous continually regards the body as a tent or tabernacle, a frail and uncertain habitation, suited to the condition of one who is only a traveller to his true home, offering no effectual protection against the many dangers to which he is exposed—a dwelling-place which may be struck or taken down in a moment, opened to heat or cold, rain or lightning. Peter (1 Pet. 1. 14) regarded the putting off his tabernacle as emancipation. This short life is the first steps of a ladder, the top of which, like Jacob's, is lost in the glories of heaven.

Hebrew.—The corruptible body presseth down the soul;
The earthly tabernacle weigheth down the mind.

Bhagavatgita.—
As men abandon old and threadbare clothes to put on others new;
So casts the embodied soul its worn-out frame to enter other forms.

Telugu.—Though a vessel be broken a new one is easily procured. Is it, then, marvellous that after a man's death he should acquire a new body? 2 Cor. 5. 2.

Bengal.—When a cow dies, she is taken up and carried to the river. When a man dies they cover him up too, and do the same.

Turk.—The Tartar who lives in a city believes himself in prison.

Probodh Chandroday.—You should consider the society of friends as a momentary flash of lightning.

Shánti Shatak.—Our place is like a terrible wilderness; our body like a building with much fleshy lattice-work in it; our earthly friends are like travellers whom we meet by chance and are soon separated from.

Life a Vapour.—Jas. 4. 13, 14.

The *Lalita Vistara* compares life to the view of a dance—to the lightning—to a torrent rushing from the mountain,—and so said Sakhya Muni, the Budhist, when tempted to remain in his father's palace.

Shánti Shatak.—Human existence is like a bottomless gulph, and human life like the fleeting scum of its rolling waves.

Maha Mudgar.—Life is quivering like a drop of water on a lotus-leaf.

Firdusi.—
Look at the heavens, how they roll on,
And look at man, how soon he's gone;

A breath of wind and then no more—
A world like this should man deplore.

Bengal.—An employ the shadow of a cloud.

The Wages of Sin is Death.—Rom. 6. 23.

The wicked are said to be holden with the cord of their own sins, Prov. 5. 22; such was *Saul* : hence death to the wicked is called the king of terrors, Job 18. 14; it is likened to a wolf, Ps. 49. 14; a flood, Ps. 90. 5; darkness, Job 10. 22.

God's punishment of sin or wages is compared to dashing in pieces like a potter's vessel; treading down as the mire of the street or ashes; grinding to powder; melting as a snail; gnashing of teeth. Even in this life the wages are—sickness, Deut. 28. 59; famine, Mat. 24. 7; war; fear, Job 18. 11. In the next it will be the blackness of darkness, 2 Peter 2. 17; the wine of God's wrath, Rev. 14. 10; everlasting contempt, Dan. 12. 2.

The devil is a bad master; his servants work hard, they are fed with husks in this life, Luke 15. 16. The pay of sin is sickness, Lev. 26. 16; famine, Lev. 26. 19; war, Lev. 26. 17.

China.—Unjustly got wealth is snow sprinkled with hot water; lands improperly obtained are but sand-banks in a stream.

China.—When the melon is ripe it will drop of itself.

China.—The day will come when the tumour will be punctured.

Urdu.—The cow will speak in the thief's belly, Gen. 4. 10.

Malay.—When is it the ants die if not in sugar?

Providence a Wall of Fire to protect the Good.
Zech. 2. 5.

Babylon had walls 300 feet high and 70 feet thick, so that six carriages could drive abreast, yet the city was taken owing to the gates having been left open when the people were drunk. The walls of Gaur in Bengal were

100 feet high. The walls of *Jericho* were high, but they fell down at the command of God, Jos. 6. 20, who often destroys walls by earthquakes.

Eastern shepherds and travellers, to protect themselves and their flocks from wild beasts at night, make fires all around them, over which the most furious animals dare not pass, not even the tiger,—being afraid of fire.

The righteous is travelling as a pilgrim through this world, a howling wilderness; the devil is a dragon, and the wicked as lions are ready to devour him, but he sleeps secure, surrounded with God a Wall of Fire; so the Jews walked through the Red Sea, the waters standing up on both sides as a wall, Ex. 14. 22.

Turk.—The nest of a blind bird is made by God.

Russian.—Without God not to the threshold, with him beyond the sea.

Veman.—Just as a showman plays his puppets, while he lies hidden, so does the Deity, while he conceals himself, admirably govern man.

No Discharge in Death's Warfare.—Eccl. 8. 8.

Death is a warfare in which the arrows of pain and fear are discharged, Eccles. 8. 8. The wicked are driven away by death, and all their joys end; the righteous desire to depart, and all their sorrows end. Death is abolished by taking away its sting—sin, 2 Tim. 1. 10.

Turk.—Death is a black camel which kneels at every man's gate.

Arab.—Caution secures not cowards against death; it comes from the sky.

Urdu.—He who is prepared to die, what will he not attempt?

Arab.—When fate arrives the physician becomes a fool.

Tamul.—The ocean is knee deep to him who is dying.

Turk.—There are two things which no man fixedly regards, the sun and death.

Sanskrit.—All rivers go to the ocean.

Bengal.—The rain never streams up the thatch.

Bengal.—The milk once drawn never enters the cow's dug again.

Afghan.—My father died and his fever ended—*i.e.*, death settles all accounts.

The Beginning of Strife, the Letting out of Water.

PROV. 17. 14.

A narrow channel cut in a dam will soon enlarge itself and make a wide breach. So with strife. The strife between the herdsmen led to the separation of Abraham and Lot, Gen. 13. 5; Paul and Barnabas separated, Acts 15. 39. Daniel, dreading the beginning of sin, would not take even the king's meat, Dan. 1. 8–16. They felt that sin was first thin like a spider's web, but soon becomes thick like a cart rope.

Urdu.—Let him touch your finger he will soon seize your wrist. So Solomon, 2 Kings 23. 13; Peter, Mat. 26. 34, 58, 64.

Tamul.—Will the flood that has burst the dam return to it at one's cry?

Persian.—The tree that has just taken root may be pulled up by the strength of a man.

Veman.—If there be one dry tree in a forest, it will produce flame by friction and sweep away the rest; thus if a base wretch be born in a noble race, he will destroy it all.

Bengal.—Going in a needle, coming out a ploughshare.

Bengal.—One drop of filth from a cow will spoil a vessel of milk.

Chanak.—To pay off debts, quench a fire, and remove disease is good, for should they increase, they will not be stopped.

Italian.—If thou suffer a calf to be put on you, they will soon put on the cow.

Spaniard.—Give me to sit down, I shall soon make a place to lie down.

Tamul.—Where there are dogs there is quarrelling.

Servian.—Out of one quarrel one hundred sins.

The Dead as Water spilled upon the Ground.

2 Sam. 14. 14.

The dead return no more to this world; they are as water spilled on the ground which cannot be gathered up again, like Pharaoh and his host which went to the bottom of the Red Sea (Ex. 15. 10), or David when he lost his child, and stopped weeping, saying—I shall go to him but he shall not return to me, 2 Sam. 12. 23; Job 14. 1–21.

Solomon uses a similar emblem of the *tree* fallen rising no more, Eccl. 11. 3. The sound of the woodman's axe gives note that some giant of the forest is about to fall: soon the crashing boughs tell plainly that the work is done, and the pride of the summer foliage is brought down to the ground. A gap is made in the screen of wood, and the eye can now wander over the soft meadows, and the distant village, that were hid before. The fallen tree lies in the direction in which it fell. While it still flourished in its pride and glory, the direction as well as the period of its fall was uncertain. It was possible that it might fall toward the north, or toward the south: nor was there any reason why it should not enjoy the sunshine and the rain through many a verdant summer. But the word was given that the axe should be laid unto its root; and now the direction in which it should fall is no more a question. It is a fixed and unalterable fact. The period during which one or the other direction could have been given to its fall is past and gone for ever. So the stroke of death fixes the direction and the character of our future state of being,

Malabar.—Can you draw out the water that has been absorbed by a piece of iron?
Japan.—A fallen blossom does not return to the twig.
Gujerat.—The deed is forgotten, but not what is written.
Tamul.—If rice be spilled it may be picked up, but can water?
Gujerat.—Drowning yourself the world is drowned.

China.—The roots of an old tree in the earth you may find;
But a dead man is fully cut off from his kind.

Badage.—As long as you hold it in your hand it is a vessel, fling it on the ground you have only useless pieces.

The Wicked pass away as a Whirlwind.—PROV. 10. 25.

In eastern countries so rapid and impetuous sometimes is the whirlwind, that it is in vain to think of flying; the swiftest horse, though running a mile in two minutes, or the fastest sailing ship, could be of no use to carry the traveller out of danger. Torrents of burning sand roll before it, the firmament is enveloped in a thick veil, and the sun appears of the colour of blood. In the frightful deserts of Senaar is pointed out a spot among some sandy hillocks, where the ground seemed to be more elevated than the rest, where one of the largest caravans which ever came out of Egypt, to the number of several thousand camels, was covered with sand, and every one perished.

The destruction of Sennacherib's army was probably effected under the direction of an angel by the blast of the hot pestilential south wind blowing from the deserts of Lybia, called the simoom. Sennacherib and his immense army had come like a whirlwind, threatening to bear down all before them, but they quickly vanished; 185,000 Assyrians being destroyed in one night, 2 Kings 19. 35. The world of the ungodly perished by the flood, Gen. 7. 21. In one day 23,000 Israelites who had joined Baal-peor, were killed, Numb. 25. 4.

Afghan.—Priority is good in all things but death. Sinners often die in a rage, like a poisoned rat in a hole.

The life of the wicked like a whirlwind rises *suddenly*, Acts 2. 2. Jonah's ship was caught in a whirlwind, Jon. 1. 4; it is very *swift*, hence said to have wings, 2 Sam. 22. 14; *very destructive*, 1 Kings 19. 11; yet God who holds the winds in his fists, Pro. 30. 4, made a whirlwind to serve as Elijah's chariot to heaven, 2 Kings 2. 11.

Canara.—When the washerman's corpse is brought out, his secrets may be discovered—*i.e.*, in the clothes he has stolen, Is. 15. 4.

Veman.—How long does the ball retain its elevation?

Afghan.—When the knife is over a man's head, he remembers God.

Hebrew.—The hope of the ungodly is like dust (thistledown), that is blown away with the wind: like a thin froth that is driven away with the storm; like as the smoke which is dispersed here and there with a tempest, and passeth away as the remembrance of a guest that tarrieth but a day.

What wicked army passed away as a whirlwind?

The Worm of Conscience.—Mark 9. 48.

Conscience compared to a worm in three points.

1. Sprung from *filth;* earth is a dunghill; 2. *produce death* by gnawing the internals, so Herod was eaten up of worms; 3. source of great *pain,* Acts 12. 23; 4. *medicine,* required, otherwise no internal cure.

Conscience is compared to a candle; such Joseph's brethren found it; Gen. 42. 21, 44. 16; Pharaoh, Ex. 9. 27, 10. 17; Saul, 1 Sam. 24; Herod, Mark 6. 26; Judas, Matt. 27. 4; Felix, Acts 24. 25. It is called a witness, Rom. 1. 9, as Cain's wounded spirit led him to wander as a vagabond.

Bengal.—No sin is hidden to the soul: only strike the ground, and the guilty start up in terror.

Russian.—The horse may run quick, but he cannot run away from his tail.

China.—Men who never violate their consciences are not afraid if you knock at their door at midnight.

Telugu.—When the thief, who stole the pumpkin, was spoken of, he felt his shoulders—*i.e.*, thinking some mark might have been left there.

Arab.—The worms of the vinegar are from the vinegar itself—*i.e.*, family disagreements are from the family itself.

Tamul.—To a gloomy eye all obscure things are demons.

Man a Worm—Job 25. 5, 6.

(*Man like a worm in five points.*)

The *Shánti Shatak* compares the wicked to dogs who delight in swallowing human bones filled with worms and moisture, eagerly licking the putrid juice as if it were palatable. Man is compared in the Bible to earth, dust, grass, a lie, vanity, in this text to a worm.

The butterfly spreads its wings, and the sun shines upon its plumes! The wisdom of the Creator has adorned it with beautiful lines, and painted it with glorious colours! It flies about and finds the plant which is proper to feed its brood of caterpillars; and there it lays its eggs to be hatched by the sun. In its infant state it crawls about as a helpless worm, and feeds upon green leaves. Then it folds itself up in a case like a coffin, where it lies, as it were, asleep, till the time of its change: when it breaks this covering, it comes forth with wings and feathers like painted birds, to fly about the air, and the dew of the fields and meadows, and visit every sweet and pleasant flower. The white ant in India also has its change when it gets wings.

We are now like the infant worms crawling about upon this earth. But if we go on in the ways of God we shall at length be changed from a worm into an angel. But first we must be shut up in the grave, and hide ourselves in the state of death till the resurrection. Then we shall be raised to life and liberty, and put on a spiritual body, and be able to visit and enjoy all the wonders of God's works, such as poor helpless mortals cannot now see or understand. O! let us not forfeit this expectation for the sake of such low enjoyments as caterpillars are capable of—grovelling on the earth!

The worm of the text means that kind which breeds in flesh, such as the worms that came out of the manna which was reserved contrary to God's commands, Ex. 16. 24.

1. *Earth sprung,* from corruption and putrefaction, so man was made of clay, Gen. 2. 7; he loves earthly things, and feeds like swine on the dunghill of vice.

2. *Mean looking,* so is man by sin, though once in God's image and very beautiful.

3. *Frail,* trod on easily: so man's life is sometimes ended by a fly or a bit of bread; a worm cannot easily escape from dangers, it becomes like seed a prey to fowls, Mat. 13. 4; Herod was eaten up of worms, Acts 12. 23; great men, like glowworms at night, may seem great, but in the morning they are like others.

4. *Various kinds,* but all are worms, so the silkworm which spins its dress out of its own bowels, the muck-worm, the glowworm, the caterpillar, Joel 1. 4, the palmer-worm, Am. 4. 9.

5. *Abode* means suitable to those who dwell in it. Job calls the grave his house, Job 17. 13; yet God says, fear not, thou worm Jacob, Is. 41. 14; though man is now a worm yet he will hereafter nestle above the clouds.

The Tongue fires the Wheel of Nature.—Jas. 3. 6.

"This course of nature," means the *wheel* of nature; and refers to a wheel catching fire from its rapid motion, spreading its flames around, and so destroying the whole machine, if not carefully greased or oiled to prevent friction or hard rubbing; so will the words of the tongue inflame the mind, and burn up the whole body with the fever of passion, and the whole heart with anger, if the oil of love and humility be not applied. The tongue sets on fire the wheel of human life, and thus destroys the whole life. So Korah's party, speaking evil of dignities, were punished, Num. 16. 1.

Modern Greek.—The tongue has no bones, yet it breaks bones.

Afghan.—May you never eat that leek which will rise up in your own throat—*i.e.*, eat your own words.

Turk.—The tongue kills more than the sword.

Turk.—Two ears to one tongue, therefore hear twice as much as you speak.

Turk.—A laden ass brays not.

China.—A word once spoken an army of chariots cannot overtake it.

Urdu.—You might hold the hand that strikes you, but you cannot hold the tongue.

Persian.—A bad word is like the sound of a dome—*i.e.*, it echoes back.

Arab.—The heart is the treasury of the tongue.

Japan.—The tongue, only an ell long, is angry with the body, five feet long.

Bengal.—His tongue is a sweeper's shovel.

Telugu.—If your foot slip you may recover your balance, but if your mouth slips you cannot recall your words.

Syriac.—A foul-mouthed man is like a cobbler's scissors, which cuts nothing but impure leather.

Turk.—We heal the wounds of a knife but not those of the tongue.

Turk.—The tongue has no bone yet it crushes.

Turk.—The fool has his heart on his tongue: the wise his tongue on his heart.

Turk.—An eye without light as a tongue without reason.

Bengal.—Days go, words spoken remain.

Persian.—A long tongue makes life short.

Persian.—Take care lest your tongue should cut off your head.

Kural.—

> The burn will heal: but festering stays
> The wound a burning tongue conveys.

Badaga.—A famine may cease, but abusive words will be always remembered.

Hebrew.—To slip on the pavement is better than to slip with the tongue.

Badaga.—You may close a well, but you cannot shut the mouth of another.

Turk.—Who masters his tongue saves his head.

Tamul.—A slip of the tongue is worse than that of the feet.

PART II.

The Wicked deaf as an Adder to the Charmer's Voice.—Ps. 58. 5.

SUCH were Pharaoh; the Jews, Mat. 23. 37, Mark 8. 18.

The wicked are said to have *uncircumcised* ears, Acts 7. 51, heaping up teachers they have *itching* ears, 2 Tim. 4. 3, stopped at the cry of the poor, Pr. 21. 21.

There are four different kinds of hearers, those like a *sponge* that suck up good and bad together, and let both run out immediately—having ears, and hearing not; those like a *sand-glass* that let what enters in at one ear pass out at the other—hearing without thinking; those like a *strainer*, letting go the good and retaining the bad: and those like a *sieve*, letting go the chaff, and retaining the good grain.

Profession without practice is compared to failing fountains, shells empty of kernels, tares among wheat, Matt. 13, foolish virgins without oil, Mat. 25. 13, the mirage; lilies fair in show, foul in scent; dead fish which float down the stream, while living fish struggle against it.

Bengal.—In name he is *Dharmadas* (a servant of righteousness), but he has no virtue.

Chanak.—Knowledge only in books (without practice), and wealth in the hands of others, are of no use, as in the time of action they are not available.

Tamul.—The toad living near the lotus tastes not its

honey; the illiterate living near the learned remain ignorant.

Tamul.—Reciting from the Vedas to a cow about to gore you.

Telugu.—A bad man with your money, no men hear you call them to eat with you food.

Arab.—As food is useless to a sick body, so is advice to one in love with the world.

Tamul.—Will the cobra be affected by kindly intercourse?

China.—A word is enough for the wise; a stroke of a whip for a good horse.

Sanskrit.—Who are destitute of sight? Those who perceive not the future world. Who are the deafest? Those who listen not to good advice.

Malabar.—By closing the eyes it has become dark.

Sanskrit.—Who has no sense of his own, what will the Shastra do for him? What will a mirror do for him who has lost his eyes?

Sanskrit.—To address a judicious remark to a thoughtless man is merely threshing chaff.

Mahabharat.—He merely learned without understanding of his own learns not the sense of books; as a spoon does not taste the flavour of broth.

The Anchor of Hope.—Heb. 6. 19.

Every man has some kind of hope.

This world, full of uneasy cares and unlimited desires, is likened to the sea, which is ever restless; treacherous in its smiles; swept by frequent tempests; full of hidden rocks and quicksands, the ruin of many a gallant ship. Some on this sea make shipwreck concerning faith, 1 Tim. 1. 19; the Church of God has, however, to cross its wild and stormy waves before it can reach "the haven where it would be." The ark of Noah, borne up in safety above the waters of the flood, was in this respect a type of the Church of Christ.

Hope is also compared to a house built on the sand, Job 15. 2; or to a *helmet*, 1 Thes. 5. 8, protecting the head against spiritual enemies. The Arabs call a water-melon hope, because of its tendrils which cling to a prop. The merchant trades and the ploughman ploughs in hope. Hope deferred makes the heart sick, Prov. 13. 12, and the hope of the wicked is as the giving up of the ghost, Job 4. 20—*i.e.*, like the last puff of breath when the person is dying.

Hope is like an anchor in three points:—

1. The anchor *secures* the vessel against tides or storms, Heb. 6. 19.

2. The anchor is *out of sight,* so hope dwells on things invisible, as Abraham hoped against hope in reference to the birth of Isaac, waiting 25 years, Rom. 4. 18. So Paul in the case of shipwreck, Acts 24. 15.

3. This anchor *rests* on the ground: the spiritual anchor is fixed not on the mud of this world, but on the rock of ages.

Maha Mudgar.—Day and night, evening and morning, winter and spring come and go; time sports with our passing age, still the wind of hope ceases not. The body dissolves, the head gets grey, the mouth becomes toothless, the handsome stick trembles in the hand, yet hope ceases not to jest with us.

Arab.—He delighting in the world drinks the milk of vain hopes.

Bengal.—Dancing on an unbaked water-vessel.

Telugu.—Mountains are smooth at a distance and rugged when near.

Arab.—Worldly hope is like the mirage, deceiving him that sees it and hopes from it.

Telugu.—Measuring the air.

Talmud.—Be very humble, the hopes of men are worms.

Arab.—Hoping from the vile is seeking fat in a dog's tail.

Tamul.—The crane hoping to eat dried fish when the sea should be dried up, wasted away in vain hope.

Arab.—The more you hope the more you suffer.

The Arrows of God's Punishment.—Deut. 32. 42.

"Arrows" mean God's judgments on the wicked, which often fly through the world to punish them. The lightning and tempest, war, pestilence, and famine, all may be his arrows to slay the ungodly, and to cut them off from the earth. So God threatened the inhabitants of Jerusalem by his prophet, Ezekiel, and assured them that for their wickedness he would "send upon them the evil arrows of famine," Ez. 5. 16.

Arrows wound quickly and unexpectedly; no noise is made; they stick sharply in the wounds; such are God's arrows of *pestilence*, Ps. 91. 5; *famine*, as in David's case, and the *sword*; Job said (6. 4) God's arrows of *disease* and the sword were within him; God's arrows for crushing the wicked are compared to treading down the grapes in a wine-press, Rev. 19. 15.

Persian.—God's club makes no noise, when it strikes there is no cure for the blow.
Arab.—The corn goes from hand to head, but at last falls into the mill.
Turk.—Even the Indian elephant fears the gadfly.
Mahabharat.—When men are ripe for slaughter, even straws turn into thunderbolts.
Japan.—No escape from the net of heaven.

The Axe of Punishment at the Root of the Tree.
Mat. 3. 10–12.

Time has been figured as a scythe mowing down the grass; here God's vengeance is compared to an axe. The King of Assyria is so called, Is. 10. 15.

The Church of God is often likened to a vineyard or garden of fruit trees, from which the owner looks for fruit in due season, and too often finds none. He is unwilling, however, to relinquish his hope of a return for all his labour, and continues year by year to prune with the greatest skill, as well as patience, the plants which so ill-repay his toil.

However high and stately may be the tree, and however green and luxuriant its foliage, the time comes when the owner is tired with waiting for fruit, and trying the effect of only cutting off branches; he determines that he will lay the axe to the root, and remove the tree itself from the ground which might be so much better filled. See parable of Barren Fig Tree, Luke 13.

How fearfully the event, thus figuratively described, was accomplished, when the temple of Jerusalem was burnt, and the city taken by the Roman General; and how afterwards, when the nation rebelled against their conquerors, Jerusalem was utterly destroyed; and the miserable survivors sold in vast numbers as slaves!

What God wants is fruit, not leaves; however rich may be the foliage—in other words, however high the profession—it is utterly worthless in His sight, if there be not the true fruits of repentance.

The Soul bartered for the World.—MAT. 16. 26.

Buddhagosha.—Evils follow the fool, smouldering as fire covered by ashes.

Malay.—The loss of a little mustard-seed is observed, while that of an elephant is unknown.

China.—To gain a cat but lose a cow.

Badaga.—In trying to save a drop of ghe he upset the ghe pot.

Tamul.—Is the foot to be cut off to try on a shoe?

Badaga.—For the nourishment of a day he sacrificed the food of a year.

Tamul.—Like burning down the house for fear of rats.

Shánti Shatak.—How vainly have I passed the whole of my life! Alas! how inestimable a jewel have I bartered for mere glass.

Panchatantra.—The fool, in seeking riches, suffers one hundredfold more than he who strives to attain eternal happiness.

Hitopadesha.—It is right to sacrifice one person for a

household, a family for a village, a village even for one's country, but for one's soul we should give up the world.*

Turk.—For to save the head we sacrifice the beard.

Sinners are Blind.—Rev. 3. 17.

The *Atmabodh* states, "The eye of ignorance does not behold God, as a blind man does not see the light." Sinners are like the blind, who are not able to see the sun, to know what colours and lights are; they see not the dangers in the road, Mat. 15. 14. Those naturally blind regret not seeing the light of the sun, and desire a guide; not so those spiritually blind; the eyes of the rich man's understanding were not opened till he reached hell, where he lifted up his eyes, being in torment, Luke 16. 23.

The man in the tombs was naked; the wicked are also blind; they see not the light of life, discern not the sun of righteousness; have no true knowledge of spiritual objects; nothing is nearer them than God, his unspeakable gifts, and their own heart, yet nothing is less known. How oft they stumble and fall into sin without any proper cause! How constantly they wander out of their proper course, and mislead those who follow them! How useless is the clearest light of the Gospel to them!—hence they feed on the wind, Hos. 12. 1, and on husks, Luke 15. 16, Deut. 28. 29. Diseased in every way the wicked have the *blindness* of ignorance, the *deafness* of spiritual unconcern, the *fever* of impurity, the *jaundice* of malice, the *swelling tympany* of pride, the *vertigo* of inconstancy, the *dropsy* of covetousness, the *palsy* of stupidity, the *rottenness* of envy, the *rheumatism* of discontent, the *delirium* of constant levity, the moonstruck *madness* of passion and rage, hardness of heart, and the stings of conscience.

Chanak.—He who has no sense, what does the Shastra do for him? What does a mirror do for a man without eyes? What does an eloquent man

* *English.*—Sometimes the best gain is to lose. Mat. 5. 29.

where there are no hearers? What do washermen in a country of naked *fakirs?*

Sanskrit.—Is a lamp pleasing to the blind, a song to the deaf, or science to the fool?

Sanskrit.—He who regards other men's money as clods of earth, and all creatures as himself, he sees.

Persian.—He asked the blind man what did he want; he said the sight of my two eyes. Mat. 10. 46.

Servian.—Better sometimes a woman blind than one too beautiful.

The Book of Life.—REV. 20. 12.

There are the books of Nature, Providence, Revelation, and here "the Book of Life"—an allusion to the register book in which the names of all the tribes and families of Israel were entered from generation to generation, so that their claims to property and to the privileges of their fathers could not be disputed, or a reference to a custom in the courts of princes, of keeping a list of persons in their service, of the officers in the armies, and even of the names of their soldiers. When it is said that any one is "blotted out of the book of life," this signifies erased from the list of God's friends and servants, like as those guilty of treachery are struck off the roll or list of officers belonging to a prince. There are also books of *judgment,* which are said to be opened, and the dead judged out of them according to their works, Rev. 20. 12; alluding to a custom of the Persians, to write down every day what had happened, the services done for the king, and the rewards given to those who had performed them, as we see in the history of Ahasuerus and Mordecai, recorded in the Book of Esther. Ex. 32. 32.

This book of life is the *oldest* book, Rev. 13. 8; it is written in Heaven, Heb. 12. 23; time destroys not its writing as it does that on tombs or pillars. The life it writes of is spiritual life, which differs from natural life in —(1) the *Holy Spirit* being the parent, 1 Cor. 15. 45; there is hidden manna to eat, John 6. 55; (2) *eternal.*

Natural life is common to devils, worms, trees, flies; man dies as the beast, but lives for ever in his soul. Life preserves from corruption, so does spiritual life.

Who are Brands plucked from the Burning.—ZECH. 3. 2.

The fire is already blackening and scorching the brand; but there is yet time to snatch it from the flame, and to save it for some nobler use. Linger not, but seize it, ere too late. Another minute, and you could not have plucked it from the fire. It bears the marks of the peril from which it has been scarcely saved; but having thus far concerned yourself to preserve it, you will not lightly throw it back again in to the flame. All we are as brands plucked out of the fire, and bear indeed the marks of the scorching flame; but God has not plucked out the brand only to cast it into a yet fiercer furnace. The Apostle Judas bid us, "save others with fear, pulling them out of the fire." Each of us is as a brand plucked out of the fire; and it is owing to the distinguishing mercy of God that we were not left in the guilt of original sin, or were not left to perish in our sin's fuel for hell fire.

Persian.—**He should be exposed to danger of death in order that he may be content with fever.**

Doing Good is Bread cast on the Waters.—ECCL. 11. 1.

In the East rice is sown upon the waters, but before sowing, the ground, while still covered with water, is trodden by oxen which go mid-leg deep; and as the rice is sown on the water so it springs up through the water, and the height of its stem is generally in proportion to the depth of the water on the surface of the soil.

It is in reference to this practice of the rice in the rains being formed into balls, and sunk in water, that the passage in Is. 32. 20, is to be explained, "Blessed are ye that sow beside all waters." In Egypt a rice crop comes up in six months.

The relief given in secret to a stranger, who may never be seen again, shall be blessed not only to him, but still more surely to the donor; it shall be found after many days; so Abraham entertained angels, Heb. 13. 2, who afterwards requited him. And the same may be said of the word of good advice, given "in season" to some one at a period of brief intercourse; nor shall any effort fail of due fruit, by which persons have shown forth their love to Christ their Saviour, Mat. 10. 42, Luke 19. 16.

The corn-seed thrown into the mud, at the subsidence of the Nile, seems lost, but nothing is lost that is done for God. The fruit will be found at the resurrection of the just, Luke 14. 14; so also is the case with instruction, Is. 55. 10, Prov. 19. 17, charity is loan to God.

Persian.—Give in this world, receive in the next (Mat. 10. 42).

Turk.—What you give in charity in this world you take with you after death. Do good and throw it into the sea—if the fish does not know it God does.

Russian.—Throw bread and salt behind you, you get them before you.

God a Builder.—Heb. 11. 10.

God as a builder different from earthly builders in five points.

A good builder must be clever to *plan*, so known to God are all his works; there was the pattern on the Mount, Heb. 8. 5; he lays a *good foundation*, so God laid the pillars of the earth; man's foundation has often bad materials in it; employ a variety of *workmen*, so God has angels, men, Nature, the firmament, in his hands, Ps. 19. A *variety* of work—God made the fountains of the great deep, the windows of heaven, hell the prison, and paradise the garden; he tells the number of the stars.

Earthly builders are mortal; limited in knowledge; build for others: improve in their plans; require materials for a building. *Abraham* looked for a city without foundations, Heb. 11. 10. The *Telegus* compare one who uses bad agents to one scratching his head with a firebrand; but God can make the wrath of man to praise him, Ps. 76. 10.

The Burden of Sin.—Mat. 11. 30.

A burthen *presses* heavily on the chest as the tenderest part, so sin on the heart, provided it be not past feeling, Eph. 5. 14; Christ, pressed by the weight of the world's sins, sweat blood, Luke 22. 44; a burthen *impedes* action, so does sin, Heb. 12. 1; believers are to bear one another's burthens, Gal. 6. 6; not so did the priest who passed by on the other side of the way, Luke 10. 31; the Jewish law ordered one to relieve even the ass of an enemy. Sin is to be carried not as a golden chain round the neck, but as an iron chain round the feet. The devil, when he mocked Eve, did not see sin a burthen, neither did the old world when it ridiculed Noah's building the ark, Gen. 3. 4. 5. A burthen is *unpleasant*.

China.—Forethought is easy, repentance is hard.
Bengal.—Faith in God is the root of all devotion; deliverance from evil is only her servant.
Japan.—Good physic is bitter.

Trusting in Riches compared to a Camel passed through a Needle's Eye.—Mat. 1. 24.

When Christ says it is easier for a camel to go through a needle's eye than for a rich man to enter the kingdom of heaven, he meant those who *trusted* in riches rather than in God, those who use riches for purposes of pride, oppression, sensuality, Jas. 2. 6; as Haman, Esth. 5. 11, *Esau*, Gen. 36. 7; for *Abraham* was a rich man yet good,

Gen. 13. 2; so were *Isaac*, Gen. 26. 13; so *Joseph*, Gen. 45. 8; *Joseph of Arimathea*, Mat. 27. 57.

Oriental.—Unmitigated evil is as rare
As wings upon a cat, or flowers of air,
As rabbits' horns, or ropes of tortoise hair.

Bengal.—Putting an elephant into a narrow dish; a horse's eggs, or a flower in the air.

Cingalese.—Like seeking feathers from turtles.

Telugu.—Like fixing a pump in the sea.

Talmud.—To let a camel go through the hole of a needle.

Persian.—A needle's eye is wide enough for a friend; the whole world is too narrow for foes.

The Wicked are Captives.—2 TIM. 2. 26.

Truth only makes free. Christ, in his first sermon which he preached at Nazareth, stated he came as a Redeemer to purchase the captives. Men are captives to—(1) *sin*, Rom. 7. 14—26; ancient tyrants fastened captives to a dead body face to face until they were suffocated by the stench; (2) *Satan*, 2 Tim. 2. 26; (3) the *Law*, Gal. 4. 25; (4) *Death*, in Heb. 2. 15, called the king of terrors. The believer's body may be captive, but his mind is free as in Paul's case.

Captives in war were often stripped naked, and thrown into a dungeon; their eyes were put out, as Zedekiah's, 2 Kings 25. 7; or as the Mahrattas gouged out the eyes of the Great Mogul in Delhi; they were often loaded with chains, devoured by vermin, fed on bread and water, living in darkness among rats.

Bengal.—One at the will of another, an ox with his nose pierced.

Japan.—The bird that flies upward does not ruffle the water.

Telugu.—A scorpion under a shoe—*i.e.*, held under restraint.

Choked with Care.—LUKE 8. 14.

Cast thy burthen on the Lord, Ps. 55. 22; *Ruth* committed her cares to God, Ruth 1. 16, 2. 12; so *Ezra* in the desert, Ezr. 8. 21–23, 32.

China.—Past events as clear as a mirror, future as dark as lacquer.

Bengal.—Anxiety is the fever of the mind; the burning sun acts like a fever on clothes.

Turk.—To everyone his own care, the miller's is water.

Turk.—You cannot contract for the fish in the sea.

Turk.—Sorrow is to the soul what the worm is to wood.

Malay.—To grind pepper for a bird on the wing—*i.e.*, care for uncertainties.

Bengal.—Grass at a distance looks thick.

Sanskrit.—Mountains are beautiful at a distance, rugged when near.

Bengal.—My mind is troubled in collecting money to pay the rent, how then can I worship Vishnu?

Russian.—Rust eats iron, care the heart.

Arab.—A heart free from care better than a full purse.

Oriental.—The grief of the morrow is not to be eaten to-day. Mat. 6. 11.

Bengal.—The ant's wings grow to its own death.

Hitopadesha.—Strive not too anxiously for thy support, thy Maker will provide. No sooner is a man born than milk for his support streams from the breast.

Chastity.

Samson, a giant, was made a dwarf in soul through his passions; he ground in fetters of brass, Judg. 16. 20. Lot was vexed with the filthy conversation of Sodom.

Kural.—Of what avail are prisons barred,
For chastity is woman's guard.

Hebrew.—Impurity in the beginning like a spider's web, in the end like a cart rope.

Tamul.—Beauty without chastity, a flower without fragrance.

Solomon.—A bad woman's lips a honeycomb, her end wormwood. Prov. 5. 3.

Badaga.—The unchaste will vanish away like a handful of mud. Is. 51. 6.

God Chastises his Spiritual Sons.—HEB. 12. 6, 8–11.

Chastisement is compared to a *fan*, Mark 3. 12; a *pruning* hook, John 15. 2; plough, Jer. 4. 3; a *furnace*, like Egypt to the Jews, Is. 48. 10; *cords*, Job 36. 8.

In Jer. 31. 18, Ephraim is represented chastised by God as a *bullock* unaccustomed to the yoke; the bullock *rebels* against the will of his master, though nourished and supported by him; it will not *subserve* his interests; when chastised, it rebels the more; *repeated strokes* only serve to inflame its rage; nor will it ever submit until it be wearied out, and unable to maintain its opposition; thus the sinner generally fights against God.

God chastised Solomon and David for their improvement; but he punished Saul with death for his offering sacrifice and sparing Agag, 1 Sam. 15; *Peter's* denial of Christ was worse than Ananiah's denial of a portion of his goods; yet how different the punishment. Pain is God's chiselling to produce his likeness.

Christ learnt obedience from suffering, Heb. 5. 8; so the Prodigal, Luke 15. 17; and we are silly *sheep*, prosperity makes us stray the more, as sunshine on the dunghill only produces a greater stench, so Jas. 1. 2.

The Germans say a child may have too much of its mother's blessing. Better the child *weep* than the father. The Spaniards say more sprigs in the garden than the gardener ever sowed. Did God *hate* his people, he would suffer them to go merrily to hell. Calm weather lets Christ sleep; the storm rouses him.

Fruits of Chastisement:—

1. *Tests reality*, as Solomon's *sword* did the true mother, 1 Kings 3; as the *storm* did Peter's faith, Mat. 14. 30–31; a *painted faith* no more avails than a painted helmet.

2. *Fructifies*, as the palm-tree, by pressure, so prayer, as

with Manasseh in fetters, 2 Ch. 33; so Paul when blind, Acts 9. 9; the hammer of chastisement squares the stones for the heavenly temple.

3. Not a mark of vengeance for sin, Job 42. 10; Paul's, Acts 28. 4; Siloam's tower, Luke 13. 4–5. Saint *Ambrose* would not stop a night in the house of a man who had never seen chastisement, lest some judgment should seize him.

4. *Peaceable fruits:* the Prodigal, in some points, happier among *swine* than he had been in his father's house.

Unsanctified affliction *parboils* a wicked man for hell; to the righteous affliction is not a fiery, but a brazen, serpent. God beats his children as we do our *clothes* in the sun only to beat out the moths. *Manasseh* got more good by his iron chain than by his golden chain.

Hitopadesha.—On affliction's touchstone a man may learn the value of his family and of his own mind.

Persian.—Without a supple rod the ox or ass would not obey.

Malay.—As a hen pecks her chickens—*i.e.*, lightly.

Afghan.—Until you heat iron you will not lengthen it—*i.e.*, punishment makes the obstinate tractable.

Tamul.—Is it proper to tame a parrot and give it into the claws of a cat?

Afghan.—The prick of a needle on a cat's head is plenty.

Gujerat.—Water on a stone wets but enters not.

Russian.—No bones are broken by a mother's fist.

Vemana.—The washerman torments the cloth to take the stains out, and then folds it. What then though he who teaches thee chastises thee.

Prabodh Chandroday.—After mortifying the body, pure spirit is discerned by reason, as rice is separated from the husk by beating it.

Sanskrit.—A bad man, gold, a drum, a bad woman, a bad horse, stalks of sugarcane, sesamur seed, and low people, should be beaten to improve their qualities.

Tamul.—A fruit must ripen of itself, must not be beaten by a cane into ripeness.

Humble as little Children.—Mat. 18. 2.

Christ the Lord of Glory became an infant wrapped in swaddling clothes; he carried the lambs of the flock in his own bosom. When his disciples repelled them he took the little children up in his arms and blessed them, and he has used children as an emblem of humility. He was a teacher of babes, and has taught us humility by babes, and particularly when the disciples disputed about pre-eminence he set a child in the midst. See parable of Marriage Feast, Luke 14. 7–11.

The humble like little children in six points.

1. *Docile;* no prejudice, no habit to prevent its receiving impressions, "train up a child in the way he should go," Pr. 22. 6, so believers are made new men by the Spirit; the mind of a child is compared to a sheet of white paper on which you can write anything. David calls himself a weaned child, Ps. 131. 2.

2. *Confiding;* the young of animals are not so dependent in reference to the world as are infants. This, however, causes more love. The mother's smile and breast are everything to the helpless babe; so the believer depends entirely on God for many years; the father's house is its home. "Ask and ye shall receive; so Abraham went forth, not knowing whither he went," Heb. 11. 8. Jacob in the same spirit went down to Egypt. Moses forsook Egypt, not fearing the king. Paul said, I know in whom I have believed.

3. *Humble and contented with little things.* Christ said, I am meek and lowly in heart. Paul said, in whatever state I am, I have learned to be content, Phil. 4. 11; submissive obedience is easily taught to a child; so with the believer every high thing is cast down; whom the Lord loveth He chasteneth.

4. *Simple-minded;* a child tells its meaning at once, its desires and aversions; so the believer has God's glory as

his sole guide. "Behold an Israelite indeed, in whom is no guile," John 1. 47. Still, to prevent imposition in the world, the wisdom of the serpent is to be united to the harmlessness of the dove. Gentle love to be without dissimulation, anger endures only for a little. The Christian does good unto all, especially to those of the household of faith.

5. *Detached from the world*, 1 Cor. 15. 20; to it business, ambition, wealth, pleasures are nothing; on the Exchange it would find no pleasure, "not a grey head upon green shoulders; so the believer is not conformed to the world; his joys a stranger intermeddles not with; weeping as though they wept not, 1 Cor. 7. 30.

6. *Attached to its father's house.* Early recollections lead him to it as a bird to its nest; so Jacob, domesticated in Padan-Aram, longed for his father's house; so Joseph when he saw his brethern; so the believer longs for heaven, as the hart after the water brooks, for Jerusalem above is his home, we in this tabernacle groan.

China.—Who flies not high, falls not low.
Malay.—The leech wants to become a snake.
Russian.—The blind cannot see, the proud will not.
China.—A great tree attracts the wind.
Arab.—His nose looks to heaven, his legs are in the water.
Persian.—The bending of the humble is the graceful droop of the branches laden with fruit.
Turk.—A low ass is easy to ride on.
Bengal.—Can the boat bear the ship's mast?
Sanskrit.—Fruitful trees bend down; the wise stoop; a dry stick and a fool can be broken not bent.
Persian.—The humble man is like the earth which alike kisses the feet of the king and of the beggar.
Japan.—No standing in the world without stooping.
Syriac.—If you mount not on the ladder, you will not get on the roof—*i.e.*, submission to a superior, the way to be superior.

Death of Righteous as a Shock of Corn.—Job 5. 26.

Death of righteous like shock of corn in eight points.

The wicked are compared to weeds to be burned, but the righteous to corn in the harvest. See parable of Taret and Wheat, Mat. 13. Autumn after the hot season is pleasant, a time of the joy of harvest, Is. 9. 3; the righteous in death is compared in the text to the cutting of grain and to harvest home.

1. *Sown* in order to be reaped again; at first the leaf is fresh, and the stalk firm, but not so beautiful as when the stalk is thin, and the leaf sere, but grain yellow; so the body must die to be raised again.

2. *Require preparatory agency;* so *showers* of grace to nourish the sun of God's favour and harden the grain, the *dews* of the Spirit to refresh, and the *winds* of affliction to keep the roots loose. Jacob, not knowing the preparatory agency, said, All things are against me, Gen. 42. 36, when he was on the eve of great prosperity; God's chastening gives the peaceable fruits of righteousness.

3. *Only cut when fully ripe;* if cut too soon the ear is watery, if too late dried up; the sower waits for the early and latter rain, the wicked are driven away, but the righteous are always prepared by hope, Prov. 14. 32; Abijah and Josiah had their harvest in early youth; Noah and Abraham in advanced years.

4. *The ripe corn is handled with care;* the scythe of death is put to the roots, but the sheaves are bound up with care. Lazarus was nursed by dogs in life, but angels took charge of him in death, Luke 16. 21; many grains in the natural harvest are lost, but not so with the righteous, John 10. 28.

5. *When ripe housed in safety;* there may be anxiety about the weather, but harvest home is a time of joy; the grain is lodged in the granary; no more tears.

6. *When ripening hangs its head;* so with increasing humility the righteous see more of their sin and of God's

goodness; Job repented in dust and ashes, Job 42. 6; so Peter took off his coat at first through zeal, but finally *waits* to put off his tabernacle, 2 Pet. 1. 14; so Paul at first calls himself the least of the Apostles, next less than the least of all saints, finally chief of sinners.

7. *Ripening becomes weighty;* the believer, a father in grace, has a zeal and love with a steadier flame; his graces are complete; hope with joy makes not ashamed.

8. Ripening corn becomes gradually *looser*, less need of the earth, so Paul learned to be in all things content; the worldling is attached to a shadow, but Paul thinks the world only dung.

9. Ripening easily *distinguished from tares* by the smell and fruit; the righteous bring forth fruit in old age, Ps. 92. 15; tares are then distinguished from wheat.

10. Ripened corn more *susceptible of injury*, as showers or wind may lay it level, so Jacob on his bed said, My soul, come not thou into their secret, Gen. 49. 6; David wished for wings like a dove to flee away.

11. Ripened corn apt to *fall* of its own accord, so Paul wished to depart. The righteous seek a heavenly country, Heb. 11. 16; hence no tears for them, Rev. 7. 14; they are clad in white robes.

Turk.—Weep not over the dead but over the fool.

Canara.—An old man may have a youthful heart; a poor man may have a noble inclination.

Canara.—Nothing like newness in clothes, like age in men.

Oriental.—A good old man is like old wine which has deposited its lees.

Arab.—The remembrance of youth is a matter of sighing; the remembrance of death refreshes the heart.

Raghuvansa.—The men of feeble mind think the death of a friend a thorn fixed within the heart, whereas the wise men look on it as extracted—for death is the gate to happiness.

Raghuvansa.—The king performed the obsequies for his deceased wife, of whom nothing, except her virtue, was left.

Charity covers a Multitude of Sins.—Prov. 10. 12.

Love pours water not oil on the flame, so with a conciliatory demeanour; love has a large mantle to hide faults; so with Christ and his disciples, Mat. 26. 31, 41; John 20. 25–27.

Talmud.—To love a thing makes the eye blind, the ear deaf.
Arab.—Love is the companion of blindness.
Galic.—Faults are thick where love is thin.

Let the Dead bury their Dead.—Mat. 8. 22.

One of Christ's disciples asked him leave of absence to go and bury his father. He replied, Your business is to preach my religion, and let those who are dead to God attend to burying the dead. A man in England, who lived to the age of 84, but was converted when 80 years old, had the inscription on his tomb:—"Died, aged 4 years,"—*i.e.*, he reckoned that he was only really alive when he served God.

To be carnally minded is death, saith St. Paul, Rom. 8. 6; and the poor *Prodigal son* in the parable, having lived in that state of mind till his conversion, the father says of him: "This thy brother was dead, and is alive again," Luke 15. 24. Man has a soul and body, each of which dies in its own way; and so either of them may be alive while the other is dead. There is a sense in which *Adam* died on the day when he sinned; and there is another sense in which Adam lived 930 years. Adam delivered down a natural life to all us that are born of him; but the only inheritance he could leave to our spirits was that death to which he was fallen. It is this death of the spirit which makes it necessary for every man to be born again.

There are multitudes of people who seem to live but are no better than dead; they are unburied dead; in them no sight, no sense of spiritual things, no appetite, no affection for them. We may preach to them all day long, and do no more good by it than if we were to preach to a man in his coffin. If we were to cry into their ears, or blow a trumpet to give them warning of the fire of judgment, and of eternal damnation, they would hear nothing. If we offer to them the bread of life, they want it not; for a dead man hath no appetite. Were the souls of men as visible as their bodies, we should see as much difference betwixt devout believers and the children of the world as between a living, healthy body and a corpse. They are *twice dead,* as Jude 12 saith, dead once by nature and dead again unto grace. The pleasures of this world will extinguish the life of a believer; she that liveth unto this world is dead while she liveth, 1 Tim. 5. 6. All heavenly affections will die. On the other hand Abel while dead yet spoke—*i.e.,* by his works.

Sanskrit.—A man of evil repute is, though living, as one dead.

China.—Let the dead care for the dead, the living for the living; *i.e.,* in reference to excessive sorrow for the dead.

Kural.—He lives whose life in love is led:
Another reckons with the dead.

Arab.—A benefactor is alive though removed to the mansions of the dead, Heb. 11. 4.
The wicked is dead though in the mansions of the living.

Persian.—Whose soul is alive, his sensual desires are dead.

Syriac.—Seek death to obtain life.

Persian.—When I am dead the world is dead.

The Congregation of the Dead and the Fool.

Prov. 21. 16.

Eight marks of fools.

1. *Understand not* who will show them any good, Ps. 4. 6; prefer corn to peace; *beasts* in man's form.

2. *Hurt themselves;* run into a hornet's nest, play with serpents; harbour a thief in the house.

3. *Strive with one stronger;* so the potsherd with its maker, Ps. 2. 9. God has even frogs, worms, and everything at his disposal.

4. *Take brass for gold;* so the mean things of earth for heaven, Phil. 3. 8.

5. *Feed on ashes, among swine,* Is. 44, 20, Luke 15. 16; so the Prodigal son; he labours for the wind, Ecc. 5. 15.

6. *Sow when they should reap.* So a death-bed repentance.

7. *Delight in mischief,* Ps. 28. 3.

8. To save their hat *lose* their head.

Chanak.—In the dusk we lose our way, and a fallen woman is like a corpse.

Syrian.—Seek death to obtain life—*i.e.*, kill passion to save your soul.

Syriac.—Put not a candle before a wall—*i.e.*, by teaching a fool.

Turk.—The fool is a cock which sings at the wrong time.

Turk.—Making a fool understand is like making a camel leap a ditch.

Drunkenness.—Eph. 5. 18.

Exemplified in Noah, Gen. 9. 21; Belshazzar, Dan. 5. 4; Nineveh, Nah. 1. 10.

Finnish.—The anvil proves the iron, the drink the man.

Turk.—Vagabonds are at home in the drinking-shop.

Russian.—A drunkard's money is in his hand but goes through his fingers.

Russian.—Drink one day, a headache the whole week.
Russian.—A drunken peasant will fight with a turnip.

Riches have Wings like an Eagle.—Prov. 23. 5.

The eagle is the king of birds; he has long wings; he can carry off a sheep in his talons, and fly high above the storms and lightning. Wings mark speed; hence the expression, wings of the wind, Ps. 104. 3. Ships are said to have wings, Is. 18. 1—*i.e.*, their sails. The four wings of riches are, water, fire, debts, thieves. If *Nebuchadnezzar* be in the palace among his nobles anon, he is soon in the park among the beasts. *Adonijah* was one day on the throne, on another seeking refuge for his life at the horns of the altar. *Zedekiah*, on Jerusalem being taken, saw his sons slain before his eyes, then his own eyes being put out, he was bound in fetters and sent to Babylon. *Haman* had great wealth, yet in one day he was hung on a gallows sixty feet high, and thus his riches fled. *Josiah* goes forth to battle, and is slain. *Ahab* goes forth against the Assyrians, and is slain also. *Judas* got thirty pieces of silver for betraying Christ, but he went out and hanged himself.

Arab.—Riches diminish in the using, wisdom increases by use.
Turk.—Every ascent has a descent.
Afghan.—Wealth is a Hindoo's beard—*i.e.*, uncertain. The Hindoos shave when in mourning, which often occurs, as the family connexions are numerous.
Telugu.—Worldly prosperity is like writing on water.
Telugu.—Riches flourish, like the charms of women, for a season, but rapidly fade away; as moonlight dies when a cloud passes over the sky.
Bengal.—Riches are like a tree on a river bank.
Bengal.—The boat is now carried on the cart, and the cart on the boat.
Hindi.—Fleeting as the sunshine of noon.
Mahamudgar.—Boast not of wealth, family, youth; fortune takes them all away in the twinkling of an eye.

Lalita Vistara.—Everything compounded is soon dissolved; frail as a vessel of earth or a city of sand.

Prashotar Mala.—What is unsteady as the water drops on the lotos leaf? Youth, riches, life.

Education, or Bending the Twig.—Prov. 22. 6.

Japan.—Pearls unpolished shine not.

Malay.—A pestle by chiselling at last becomes a stick.

Malay.—A young buffalo need not be taught.

Malay.—Sores are not to be shown to flies, and children are not to be taught to lie.

Malay.—You may place on the lap a betel-nut but not a betle-nut tree.

Malay.—To give a calf to be brought up by a tiger.

Chanak.—Parents are the enemies of their children if they refuse them education; for they appear in society as herons among the flamingoes. Prov. 22. 6.

Bulgarian.—We bend the tree when young.

Japan.—Like learning to swim in a field.

The Righteous are Epistles not Written with Ink.
2 Cor. 3. 3.

God's writing things *in a book* denotes his perfect knowledge, exact remembrance, and continued just regard to them. His writing *bitter things* against one, signifies his gradual afflicting of him with severe and lasting troubles, as he did Job. His writing *his law* in men's heart, and sealing them with his Spirit, imports his applying his word by his Spirit to their heart, that they may be conformed to his image and law, and comforted by his influence, Rom. 2. 15. His writing men's *names in heaven* in his book of life, with the living, with the righteous, imports his particular and fixed choice of them to obtain everlasting life, Luke 10. 20. His writing his name *in their foreheads* imports his rendering them like him in holiness, and enabling them to make an open profession of his truth, Rev. 14. 1. His putting their tears into his bottle, and *marking them* in his book, imports his kind observation, and careful rewarding thereof.

Afghan.—What is white shines best amid black.

Providence guards the Righteous as the Apple of the Eye.—Ps. 17. 8.

The ball of the eye is secured by the eyebrows, which turn aside the perspiration of the forehead from the eye, while dust and insects are kept off by the eyelids; the socket of bone the eye is placed in, protects the apple or pupil of the eye, which is in the centre of this, surrounded by the white of the eye. Such is God's protection.

Bengal.—He who has given life will give food.

The Single Eye of pure Intention.—Mat. 6. 22.

Turk.—The eyes are a balance of which the heart forms the weight.

China.—A hair's breadth at the bow is a mile beside the butt.

Arab.—The contemplation of vice is a vice. Prov. 23. 31.

Turk.—The chimney catches fire from within.

Veman.—A feast given without kindness is a mere waste of flour-cakes; worship devoid of piety is a waste of the sprouts used in sacrifice; and gifts devoid of charity are a mere waste of gold. 1 Cor. 10. 31.

Oriental.—You cannot drive a straight furrow without a straight eye.

Telugu.—Observances void of purity of heart! to what end are they? to what is the preparation of food without cleansing the vessel? Mat. 15. 8.

Telugu.—Those who mortify their bodies, calling themselves saints, are yet unable to cure the impurity of their hearts. If you merely destroy the outside of a white ant hill, will the serpent that dwelt therein perish?

Telugu.—The hypocrite's meditations are like those of a dog on a dunghill.

Tamul.—Like a jackal going round the grave of a child—*i.e.*, not from respect, but to tear up the corpse.

Shânti Shatak.—Praise to the stomach which is satisfied with little food, but shame to the heart, which, though it has a hundred desires satisfied, is pursuing after more.

Sanskrit.—As the spokes of a wheel are attached to the nave, so are all things attached to life.

God our Father.—HEB. 12. 9.

Authority and dignity belong to a father, hence the rulers of Israel were called fathers. Abraham commanded his children, and was hence called the Father of the Faithful.

God like a good father in fifteen points :—

1. *Compassionate* to children, so were the Apostles, 1 Thes. 2. 11; hence Paul calls Timothy his son, Tit. 3. 4; John 3. 16; Ps. 103. 13; God treats them as lambs, Is. 40. 11.

2. *Reverenced* by children and not rebuked.

3. *Governs* with wisdom.

4. *Gives being,* so Jacob to the twelve Patriarchs, so Abraham to the Jews numerous as the sand of the sea, Acts 7. 8; believers are begotten by the word of truth, Jas. 1. 18; 1 Cor. 4. 15; God is the father of all men, especially of all regenerate, Gal. 4. 6; Eph. 4. 6.

5. *Nourishes,* believers as new-born babes receive the milk of the word, 1 Pet. 2. 2; a father gives a fish, not a serpent, Mat. 7. 10; Ps. 34. 8–10.

6. *Clothes,* so Jacob made for Joseph a coat of many colours. God clothes the grass, so will He us, Matt. 6. 30; He gives the robe of salvation, Isa. 61. 10.

7. *Protects,* covers them with his *wings,* so David, 1 Chr. 16. 21, 22.

8. *Delights* even in their lisping, so prayer the language of a sigh, Rom. 8. 26; though they chatter like a crane, Isa. 38. 14; the publican only smote on

his breast, yet God delighted in his humility, Luke 18. 13.

9. Sets a *good example,* merciful, Luke 6. 36; patient, Col. 1. 11.

10. *Loves* best those most like Him, so *Daniel* was greatly beloved, Dan. 9. 2; so David a man after God's own heart, Acts 13. 22; John the beloved disciple.

11. *Educates;* God's word makes wise unto salvation, 2 Tim. 3. 15; sends Prophets, Eph. 4. 11; in Christ hid treasures of wisdom, Col. 2. 3.

12. Ready to *hear requests,* 2 Cor. 6. 2; grants not injurious things, Jas. 1. 5, 6; but takes away hurtful things, so hedges their way with thorns, Hos. 2. 6.

13. Regards them even *at a distance,* so in the parable of the Prodigal son, Luke 15. 20.

14. *Patient;* values sincerity; the children have rebelled, Is. 1. 2–5.

15. *Chastises,* Prov. 22. 15; He rebukes transgression with a rod, sometimes he only remonstrates, Mic. 6. 3; to be without chastisement a note of bastards, Heb. 12. 8; punishment a mark of love, Rev. 3. 19; for our profit, Heb. 12. 10; even then he is pained; this chastisement is in measure.

16. Makes *provision* for. Earthly fathers, often passionate, though they be kings, yet of poor dignity, often know not the condition of their distant children, who may become poor, Is. 54. 10; cannot convert, Heb. 2. 14; Ex. 36. 26; estate divided or only given to one; are mortal.

The wickedness of a child does not estrange the heart of a parent, so God remembers we are but dust, Ps. 103. 14; he pities; Christ our High Priest is touched with a feeling of our infirmities.

Bengal.—The tree feels not its own fruit weighty.

Badaga.—Mix milk with water, it is still milk. Your mother might behave badly, still she is your mother.

Arab.—A blow from a lover as sweet as the eating of raisins.
Bengal.—If you love me do not beat my dog.
Afghan.—Though a mother be a wolf she does not eat her cub's flesh.
Raghuvansa.—The father can no more destroy his son than the cloud can extinguish by its water the lightning which proceeds from itself.

Faith without Fruits is Dead.—JAS. 2. 17.

Faith is the root, works are the fruit: to try to do works without faith is like what the Bengali proverb states, "Cutting away the root and watering the branches." The *Egyptians* painted a tongue with a hand under it, to show that knowledge and speech are efficacious and good, when that which is known and said is done. We must be golden-handed as well as golden-mouthed. Blessed are they that *do* his commandments, that they may have right to the Tree of Life, Rev. 22. 14. Knowledge without action is a man without arms; it is wine shut up in the vessel, that does good to none, and will corrupt at last and mar the vessel. Such knowledge will be like the poison that lies long in the body and at last kills without remedy. So she that liveth in pleasure, 1 Tim. 5. 6.

In *rain,* not mere water fructifies, but a secret spirit or nitre that descends with it. Doing is the noblest improvement of being. The soul's essence is *action.* Religion, if confined to the heart, is not so much entertained as imprisoned, that, indeed, is to be its *fountain* but not its *channel;* fountains would not be so much valued if they did not produce rivers. God planted religion among men as a tree of life, which though it was to spring *upward* directly to himself, yet it was to spread its branches to the benefit of *all below;* like incense, which, while it ascends to heaven, it perfumes all about it. Not like the man who tells me his heart is right with God when his hand is in my pocket.

The unripe fruit has little beauty, little flavour; is plucked with difficulty from the tree. But let the air and light, the warm sun and the fruitful showers, unite to swell it, and to ripen it; it is beautiful, it is sweet, falling from the bough into the hand of him that touches it.

In Gal. 5. 22, 23, the fruits which the righteous ought to bear are described; those of the wicked are given Gal. 5. 19–21; the barren fig-tree was cut down, Luke 13. 7.

Afghan.—Cold is not kept out with a "for God's sake," or "for the Prophet's sake," but with four seer (2 lb.) of cotton—*i.e.*, cotton is used to stuff quilts and make them warm.

Telugu.—Worship without faith is a mere waste of flowers —*i.e.*, flowers are used in worship.

Chanak.—Learning placed only in books, and wealth in the hands of others, are of no use, as not available in time of action.

Arab.—Where the mind inclines, the feet lead. Love climbs mountains.

Arab.—There are three things never hidden: love, a mountain, and one riding on a camel.

Persian.—Love and musk do not remain concealed.

China.—To come to the river wishing to fish is not enough; you must bring the net in your hand.

Sadi.—

Though the water of life from the clouds fell in billows,
And the ground were strewn over with paradise loam:
Yet in vain would you seek, from a garden of willows,
To collect any fruit as beneath them you roam.

Oriental.—Expecting good fruits from the wicked is draining *swallow's milk*, plucking a *hog's soft wool, sands* yielding pomegranates.

Bengal.—One knows the horse by his ears; the generous by his gifts; a man by laughing; and a jewel by its brilliancy.

Tamul.—Will the tiger's young be without claws?

Arab.—A learned man without works is like a cloud without rain.

Rabbins.—A basket full of books—*i.e.*, a man of knowledge, but without using it.

Sanskrit.—A fallen woman is dead.

Panch Tantra.—As shade and sunlight are ever closely joined together, so an act and the agent stick close to each other.

The Earth waxes old as a Garment.—HEB. I. 10-12.

The earth itself is millions of years old, and has changed its garment—*i.e.*, the surface—many times. The Himalayas were once islands in an ocean which covered all India, and the Bay of Bengal washed the foot of the Himalayas. India was once not a continent but an archipelago; its present mountains were then islands, while the valley of the Ganges was formed from the earth brought down from the mountains. England itself was then a tropical climate; sharks, alligators, and elephants lived there, though it is now too cold for them.

The heavens will be folded up as a scroll, Is. 34. 4, Rev. 6. 14.

Arab.—The garment of salvation never grows old, Is. 59. 17, Ps. 104. 2.

China.—The pleasure of doing good is the only one that will not wear out.

Hebrew.—All flesh waxeth old as a garment.

Bhagavatgita.—

As their old garments men cast off, anon new raiment to assume;
So casts the soul its worn-out frame, and takes at once another form:
The weapon cannot pierce it through, nor wastes it the consuming fire;
The liquid waters melt it not, nor dries it up the parching wind;
Impenetrable and unburned; impermeable and undried:
Perpetual ever-wandering, firm, indissoluble, permanent, invisible, unspeakable.

The Strait Gate and Narrow Way to eternal Life.
MAT. 7. 12.

The *Katha Upanishad* of the *Yajur Veda* states, "The way to the knowledge of God is considered by wise men difficult, as the passage over the sharp edge of a razor." Though the way to heaven does not allow the unclean or lions to pass on it, the wayfaring man, though a fool, may find it, Is. 35. 8; it is not like the broad way, crowded, or on an inclined plane, or easy like a boat going with the tide, or ending abruptly as Sodom did in brimstone; the way of transgressors is hard, as Samson, Judg. 16. 16, Saul, 1 Sam. 31. 4, and the licentious found, Prov. 2. 18, 5. 11; Josiah found the way that seemed right to him ended in death, 2 Chr. 35; the way of life goes to the eternal city, John 14. 6; the broad way has many on it and is easy, leading to death, Prov. 4. 19.

Arab.—The ascent to virtue steep; the descent to vice smooth.

Persian.—The water of life is in darkness—*i.e.*, search is necessary.

Persian.—Travel the highway, though it be roundabout—*i.e.*, short cuts are dangerous.

Hitopadesh.—A stone is rolled up a hill by great exertions, but is easily thrown down.

The Girdle of Truth.—EPH. 6. 14.

Some girdles are made of gold or fine linen, yet are perishable; but truth is immortal; as the *Russian* proverb states, *Truth is not drowned in water, nor burned in fire,* and the *Bengali* proverb, "False words and sprinkled water remain not long." Better totter in our bodies than in our words. Truth means the unleavened bread of sincerity, 1 Cor. 5. 8.

The *Shánti Shatak,* treating of the marks of the friends of truth, states "they have as a father patience, as a mother forgiveness, as a wife peace of mind, their heir truth, their sister pity, their brother temperance, the earth their bed, their garment the air, and wisdom their nectar." The *Markanda Purana* writes of truth :—

Through truth only the sun shines, on truth the earth stands,
To speak the truth is the highest duty, on truth the heaven rests;
Though we weigh a thousand Asvamedhs against truth,
Yet will truth outweigh a thousand Asvamedhs.

Hypocrisy and malice are called leaven as being sour, and making other things sour, working secretly, puffing. Leaven also, from its diffusive nature, symbolized the rapid spread of the Gospel, Mat. 13. 33.

Nathaniel was an example of sincerity, a man without leaven, John 1. 47; such was Paul.

Truth or sincerity is like a girdle in seven points :—

1. A *belt* used by soldiers to protect the stomach and vital parts. We are told to gird up the loins of our mind, 1 Pet. 1. 13—*i.e.*, restrain earthly affections.

2. *Cleaves close all round*: therefore the clothes were not easily loosed. The righteous should not turn to the right hand or the left, 1 Kings 13; as the *Bengali* proverb, "One foot on land, another on water."

3. *Strengthens the loins*: gird up thy loins, 2 Sam. 22. 40; God girds the loins of kings, Job 12. 18; sincerity strengthens, 1 Kings 20. 11; sincerity is the girdle to faith, hope, love, Matt. 6. 22.

4. A *preparation for battle*, Ps. 65. 3: a war of words necessary to contend for the faith, as the righteous is a soldier.

5. A *preparation for travelling*, as the garments were long; so Elisha's, 2 Kings 4. 29; so the spiritual pilgrims have to travel far, and the storms of persecution will blow away loose garments.

6. *Preparatory to serving*: so the servant ploughed with loins girt, Luke 12. 35.

7. An *ornament*, covers the joints of the armour, hides seams; sincerity covers low birth even in one of low descent, Is. 43. 4; it covers poverty. All are yours, 1 Chr. 3. 22.

China.—An untruthful man is iron without steel;
An untruthful woman is rotten grass and tangled hemp.
Afghan.—To lie is to leap from the house-top—*i.e.*, a leap in the dark.
Bengal.—A hero's word and an elephant's teeth remain fixed.
Talmud.—Lies have no legs.
Bengal.—Only a shrimp moves backward; only a mean person backs out of his word.
Turk.—The house of a liar is burned, but no one believes it.
Bengal.—In promise he puts the moon in your hand.
Bengal.—A lie is water sprinkled—*i.e.*, remains not.
Bengal.—Truth as a stone dissolves not in water.

Seeing through a Dark Glass.—1 Cor. 13. 11.

The eastern mirrors were made of *polished steel*, or brass, hence the *sky* is compared in Job 37. 18, to a molten looking-glass. The Moorish women in Barbary hang looking-glasses on their breasts.

There were in Paul's time no windows of glass, but talc or horn ones; through these people saw very dimly; and such is our vision now of God's attributes, and of the mysteries of religion; Providence is a wheel within a wheel, Ez. 1. 16. Ships get on the rocks in a fog.

Russian.—At night all cats are grey.
Tamul.—As the blind quarrelled about an elephant they had examined.
Afghan.—The frog mounted on a clod, said he had seen Kashmir.
Japan.—A small-minded man looks at the sky through a reed.
Japan.—To lap up the ocean with a shell.

Japan.—The frog in the well sees nothing of the high seas.

China.—Sitting in a well and staring at the stars.

Telugu.—Like one who does not know the alphabet attempting multiplication.

Tamul.—Sounding the ocean with a jackal's tail.

Russian.—They will not see all the world by looking out of their own window.

Prabodh Chandrody.—How can an answer be given to him who does not *comprehend his own spirit*, any more than it is possible to inform a blind man respecting the figure of his body?

Bengal.—Many elephants cannot wade the river; the mosquito says it is only knee deep. Is. 45. 9.

Persian.—The legs of those who require proofs of God's existence are made of wood.

Telugu.—We cannot see our own forehead, our ears, or our backs; neither can we know the hairs of our head; if a man knows not himself how should he know the deity?

Sanskrit.—He who does not go forth and explore all the earth is a well frog.

Arab.—The man is strange—who seeking a lost animal, suffers his own soul to be lost—who ignorant of himself seems to understand God—who doubts the existence of God when he sees his creatures.

Hearers not Doers gazers in a Looking-glass.

JAS. I. 23, 25.

God has given us a mirror in which we may see the true character of our soul; we may thereby grow in self-knowledge, and may adorn ourselves, not with what ministers to pride and worldly vanity, but with the ornaments of meekness and holiness, which are of great price in God's sight. This mirror is his holy Word, which holds up to us the true lineaments and features of the soul, and shows us how greatly it has lost the beauty of the image and likeness of God, and how it is disgraced and deformed by spots and blemishes of sin. The swellings of pride, the lines of envy and care, the shades of sensuality, sloth, and earthliness appear too plainly, when we look into this faithful mirror, which is not like flattering friends who say smooth things to us, and sometimes puff us up with the notion that we are clothed with various graces; but it tells us the very truth concerning our spiritual state; and no veil of false excuses, or artful cloaking and colouring of our faults, will disguise from us our true state, if only we never neglect to consult this mirror in sincerity and with earnest prayer.

There is looking without helping, as the Levite did, Luke 10.

Hearers not doers are also compared to those leading captive silly women ever learning never coming to the truth, 2 Tim. 3. 7; or to those hearing a fine song, Ezek. 33. 32; children with rickets have large heads, but weak joints. God's word was designed as milk to enable persons to grow, 1 Pet. 2. 2. A fresh corpse can have the image of an object painted on the eye, but it reaches not to the heart. Some hearers are like a sponge which suck up everything, but all goes out again; others like a strainer letting go the good and retaining the bad; while some are like a sieve dropping the chaff and retaining the good grain.

China.—The doctrine that enters only into the eye and ear is like the repast one takes in a dream; Ez. 33. 32.

China.—Better return home and make a net than go down the river and desire to get fishes.

China.—To look at a plum is not to quench one's thirst.

Bengal.—One man is being impaled, while the other counts the joints on the stake.

Veman.—Let the sinner listen to holy texts he will not relinquish his vile nature: though you wash a coal in milk—will the blackness be removed?

Veman.—Whatever he devoid of understanding may read, his virtue continues only so long as he is reading; even as a frog is dignified only so long as it is seated on a lotus leaf.

Turk.—It is not in speaking continually of honey that sweetness comes into the mouth.

Arab.—Experience is the looking-glass of the intellect.
Persian.—A mirror in an Ethiopian's hand.
Urdu.—If the camel could see his hump, he would fall down and break his neck.
China.—Without striking the flint there is not even smoke.
Tamul.—If the men be ugly; what can the glass do?
Arab.—A learned man without practice, a cloud without water.
Persian.—One pound of learning requires ten of common sense to apply it.
Buddhagosha.—A reciter of the law, but not a doer, is like a cowherd counting the cows of others.

The Wild Goat on the Mountains protected, so the Righteous.—Ps. 104. 18.

How safely does the wild goat rest on the side of the precipitous mountain, or climb the dizzy height, where man's brain would turn, and his feet would inevitably slip! How freely and fearlessly does she leap from rock to rock! Her eye is as true, and her foot as sure upon the steep and slippery crag, as on some beaten road! God has fitted her for "the high hills" on which he has appointed her to live, and has endued her with those faculties of the foot and of the eye, which enable her, even in the darkest night, to walk on rocks and precipices where man could not tread securely under the noonday light.

The lesson taught is God's protecting providence, which tempers the wind to the shorn lamb; it is like *Jacob's ladder,* extending from heaven to earth, though God's way to us may be in the sea, Is. 43. 16—*i.e.,* leaving no track. God's acts are like *clouds,* which though black have the rainbow of hope from Christ the Sun of Righteousness, or like *wheels* of quick and easy motion, which, though wheel within wheel, are regulated by the main wheel.

The Tongue an Helm.—JAS. 3. 2–5.

We are told to keep the *door* of our lips; the tongue is little like a helm, or a bit in a horse's mouth, yet it guides. Sennacherib's tongue brought death on 185,000 soldiers, 2 Kings 18. 28; so Ananias and Sapphira's tongue brought death, Acts 5. 8–10.

Bengal.—His tongue is a sweeper's shovel.

Solomon.—A soft tongue breaketh the bone; a wholesome tongue is a tree of life.

Telugu.—If your foot slip you may recover your balance, but if your mouth slips you cannot recall your words.

Providence as a Hen sheltering her Chickens.
MAT. 23. 27.

A hen, on seeing the hawk that is hovering over her young, hastens forward to meet her frightened brood. Fearless in that defence she places herself in front of the danger. She gathers her chickens under her wings. Not one of them is denied admission to that hiding-place, which they all so fondly seek, under a sense of their own utter helplessness.

Christ had previously called the Pharisees the Gurus (teachers) of that day—hypocrites, blind guides, serpents; in this text all is love to the people of Jerusalem, 700,000 in number.

Man is more inconsiderate than animals, than an ox or ass, Is. 1. 3.

1. *A hen is very compassionate to her young;* so Christ wept over Jerusalem, Mat. 23. 13. The hen even flies at a dog approaching to her young; so Christ resisted the devil, Mat. 4. 6, 8.

2. *A hen becomes weak from nourishing her young;* so Christ sweat great drops of blood, Mat. 26. 30; he bore the heavy cross, Luke 23. 14.

3. A hen *clucks* to warn her young of danger; so God pleads—why will you die? Ez. 14. 6.

4. *A hen's wings receive her young,* Ps. 91. 3. God says, I have spread out my hands, Is. 65. 2, come to me all that labour, Mat. 11. 28, 29.

A hen *scratches* to get meat for her young; she fasts herself to give meat to them; so God says, Ho every one that thirsts. Is. 55. 1. A hen soon forgets *her young* when grown. Not so God. Can a woman forget her sucking child? Is. 49. 15. A hen loses her young in spite of herself, God's people never perish, John 10. 28.

Telugu.—Will he who planted the tree not water it? Luke 12. 24.

Persian.—The provider of food (God) gives to daily food wings in order to come.

Honesty.—Rom. 13. 13.

Christ gave the golden rule, Mat. 7. 12.

Bengal.—The thief and the hog have one path.

Hebrew.—He that builds his house with other men's money is like one that gathers himself stones for the tomb of his burial.

Hospitality.—Rom. 12. 13.

Justus was hospitable to Paul, Acts 18. 7.

Badaga.—He does not ask his friend to go away, but he makes such a smoke in the house that his friend is obliged to leave.

Telugu.—A kind reception is better than a feast.

Who are God's Jewels.—Mal. 3. 16, 17.

Jewels are much valued in every country; hence the New Jerusalem's gates are represented as made of pearls, Rev. 21. 21. The jewels on the High Priest's breast-plate symbolized the twelve tribes as dear to him. An esteemed wife is called by the Hindus a jewel of a woman. See parable of the Pearl, Mat. 13. 45.

The righteous are like jewels in seven points :—

1. *All jewels are dug out of the earth* from rubbish, except the pearl found in the oyster; the diamond is only crystallized carbon or coal hardened in the earth; so believers at first of the earth earthy (1 Cor. 15. 49) dead in trespasses.

2. *Jewels receive a fine polish*, which requires a long time. A wheel is used for this purpose, so adversity polishes believers to put on the new man as it did to *Job* and *David*; the polishing continues till all the flaws are removed, thus the Church hereafter by affliction's rubbing, will be without spot or blemish.

3. *Jewels are rare.* Many stones and metals are not equal in value to a small one, so believers a little flock, Luke 12. 32, not many wise called. Silver and gold were, however, as stones in Solomon's times, 1 Kings 10. 27, so again in the New Jerusalem.

4. *Jewels are very beautiful*—yellow, green, purple; so the graces are beautiful—as love with *John*, humility as in *Mary*, patience as in *Job*—whatever things are lovely, Philip. 4. 8. Believers like jewels shine in the dark, so believers are the light of the world, so Peter and John's boldness was admired, though they were ignorant men, Acts 4. 5. Stephen's face shone when dying. *Jewels are ornamental, set in a crown, ring, or seal*, used by brides and kings; so the believer's crown will be an ornament to Christ's crown, Ex. 28. 29. To angels is manifested the love of God to man.

5. *Jewels are durable*; such as the Kohi Nur of Ranjit Sing. This is one cause of their value, so the hidden man of the heart, 1 Peter 3. 4; when earthly jewels shall be destroyed at the last day the righteous shall shine forth, Mat. 13. 43; many seeming jewels are only glass, so with hypocrites.

6. *Jewels are very valuable;* so the righteous are the pearls of creation, of great price, Mat. 13. 45, redeemed not with corruptible things, 1 Peter 1. 17, the precious sons of Zion were esteemed by the Chaldeans as earthen vessels, Lam. 4. 2, yet regarded as the apple of God's eye, Deut. 32. 10. Ten jewels—*i.e.*, good men—would have saved Sodom could they have been procured.

7. *Jewels are kept carefully;* so believers are kept by the power of God; angels have charge over them, Mat. 4. 6. The Lord is their shade.

Chanak.—That jewel knowledge, which is not plundered by kinsmen, nor carried off by thieves, which does not decrease by giving, is great riches.
Urdu.—Among men some are jewels and some are pebbles.
Sanskrit.—The sandal grows not in every wood.

God a Judge.—Rev. 20. 12.

From God's judgment-seat there is no escape by bribery. God spared not the devils, neither Nebuchadnezzar nor Pharaoh. He is the Father of Lights, and knows the law he himself made; he is patient, because he is eternal; he spared the world in Noah's time 120 years; and the world has been spared now 6,000 years.

The eyes of the Lord are in every place, beholding the evil and the good. There is no secret place in which the sinner can hide himself; for God, who is present everywhere, sees in the dark as well as in the light. He hears us when we do not speak, because he hears our thoughts. As the light of the sun reaches to the ends of the world, so his power is everywhere, Ps. 139.

God differs from earthly judges in four points:—

The judge, who punishes sins in a court of justice, receives his information from *others*, and can know only that which the witnesses tell him. But God is both judge and witness, and knows all things. When the judge has condemned a man and he is put to death, he has no more that he can do; but the power of God reaches *beyond the grave,* for he can destroy both the soul and body in hell. His hand shall find out those whom the grave has hidden from our sight, and they shall be brought forth, and placed before his judgment-seat to be judged for their past lives. Thefts, murders, and other sins which were committed in the *dark,* and were hidden from men so long as the offenders lived, shall then all be discovered, and made known. With the fear of this, the guilty shall tremble when they rise from their graves; then shall they call upon the mountains to fall upon them, and hide them from the face of their judge, Rev. 6. 16.

Bengal.—Sand sharpens a knife, a stone the axes, good words a good man, a thrashing a rogue.

Bengal.—Before a turning-lathe a thing cannot remain crooked.

Knowledge.—1 Sam. 2. 3.

Empty knowledge puffs up, 1 Cor. 8. 1, 2.

Menu.—A wooden elephant, an antelope of leather, and a Brahman without knowledge—these three things only bear a name, Rev. 3. 1.

Atmabodh.—By ignorance the soul is ruined; when this is removed, the soul shall shine forth as the sun when the clouds disappear.

Atmabodh.—The flame of knowledge which blazes forth when the contemplation is unceasingly rubbed upon the fuel of the soul, consumes all the stubble of ignorance.

Atmabodh.—Knowledge alone effects emancipation, as fire is indispensable to cooking.

Avyar.—He without knowledge is blind.

Kural.—Those who know have eyes and see; those who know not have only two holes in front.

Sanskrit.—The gem of learning is great wealth; it cannot be shared by cousins, nor lost by robbery, nor exhausted by liberality, Mat. 6. 19.

Sanskrit.—A reasonable word should be received even from a child or parrot.

Arab.—Ignorance is the greatest poverty.

Sanskrit.—One void of learning is a beast.

Sanskrit.—The spring is the youth of trees, wealth is the youth of men, beauty is the youth of women, intelligence is the youth of the young.

Arab.—One day of a wise man is worth more than the life of a fool.

Niti Shatak.—The man without learning is a beast.

Sin, a Leprosy.—Is. 1. 6.

Disease called an arrow flying at night, Ps. 90., such as cholera. David was a man after God's own "heart;" though living in a palace of cedar, he could not prevent disease, the fruit of sin, from entering; no soundness in his flesh, no rest in his bones, an emblem of sin; this was the man once so lively who danced before the ark, Ps. 38. 7.

Sin is like leprosy in twelve points:—

1. *Painful.* Pain is often useful in warning of danger to the body; thus fire warns, but the absence of mental pain is often an opiate to the conscience; thus Cain did not feel at first that he was guilty of murder; he said, Am I my brother's keeper? Gen. 4., 9. So when David committed murder he slept well. On another occasion, however, he states the arrows of the Almighty are within him. A pain often points out the seat of disease; opiates are not good in such a case. The pain of future punishment should be anticipated like as in the case of the men that heard Peter, and who were pricked to the heart, Acts. 2. 37, others, however, as in Judas's case suffer pain without any benefit.

2. *Wastes the body and beauty.* His beauty consumes like a moth, Ps. 39. 11. The Nazarites, whiter than snow, became black as a coal, Lam. 4. 8. God saw once every thing he made was good, even man's body, but sin has

dimmed the fine gold. "They are altogether become filthy." The jaundiced eye does not always see its own ugliness; so with the sinner.

3. *Impairs the strength of the limbs.* The strong becomes very weak, so the sinner—"sin revived, I died." The sick man tries to walk, but falls; he has the will, not the power. The law in the members warring against the law of the mind, Rom. 7. 23.

4. *Spoils the appetite.* Food is necessary, yet there is no relish, hence death ensues; the manna of God's word is despised; the honeycomb of the promises is loathed; the wine and milk of Gospel truth are rejected; he turns as a dog to his vomit, and eats husks, Job 31. 21. Behold he prayeth, was the sign of Saul's spiritual appetite, Acts 9. 11.

5. *Blasts the comforts of life.* The ear enjoys not music; Job when a leper said, My soul chooseth strangling rather than life, Job 7. 15. Vanity of vanities, says Solomon, Eccl. 1. 2; as vinegar upon nitre, so songs to a heavy heart, Prov. 25. 20.

6. *Unhinges the whole body.* The heart and limbs feel local complaints. I am poured out like water, Ps. 22. 14; so the conscience calls bitter sweet, the whole head is sick, Tit. 1. 5. The imagination is only evil.

7. *Terminates in death.* The blood is affected, and then the dust returns to dust; he that liveth in pleasure is dead, 1 Tim. 5. 6. How fearful are plagues, such as small-pox, cholera, yet how much more so the disease of sin.

8. *Deeply seated.* Not skin deep, but affecting the vital parts of the blood and the heart, which is deceitful above all things.

9. *Widely spread* since Adam's time; small-pox, leprosy are spread to every part of the body, so man's members are made instruments of unrighteousness; "his tongue, a world of iniquity;" his eyes full of covetousness; his hands defiled with bribes; his feet swift to shed blood.

10. *Extremely complicated.* Now the fever of agitated passion, the palsy of want of natural affection, the decay of spiritual affection—a complication of disorders, so that what is a remedy in one case is a poison in another.

11. *Hereditary.* "What is born of the flesh is flesh." "In sin did my mother conceive me," Ps. 51. 5. By one man sin entered into the world, Rom. 5. 12; so Gehazi's family inherited from him the leprosy, 2 Kings 5. 27.

12. *Most infectious.* The atmosphere of the earth is charged with disease which is caught from the air of a room or from clothes; but sin from a glance, or a word, as in David's case. Evil communications corrupt good manners. Only Christ was exempt from this infection; like a sunbeam he could penetrate impurity without being soiled.

13. *Very loathsome and malignant.* The drunkard's and libertine's complaints are such. The body, as in leprosy, is often a putrid mass, so that friends cannot come near. Paul says, "Who shall deliver me from the (putrid) body of this death?"

14. *Incurable by human means;* sin, when it hath conceived, brought forth dead. Quack doctors will not do. No doctors can cure this leprosy.

Russian.—The fleetest horse escapes not from its tail.
Tamul.—Is the young jackal to be trained to howl?
Arab.—The shadow of the deformed is deformed.
Tamul.—A lame man is a hero before a cripple.
Tamul.—As if one changed his pillow to cure the headache.
Persian.—If you keep sour milk in a leathern bag 100 years, it will still be sour milk. John 3. 5–7.
Urdu.—Put a dog's tail into a straight pipe for 1000 years, it will still be as crooked as ever.

God's People graven on the Palms of his Hands.

Is. 49. 15, 16.

God says a mother may forget her sucking child, but he will not forget his people, Is. 49. 15. An engraving is not impressed on the surface as writing but is cut in or graven with a pen of stone or of writing iron; this impression is not rubbed out like that of ink or on palm leaves, but remains like the impression of the style on leaves. God's having his people graven on the palms of his hands, means their being in a secure place, and one easily observed by the individual.

Hitopadesh.—He by whom swans are made white, and parrots green, and peacocks variegated, will provide thy subsistence.

Sanskrit.—A mother curses not her son; the earth suffers no harm; a good man does no injury; God destroys not his creation.

Light.—Ps. 36. 9.

God the sun, the source of light, Jas. 1. 17; communicated to the body through the eye, Mat. 6. 22; the path of the just like the shining light, Prov. 4. 18; the favour of God is light, Ps. 27. 1, and is therefore agreeable, Ecc. 11. 7.

Upanishad.—It is through God's shining that all else shines; by his lustre the universe is illuminated.

The Righteous Bold as a Lion.—Prov. 28. 1.

The roaring of a lion in quest of his prey resembles the sound of distant thunder, and being re-echoed by the rocks and mountains, appals the whole race of animals, and puts them instantly to flight. So great are the terror and dismay which his roaring produces, that many animals, which by their swiftness might escape his fury, astonished and petrified by the sound of his voice, are rendered incapable of exertion. He never flies from the hunters, nor is frightened by their onset; if their numbers force him to yield, he retires slowly, step by step, frequently turning upon his pursuers. He has been known to attack a whole caravan, and when obliged to retire, he always retires fighting, and with his face to his enemies. "An army of deer with the lion as leader is more terrible than an army of lions with a deer as leader."

A lion was the symbol of a king; Judah is called, from its brave character, a lion's whelp, Gen. 49. 9; Babylon is called a lion on the eagle wings of conquest, Dan. 7. 4; Paul was delivered out of the lion's mouth—*i.e.*, from the wicked—2 Tim. 4. 17; Nebuchadnezzar was called a lion, Jer. 4. 7; Christ called the lion of the tribe of Judah, Rev. 5. 5.

A lion is

1. *Courageous;* such was David, Ps. 27. 3; so Nehemiah said, shall such a man as I flee, Neh. 6. 11; so Paul boldly avowed his doctrine to be what the governor called heresy, Acts 24. 14; he fought with beasts, 1 Cor. 15. 32; the Apostles said they must speak of the things they had seen, Acts 4. 20; so Elijah, 1 Kings 10. 15, 19; Is. 41. 14. The lion called the king of beasts, so believers are more than conquerors, Rom. 8. 3; other beasts fear it, so Herod feared John, Matt. 15. 5.

2. *Strong.* Samson says, out of the strong lion came forth sweetness, Judg. 14. 14; Christ as a lion is mighty to save, Is. 9. 6; at times the lion is still when he crouches down before his spring; Christ is now a lamb, but afterwards will be a lion, on the last day, Am. 3. 8.

3. *Mild:* to these submissive, yet firm; so John before Herod; Paul before Felix; so Moses.

Russian.—Fear has many eyes; he fearing the wolf enters not the forest.

China.—Men who never violate their conscience are not afraid of a knock at their door at midnight.

Urdu.—The leaf cracked, and your servant fled.

Persian.—He fled from his own shadow.

Arab.—No religion without courage.

Turk.—Among ten men nine are women.

Canara.—An elephant fears not fishes, neither do the good the bad.

African.—If a mouse were as big as a bullock, yet it would be the slave of the cat.

Time like a Mail-post, Swift Ships, Eagles.—Job 9. 25, 26.

Time, in its rapid devastating course, is compared to a flood, Ps. 90. 5; to a *tale* that is told, Ps. 90. 9; a *hand-breadth,* Ps. 39. 5; a *dream,* Ps. 73. 20; a weaver's shuttle, Job 7. 6.

In Job's days human life had been gradually shortening from 500 to 70 years.

The dromedary post, though not as quick as a horse in a given space, yet maintains an uniform continued progress.

Time is like a mail-post, in four points:

1. The postman rides on *swift horses* 150 miles a day, while the caravan moves only at two miles an hour.

2. *Changes* in order to increase speed.

3. *Delays* little for rest or mere salutation, Luke 10. 4.

4. *Allows no obstruction on the road.* The Persian messengers could, by royal authority, press horses, men, or ships, so as to expedite them, Esth. 3. 15.

The post may be stayed, but the sun never stops.

Swift ships—*i.e.,* made of papyrus of the Nile—which cut through the water with easy speed.

Italian.—Time is an inaudible file.

Greek.—Man is a bubble.

Bengal.—There is no hand to catch time.

Canara.—Life is a lamp exposed to the wind, Jas. 4. 14.

Arab.—Who is able to restore what was yesterday, or to plaster over the rays of the sun?

Persian.—The best teacher is time.

China.—As wave follows wave so new men take old men's places.

China.—Men live like birds together in a wood:
When the time comes each takes his flight.

China.—A generation is like a swift horse passing a crevice.

China.—When we take off our boots and stockings to-day,
That we shall wear them to-morrow who can say?

Canara.—The pearl though originating in water does not become water again, Prov. 4. 18, 1 Cor. 13. 11.

Oriental.—The world has nothing constant, but its instability.

Arab.—Every day in thy life is a leaf in thy history, Prov. 27. 1.

Kathá Saritságar.—The rivers, the flowers, the moon's phases, disappear but return, not so youth.

An Oppressor like a Crouching Lion.—Ps. 10. 9.

A lion is proud, strong, and crafty, lying in wait for the prey; such were *Nebuchadnezzar*, Dan. 3, *Manasseh*, 2 Kings 21. 16, *Rehoboam*; *Satan* is compared to a roaring lion, 1 Pet. 5. 8, active as with Job, knowing his time is short, Rev. 12. 12.

Oppression is an abuse of power, the practice of unjust and uncharitable actions as to a hired servant, Deut. 24. 14, or widow, Ex. 22. 21–24. Oppression makes a wise man mad, Ecc. 7. 7; grinds the face of the poor, Is. 3. 15; flays the poor, Mic. 3. 1–3. Envy one cause of oppression, as in Ahab and Naboth's case; pride another, as in Jezebel's case.

Telugu.—There is no justice in oppression, and no sight in a blind eye.

Bengal.—The landlord loves the peasant with the same love as the Musalman has to the fowl—*i.e.*, which he fattens in order to kill.

A Living Dog better than a dead Lion.—Ecc. 9. 4.

"*Half a loaf* is better than no bread."
"He with *one eye* sees the better for it."
"A standing *thistle* better than the falling cedar."
"*A living sheep* better than the dead camel."
"*A living hodman* better than the dead Emperor."

This text points out the value of life, using as an emblem the dog, the meanest of animals, Matt. 15. 26, and the lion, the noblest, Prov. 30. 30.

Man and Wife one Flesh.—Matt. 19. 5.

There is an union, but not like the one in Nebuchadnezzar's image, Dan. 2. 33. No bitterness is to be shown, Col. 3. 19. The Egyptians represent a man without a woman by a single mill-stone, which cannot grind alone.

Talmud.—Even though the wife be little, bow down to her in speaking, *i.e.*, do nothing without her advice.

Jainwriter.—The husband and wife must, like two wheels, support the chariot of domestic life, otherwise it must stop.

Arab.—Women are parts cut out of men. Gen. 2. 23.

China.—Husband and wife in perfect accord;
Are the music of the harp and lute.

China.—A good man will not beat his wife;
A good dog will not worry a fowl.

Badaga.—If you yoke a buffalo and an ox together, the one will push for the swamp and the other for the hill.

Arab.—A mule yoked with horses. 2 Cor. 6. 14.

Persian.—Tied by the neck, *i.e.*, married to a bad woman.

Persian.—A bad wife is a tree growing on the wall, *i.e.*, like the fig tree which undermines the wall by its roots.

Russian.—A wife is not a guitar, *i.e.*, which having done playing with you hang on the wall.

Telugu.—The house is small and the wife like a monkey.

China.—A widow is a rudderless boat.

Basque.—He who marries a wolf often looks towards the forest.

Talmud.—God did not make woman from man's head, that she should not rule over him; nor from his feet, that she should not be his slave; but from his side, that she should be near his heart.

Bhagavalgita.—Women like flowers are of tender fabric; and should be softly handled, Eph. 5. 25.

Badaga.—A passionate wife is as bad as a house that leaks.

Bartrihari.—This is the fruit of love among married people, one mind among two persons; where there is discord, it is the marriage of two corpses.

Mrichhakati.—

Look round the garden, mark these stately trees,
Which duly by the king's command attended;
Put forth abundantly their fruits and flowers,
And clasped by twining creepers; they resemble
The manly husband, and the tender wife.

The Miser.—Luke 12. 19.

Sanskrit.—A miser's wealth goes by fire, robbers, and kings.

Telugu.—Practising the humility of a fox, he heaps up wealth and does not use it; thus is rice sprinkled at the mouth of a bandicoot trap, Prov. 13. 11.

Badaga.—A miser is a tree with fruit you cannot get.

False Peace like Untempered Mortar.—Ezek. 13. 10.

In Persia, proper mortar is made of plaster, earth, and chopped straw well kneaded together; but often to save expense they put much water to a little plaster, which *looks* as well but is not plaster. There is no cement in a house so built; it is like the house on the sand, which the whirlwind or flood breaks down, Mat. 7. 27, like some of the bridges in India, cemented by rubbish, not by mortar, or like the virgins without oil, Mat. 25. 1–13. Such is all false peace without repentance and faith in the atonement of Christ, like that of the rich fool, Luke 12. 19.

Bhagavadgita.—The soul floats like the lotus on the lake unmoved, unruffled by the tide, Acts 20. 24 16–25.

Modern Greek.—No one is disgusted with his own bad smell.

Telugu.—Like sprinkling rose-water on ashes.

Arab.—Temperance is a tree which has contentment for its root, and peace for its fruit.

Malayalim.—Time shows the value of a bridge built of wood, Prov. 5. 3, 1 Cor. 3. 13.

Modern Greek.—Neighbour! your house is on fire. Impossible, I have the keys.

Russian.—The bell calls to church, but goes not in itself.

Oriental.—The prosperity of an ignorant man is like a garden on a dunghill.

China.—We never wander so far away as when we think we know the way.

Cingalese.—Like changing the pillow when suffering from headache.

Modern Greek.—He who eats flax-seed eats his own shirt—*i.e.*, the future sacrificed to the present.

Tamul.—As quiet as a snake in a box.

Bhagavatgita.—Without quiescence there can be no bliss.
E'en as a storm-tossed ship upon the waves,
So is the man whose heart obeys his passions,
Which like the winds will hurry him away.

Buddhagosha.—Who subdues his passions is a lake without mud.

Arab.—Patience is the key to joy.

Mountains.—Dan. 2. 45.

Their solid strength, untouched by visible decay, gave mountains the name of the pillars of heaven, Job 26. 11. Their majesty defies the turbulence and confusion of the world at their feet, yet God weighs them in a balance, Is. 40. 12.

Raghuvause.—The storm may uproot the trees, but not the mountains, Ps. 125. 2.

Arab.—When we cross one mountain, another appears.

The Spiritual Net.—Mat. 13. 47.

As the sea is a frequent type or emblem of the world, so "the fishes of the sea," which take their course at will, and so often prey upon one another throughout that waste of waters, represent the vast numbers who know not God, and walk in the way of their own hearts, without any sure guide or rule of conduct, and too often only envying and provoking, hating and devouring, one another. Into this broad sea of the whole world a net was to be cast; and instead of their lowly labours on the little sea of Galilee, the Apostles were to be employed in gathering men out of every clime and country into the Church of God, and in drawing them under the blessed restraints and holy discipline of "the obedience of faith." A net will indeed gather of every kind, and when it is drawn to the shore, a separation is made of the fishes which are worth the pains of taking out of the sea, and of such as are nothing worth, and may be cast away. Thus among those who are gathered into the visible Church of Christ, there "are good and bad," many false professors as well as sincere servants of God; nor will the good be separated from the bad until the net is drawn completely to the shore, which will not be till the end of the world. The fish, whether big or little, are taken out of the sea of this world, a stormy place full of rocks, subject to tempests.

The Night of Life and Day of Eternity.—Rom. 13. 12.

The *Shánti Shatak* states, "The world is like a wild desert, the house of our body is full of holes, our fancies are a night which throws the veil of illusion over us: be watchful and defend yourself with the sword of knowledge, the shield of resignation, and the armour of caution."

Morning comes after night, so the morning of eternity,

Ps. 49. 14; morning longed for, Ps. 130. 6; morning makes things manifest, Isa. 58. 8, 1 Cor. 4. 5; morning brings joy, birds sing, flowers are fresh, Isa. 26. 19; morning foreshows the king of day.

Life like night in four points:—

1. A state of *darkness;* whereas light symbolizes knowledge, Is. 8. 20; holiness, 1 John 1. 7; comfort, Ps. 97. 11; and glory, Col. 1. 12.

2. The time of *sleep,* 1 Thess. 5. 7, hence sleep is called the son of night. Half our days we pass in the shadow of the earth, and the brother of death (sleep) extracts a third part of our lives.

3. Time of *danger* beasts and thieves prowl about, Is. 21. 12; heaven is light, "the inheritance of the saints in light."

4. *Inactivity,* ignorance, Luke 1. 79, night an emblem of death, John 9. 4. The Arabs say he who has done justice in the night has built himself a house for the next day.

Afghan.—When night comes fear is at the door; when day comes fear is on the hills.
Arab.—Night is blind, 1 Thess. 5. 7.
Russian.—At night all cats are black.
Oriental.—The prosperity of the ignorant is like a garden on a dunghill.
Arab.—Nightly prayer makes the day to shine.
Bengal.—Where there is fear of the tiger it is evening.
Arab.—The day blots out the dread of night.
Turk.—Night is the day of the wicked.

The Sensualist's Old Age.—Eccles. 12. 1–7.

This is a description of the dreary old age of the man who when young would go on in the way of his heart; not as the good old age of Abraham and David, Gen. 15. 15, 1 Chron. 29. 28, or the serene old age of Isaac, Jacob, Moses, and Joshua, Is. 40. 30–31. The pious old renew their youth as the eagles, they bring forth fruit in old age, Ps. 92. 15.

In the 12th chapter of *Ecclesiastes*, the Preacher Solomon admonishes to dedicate youthful days to the service of our *Creator*, considering the *evil days* of the winter of life which are coming on, when the faculties of our minds and bodies often fail. For then, *the sun and the moon and the stars are darkened—i.e.*, the superior powers, which rule in the body of man, as the heavenly luminaries do in the world—viz., the understanding and reason, the imagination and the memory—are obscured as when the clouds interpose between us and the lights of the firmament. In the earlier season of life, the clouds of affliction having poured down their *rain*, they pass away, and sunshine succeeds; but now the *clouds return after the rain—i.e.*, old age itself is with the wicked a continual sorrow, and there is no longer any hope of fair weather. *The keepers of the house*, the arms and hands, which are made to guard and defend the body, begin to shake and *tremble;* and the *strong men*, the shoulders, where the strength of the body is placed, and which were once able to bear every weight, begin to stoop and *bow themselves;* the *grinders*, the teeth, begin to fall away, and *cease* to do their work, *because they are few. Also those that look out of the windows are darkened—i.e.*, the eyes, those windows of the soul, through which we look at all things abroad, become dim; and he that uses them is as one who looks out of a window in the night. *The doors are shut in the streets—i.e.*, difficulties and obstructions attend all the passages of the body, and digestion becomes weak when the *grinding* is low. The youthful and healthy sleep soundly, and are apt to transgress by taking too much rest; but the aged sleep with difficulty, and *rise up at the voice of the bird*, at the crowing of the cock. *The daughters of music are brought low;* the voice falls, and becomes hoarse; the hearing is dull; and the spirits, now less active than they used to be, are less affected by the powers of harmony; and so the old sit in heaviness, hanging down their heads, as virgins drooping under the sorrow of captivity. Old age, being inactive and helpless, becomes *afraid of that which is high;* it is fearful of climbing because it is in danger of falling; and, being unfit to endure the hardships of fatigue, and the shocks of a rough journey, the *fears* which are *in the way* discourage the old from setting out. Then the *almond tree flourishes*—*i.e.*, the hair of the head becomes white as the early almond blossoms in the hard weather of the winter before the snows have left; and even the *grasshopper becomes a burthen*—*i.e.*, the legs, once light and nimble to leap, as the legs of that insect, and which used with ease to bear the weight of the whole body, are now become a burthen, and can scarcely carry themselves; and, when the faculties thus fail, the *desire fails* along with them, for nothing is desirable when nothing can be enjoyed.

Such are the *evil days* which come upon many when their youth is passed in sin, and prepare the way for death, when *man goeth to his long home.* Then the *silver cord,* the nerves, whose coat is white and shining as a cord of silver, is loosed, and no longer does its office. The circulation of the blood stops at the heart, the fountain of life, as when a *pitcher,* which draws water, *is broken at the well,* or the watering *wheel,* circulating with its buckets, which it both fills and empties at the same time, *is broken at the cistern.* Thus do the vital motions all cease in death; and the *dust returns to the earth,* to become such *as it was* before man was made out of it; and his immortal *spirit returns unto God,* the fountain of immortality from whom it proceeded.

Arab.—Hoary hairs are death's messengers.

Arab.—The gravity of old age is fairer than the flower of youth.

China.—In clothes we value novelty: in men old age.

China.—A wall is cracked and lofty, its fall must be speedy.

Afghan.—Oh! greybeard, thou eatest earth—*i.e.*, money to an old man is as useless as earth.

Afghan.—The ass grown old did not know his master's house.

Arab.—The cat became blind but still was hankering after mice.

Bengal.—Plastering an old hut with clay and cow dung—*i.e.*, passing off a vile article as excellent.

Hebrew.—Old age is a crown of nettles: youth is a crown of roses.

Sanskrit.—The old who cannot enjoy sensual objects nor yet abandon them, resembles a toothless dog licking a bone.

Sanskrit.—Wealth stops at the house, friends and relatives at the grave, good and evil deeds follow the dying man.

Oppressing the Poor a Sweeping Rain.—PROV. 28. 3.

The periodical rains which follow the long-continued drought of summer in Eastern countries, sometimes occasion a devastation unknown in a European climate. The rivers and brooks, in consequence of the periodical rains, overflowing their bounds, carry ruin into the most cultivated districts, but especially among the dwellings of the poor, which, being usually built of mud, or of bricks burnt only in the sun, are the first to fall before the torrent, involving the inhabitants in destruction.

The giants before the flood were oppressors, Gen. 6. 4, 12, 13; so were the *Egyptians*, Ex. 1. 13; so *Jezebel*, 1 Kings 21. 7–13, devoured by dogs, 2 Kings 9. 30–37; not so Job, 31. 13–15; or those obeying the law of Moses, Deut. 15. 7–11, 24. 10–15. See the parable of the Unmerciful Servant, Mat. 18. 30–34.

Oppression of the poor is called a *panting after* the dust on their head, Amos. 2. 7—*i.e.*, thereby the oppressors incline to rob them of everything, and crush them to the dust of death. It is represented as a *selling the poor for a pair of shoes*, Amos 8. 6, to mark how lightly the oppressor esteems them, and for how little he is disposed to ruin them. It is called a *crushing* and *treading upon them,* Amos 5. 11, to signify the grievous, afflictive, and debasing tendency thereof. It is called a *slaying* of them; a *chopping their bones,* Mic. 3. 3; a frightening and tearing them in the manner of lions, wolves, or bears; to denote the inhuman cruelty contained in it, and the utter ruin effected by it. It is represented as a *building of houses and cities by blood,* Hab. 2. 12; because oppressors rear these structures with the wealth extorted from others, to the endangering of their life. It is called an *eating of God's people as bread,* Micah 3. 3, to mark the pleasure and greed wherewith wicked men persecute the persons, ruin the character, and consume the substance of the godly.

The widow of Zarephath, 1 Kings 17. 12, was happier than Queen Jezebel, the oppressor; while the rust of the rich man's gold shall eat his flesh as fire, Jas. 5. 2–3, it shall also, like the dust, be a testimony against him, Mark 6. 11.

Solomon writes, the teeth of the oppressor are *knives* to devour the poor from off the earth, Prov. 30. 14. We are to open our mouth for the dumb, Prov. 31. 8.

Bengal.—The relation of the carving knife to the pumpkin.
China.—Unjustly-got wealth is snow sprinkled with hot water. Lands improperly obtained are but sand-banks in a stream.

The Righteous as the Palm Tree.—Ps. 92. 12.

The righteous resemble the palm tree in five points:

1. *The palm tree grows in the desert.* Earth is a desert to the righteous; true believers are even refreshed in it as a palm is in the Arabian desert; so *Lot* amid Sodom's wickedness, and *Enoch,* who walked with God amongst the antediluvians.

2. *The palm tree grows on the sand, but the sand is not its food;* water below feeds its tap roots, though the heavens above be brass. Some righteous live not as the

lily, by green pastures, Hos. 14. 5, or willow by water-courses, Is. 44. 4, but as the palm of the desert; so *Joseph* among the Cat-worshippers of Egypt, *Daniel* in voluptuous Babylon. Faith's penetrating root reaches the fountains of living waters.

3. *The palm tree is beautiful,* with its tall and verdant canopy, and the silvery flashes of its waving plumes; so the believer's virtues are not like the creeper or bramble, tending downwards; their palm branches shoot upwards, and seek the things above, Col. 3. 1; some trees are crooked and gnarled, but the righteous is a tall palm, as a son of the light, Mat. 3. 12, Phil. 2. 15. The Jews were called a crooked generation, Deut. 32. 5, and Satan a crooked serpent, Is. 27. 1; but the believer is upright like the palm. Its beautiful unfading leaves made it an emblem of victory; victors in heaven are represented as having palms in their hands, Rev. 7. 9; it was twisted into verdant booths at the Feast of Tabernacles; and the multitude, when escorting Christ to his coronation in Jerusalem, spread leaves on the way, John 12. 13. No dust adheres to the leaves as it does with other leaves; the righteous is in the world, not of it; the dust of earth's desert adheres not to his soul. The leaf of the palm is the same—it does not fall in winter, and even in the summer it has no holiday clothing; it is an evergreen: the palm tree's rustling is the desert orison.

4. *The palm tree is very useful.* The Hindus reckon it has 360 uses. Its shadow shelters, its fruit refreshes the weary traveller; it points out to water. Such were *Barnabas,* a son of consolation, Acts 4. 36, Lydia, Dorcas, Acts 9. 39, and others, who on the king's highway showed the way to heaven, as Philip did to the Ethiopian eunuch, Acts 8. 34.

The palm tree bears fruit even to old age. The best dates are produced when the tree is from thirty to one hundred years old, and 300lbs. of dates are annually yielded; so the righteous grow happier and more useful as they become older; knowing their own faults more, they are more mellow to others; like the sun setting, beautiful, mild, and large, looking like Elim in the desert, where the wearied Jews found twelve wells and seventy palm trees, Ex. 15. 27.

Perseverance as the Husbandman.—Jas. 5. 7.

Arab.—A poor man without patience is like a lamp without oil.

Arab.—When you are an anvil, be patient; when a hammer, strike.

Malabar.—You must not cast away the paddle when you approach the shore.

Bengal.—The bundle was pressed hard, but the knot was left loose—*i.e.*, business neglected at the close.

Malabar.—By practice you may lift up even elephants.

Telugu.—With a single blow he opens not nine nuts.

Niti Shatak.—The perseverance of a man of constant mind can never be overwhelmed by misfortune, as the flame of the torch turned upward never goes down, 2 Cor. 6. 10.

Urdu.—The crows keep cawing, but the corn grows notwithstanding.

Turk.—Little by little we become fat.

Telugu.—He watched the field until the harvest, and then let it go to the jackals.

Polygamy.

Malay.—Two wives under one roof: two tigers in one cage.

Bengal.—Who has two wives has much sorrow, 1 Kings 11. 4.

Telugu.—Two swords cannot be contained in one scabbard.

Afghan.—Who likes squabbles at home contracts two marriages.

Tamul.—Why fire the house of a man who has two wives; *i.e.*, the fire of anger and jealousy is enough.

Malay.—The desire of the heart might be to grasp mountains, but what use when the arm will not reach round ?—*i.e.*, a man desiring to marry above his station.

Prevention better than Cure.

Bengal—When the thief has escaped men are very wise.
Gujerat.—Diseases and delays indulged augment.
Polish.—What I see not with the eye cannot pain the heart.
Arab.—Shut the window from which a bad smell comes.
Sanskrit.—Keeping away from the mire is better than washing it off.
Tamul.—Relying on the efficacy of the proposed remedy, will you put your hand in a snake's hole ?

Pride.—Prov. 21. 4.

Exemplified in Haman, Esth. 3. 15, Nebuchadnezzar, Dan. 4. 30, Agrippa, Acts 12. 21–23, Herod, Acts 12. 21–23, Pharaoh, Ex. 5. 2.

Afghan.—To every man his own understanding is king.
China.—We fill tanks, but the heart of man who can fill?
Telugu.—Like the bat, which thinks it holds up the sky.
Canara.—He has to live on gruel, yet requires some one to wipe his moustache.
Afghan.—The fox thought his own shadow very large.
Basque.—Pride sought flight in heaven, fell to hell.
Canara.—What is extended will tear: what is long will break, Prov. 16. 18.
Telugu.—A tooth projecting beyond the lips; a wick too big for the dish.
Arab.—His head in the dirt, his tail to the sky.
Mahabharat.—
The sinner is ever like a great inflated skin;
The imaginations of conceited fools are baseless.
Turk.—He who falls from a horse or ass prepares a bed;
He who falls from a camel prepares a tomb.
Tamul.—When a sieve full of pride is sifted nothing remains.
Sanskrit.—No greater enemy than pride.

China.—

To pretend to satisfy his desires by possession,
Is extinguishing fire with straw.

Arab.—Content enjoys riches, covetousness produces cares; every ambitious man is a captive, and every covetous one a pauper.

Japan.—Be a serpent save in the poison—*i.e.*, learning without pride, Mat. 10. 16.

Punctuality and Watching opportunity.—Eph. 5. 16.

Telugu.—When the dog comes a stone cannot be found. When the stone is found the dog does not come.

Japan.—To cut a stick when the fight is over.

China.—Lighting a fire when the breeze is blowing.

Canara.—A word in season is good; out of it, like a silk cloth torn.

Arab.—To hammer cold iron.

Talmud.—While you have the shoes on your feet tread down the thorns.

Bengal.—They fetch the salt after rice is eaten.

Russian.—Hurry is good only for catching flies.

Sanskrit.—By delay (in using it) nectar becomes poison.

The Heavenly Race.—Heb. 12. 1, 2.

World's race differs from the heavenly in six points:—

It was the practice in ancient Greece to celebrate once every four years with great solemnity certain games, as trials of bodily strength or skill in wrestling, leaping, running, the quoit; these were attended by a vast assemblage of people of all ranks. The *prize* that was contended for was a crown or chaplet of leaves, with which the victor was crowned, while his name was proclaimed by heralds in the presence of the whole assembly; *judges* were appointed to decide on the merits of the candidates, and to see that the several contests were conducted according to the laws that were laid down.

The foot-race was one of the principal of these games; and St. Paul has in many places alluded to it in illustration of the Christian life, 1 Cor. 9. 24–27, as a continual strife or *contest* for victory over our manifold, corrupt, and deceitful lusts; and he encourages us to maintain the conflict by the thought that we are contending for a glorious *prize* in the presence of a great crowd of witnesses. The *crown* for which we contend is not a chaplet of fading leaves, but a crown of righteousness and glory, 1 Cor. 9. 25. The *witnesses* of our manful efforts are the great company of those cited by the Apostle, who have before us gained this mastery over sin, the world, and the devil, and have now by faith and patience attained the promises; we contend for the prize of our high calling in the presence of God and of his holy angels.

A man, who was about to contend in a foot-race, would first lay aside every *weight* that might be about his person, and would disencumber himself of every needless garment. Yet Paul ran his race in Rome, when he was a prisoner in chains. Thus we are to prepare ourselves for our course by laying aside every weight; and "the sin that doth so easily beset us." He who does not take pains to divest himself of covetousness, sensuality, pride, and other too-easily besetting sins, is as one who should lade himself with thick clay when about to start upon a race, Habak. 2. 6.

When once the candidates started on their course, they did not suffer themselves to relax in their *efforts* until they had reached the end. They did not linger on the way, nor stop to look back with satisfaction on the progress which they had made; but they thought only of what yet remained to be done; and they kept the eye steadily fixed upon the mark or goal. If they found themselves disposed to give way, they remembered the prize which was such an object of desire, and pressed forward with renewed spirit, Rev. 2. 10. It will not do for us to relax our efforts to obtain the mastery over our own lusts and passions as they will gain upon us if we give them the least advantage, Thess. 3. 13.

In the heavenly race *all* may be winners; there is no *jealousy*, the strong are to help the weak; there is *joy* in running, Ps. 19. 5; the value of the prize is an exceeding weight of glory; the spectators are angels, devils, and God; the Judge is impartial, and perfect in knowledge.

Tamul.—To advance a span and fall back a cubit.
Japan.—Fall seven times, stand up the eighth time.
Urdu.—Sweetmeats are not distributed during a battle.
Tamul.—A noisy dog is not fit for hunting.
Tamul.—He lacks sense who broods over the past.
Tamul.—When on the way to heaven do you carry a spinning wheel under your arm?
Russian.—Who hunts the bear does not sleep over the sport.
Afghan.—He who stands still in mud, sinks.
Japan.—To give wings to a tiger.

God will not Break the bruised Reed.—Mat. 12. 20.

See the parable of the Publican, Luke 18. 9–14, illustrating God's kindness to the humble and penitent.

The bruised reed, which has been crushed by some weight that has passed over it, and appears to be bowed hopelessly to the ground, is the emblem of one who has been crushed under the burthen of his sins, and of all that sorrow and remorse which are sure to follow in their train. Judas was so weighed down with remorse that he went and hanged himself, Mat. 27. 5.

" The smoking flax" is another emblem of the same case; and with this additional resemblance. If the flax which has been lighted will not burn, its smoke is so offensive, that all cry out impatiently to have it quenched as soon as possible. And this fact is elsewhere used to show how abominable are the wicked in the sight of their holy

Maker; for he says of them, and especially of such as say to their fellow-sinners: "Stand by thyself, for I am holier than thou:" "These are a smoke in my nostrils (Is. 65. 5), a fire that burneth all the day"—that is, not a quick and pleasant flame, but a mere smouldering fire; such as lingers in flax when too damp for any flame to break out, and emitting only a noxious smoke. God will not rashly snap asunder the last thread by which a spiritual life keeps its hold on the soul of one who has fallen. It is far better to be as a bruised reed (of a contrite and humble spirit), than to be as the cedars of Lebanon that are exalted and lifted up, or as the oaks of Bashan, on which the day of the Lord of Hosts shall be, Isa. 2. 13.

God a Refuge and Shield.—Ps. 17. 1; Gen. 12. 1–4; Dan. 2. 16–19.

God is a hiding place, Is. 32. 2, and a *strong tower*—*i.e.*, a refuge in time of war, Prov. 18. 10. But the name "refuge" has a very particular meaning. If any Israelite killed a man by accident, God told Moses that he must not be treated as a murderer, because he did not design to murder, Num. 35. But, lest the kinsman or relation of the person killed should take away the life of the manslayer, which was allowed to be done in the case of murder, he was to hurry off with all speed out of his way, and to take refuge in one of the six cities appointed for the protection of such persons. These cities were well supplied with water, and plenty of provisions, so that there was no occasion to go out of them to buy, which would endanger the manslayer. The roads to these places were all plain and easy of access, kept in good order, and provided, wherever it was necessary, with bridges to cross streams of water, and wherever two roads met, there were hand-posts pointing to the proper direction, on which was written in large characters, so that it might easily be read, "Refuge, Refuge." So God is our refuge, to whom we may flee in distress, as the manslayer did to the city of refuge.

Rend the Heart, not the Garment.—JOEL 2. 13.

Rending the garment was a sign of grief, as Jacob did, Gen. 37. 34, Job. 1. 20.

The Russians have a proverb "People sometimes sin like David, but do not sorrow like him," 2 Sam. 12. 13. Repentance is compared to *awakening*, Eph. 5. 14, a *pricking* at the heart, Acts 2. 37, *smiting*, Luke 18. 13, coming to oneself, Luke 15. 17. The tear of repentance is dropped from the eye of faith; repentance consists in attrition, as when a rock is broken in pieces, and in contrition, as when ice is melted in water; the former is the work of the law, the latter of the Gospel—the one is like a hammer, the other like dew. Ice must not only be broken, but melted, so the coldness must be taken out of the heart. False repentance is the sudden torrent after rain in the mountains; or like people who throw their goods over in a storm, and wish for them again in a calm. False *repentance* is also compared to the sow returning to wallowing in the mire, 2 Pet. 2. 22. See parable of Prodigal Son, Luke 15. 11–32. The true is the stream flowing from a living fountain.

Divinely applied to our heart, the Gospel is not only a net but a *plough*, breaks up the fallow ground, tears up the roots of corruption, and prepares us for receiving the good seed of grace. How proper for its operation, the winter of adversity and spring-tide of youth! How necessary that every application be attended with the dewy influence of the Holy Spirit!

The hypocrite's repentance is like Jonah's gourd, which came up in a night and perished in a night, Jonah 4. 10, or a deceitful bow, Hos. 7. 16.

Examples of true repentance in rending the heart are met in Manasseh, 2 Chr. 33. 12–13, Nineveh, Jonah 3. 5–8,

Peter, Mat. 26. 75, the thief on the cross, Luke 23. 40–41, Ahab rent his clothes and his heart, 1 Kings 21. 27–29. Examples of false repentance in Pharaoh, Ex. 9. 27–34, Saul, 1 Sam. 15. 24–30, Judas, Mat. 27. 3–5, Jews pricked to the heart, Acts 2. 37. The furrow will be crooked if the eye looks back. The plough of repentance breaks the hard stony soil of the heart, kills the weeds; Luke 9. 62.

Arab.—The fasting of desires after worldly pleasures the best fasting.

Afghan.—Paradise is a good place, but the getting there is by lacerating the heart.

Arab.—It is more useful to fly from yourself than from a lion, Rom. 7. 24.

Arab.—The best part of repentance is little sinning.

Turk.—Only a fool falls twice into the same hole.

Arab.—The tears of repentance are cool, and refresh the eyes.

Russian.—Are there tears, there is conscience.

Mrichhakati Natak.—

Why shave the head and mow the chin
Whilst bristling follies choke the breast:
Apply the knife to parts within,
And heed not how deformed the rest:
The heart of pride and passion weed,
And then the man is pure indeed, Mat. 23. 25.

Resignation.

See Job's case, Job 1. 20–22; Moses, Ex. 3. 23–27; David, 2 Sam. 23. 25. 16. 10–12; Jacob, Gen. 43. 14.

Persian.—God rights him that keeps silence.

Talmud.—Be as strong as a leopard, light as an eagle, quick as a goat, and brave as a lion, to do the will of thy heavenly father.

God's Grace a River.—Rev. 22. 1.

The river of God's grace differs from earthly rivers in nine points:—

In this text, as in various others in the Bible, there is an allusion to the flowing rivers, on the banks of or near which the eastern gardens were planted and cities were erected; and the church of God is called a city, because like a city it is composed of many individuals living together, having the same common privileges; which is refreshed and delighted by this river common to all—*i.e.*, by the spiritual blessings which God bestows upon it, regaling all its spiritual senses, and supplying all its spiritual need.

A flowing river is often spoken of in Scripture, when it is intended to describe the *abundance* of anything, Job 29. 6. "The rock poured me out rivers of oil"—*i.e.*, great plenty and abundance of oil, Ps. 36. 8; "Thou shalt make them drink of the river of thy pleasures;" that is, thou shalt make them partake of that abundant pleasure, delight, and satisfaction which thou didst not only enjoy thyself, but bestowest upon thy people. In Job 40. 23, it is said of the hippopotamus, "He drinketh up a river"—*i.e.*, a great quantity of water. "Thou waterest the earth with the river of God," Ps. 65. 9; that is, with plentiful showers of rain from the clouds; and "river" may denote the constancy and *perpetuity* of these pleasures as well as their plenty, John 7. 38. "He that believeth on me, out of his belly shall flow rivers of living water"—*i.e.*, he shall be endued with the gifts and graces of the Spirit in a plentiful measure, which shall not only refresh himself, but shall break forth and be communicated to others also for their refreshing. In Psalm 46. 4, the words mean the gracious presence of God, and the blessings following thence, which shall make Zion, or the Church of God, glad.

God is compared to a place of *broad* rivers, Is. 33. 21; by him saints, in their situation and blessings, are *adorned* and beautified; by him the air—*i.e.*, the soul's breathing, is rendered *pure* and *wholesome;* by him they are completely *defended* from every foe; by him they have full *access* to the profitable *commerce* of the celestial country; in him how wide their prospect into eternity, into things in heaven and on earth! How inexhaustible his fulness to *quench* their thirst; to satisfy their desires, *refresh* their souls, and *purge* away their filth.

A river, however large, like the Amazon, which is 180 miles wide, springs from a small *fountain*, scarcely seen, like the founts of the Ganges at Gangautri; the river of grace *rises far away in heaven* from the throne of God. A river, not like a tank, has much water constantly flowing; all may come to it, Is. 55. 1;—it sometimes overflows, so at Pentecost, and in the time when God's knowledge shall cover the earth. In its course it is impetuous, carries away impediments; so Paul went out a lion, came in a lamb, Acts 9. 6; it *fertilizes*, the righteous are compared to willows by the watercourses, Is. 44. 4; the banks of Indian rivers are very fertile; its waters are *carried to the ocean*, so all grace ends in God; the water is always *new and fresh*, hence grace compared to a tree of life bearing twelve manner of fruits every month.

The river of God's grace differs from earthly rivers in these points—it never dries up; is never frozen up; breeds no noxious animals; its channel is not shifted; never muddy; cleanses the soul; its fountain—the Holy Spirit—is eternal; its waters as clear as crystal; no trail of the serpent; no tigers near this river; no gold alloyed; no blighted flowers.

The Sacrifices of the Body and of Praise.—ROM. 12. 1.

Paul wished to be delivered from his body of death, referring to the custom of fastening a living body to a dead one until the criminal so fastened died from the stench of the putrefying corpse; and yet this vile body, which will be glorified, is to be used in God's service,—but the sacrifices to God are a broken spirit. Sacrifice was the immediate commerce of a creature with its God, in which the Lord of all condescended to receive offerings at our hands. Paul in this view offered his body as a sacrifice, and he was beheaded, 2 Tim. 4. 6. We are to offer the meat-offering of charitable distributions, the drink-offering of penitent tears, the hen-offering of prayer, the peace-offering of praise, and the whole burnt-offering of worldly desire. The priests before offering sacrifices must be washed, annointed, and put on white garments; they must have clean hands, Is. 52. 11, so must we spiritually. The sacrifice was not to be offered with strange fire; Nadab and Abihu were killed for doing so; neither were the blind to be offered, Lev. 22. 22. The sacrifices of the wicked are an abomination, Prov. 21. 27; so Absalom found, 2 Sam. 15. 7–13; Jeroboam in his worship, 1 Kings 12. 26–33; Jezebel's fast, in order to murder Naboth, 1 Kings 21. 9–12; the Pharisee in his prayer, Mat. 23. 14.

Tamul.—Flowers beyond reach are sacred to God; those within reach are for themselves.

The Troubled Sea of Evil Passion.—Is. 57. 20.

Passions, like the sea, are generally considered as terrible, yet they have their use. Men do not reflect on the wonders and blessings which the sea presents to us in so visible a manner; it conveys ships, cools the air, yields plenty of fish, supplies water to the clouds, and salt; the saltness of the sea is such that a pound of its water contains two ounces of salt. The sea salt appears to be lighter than that which we use in common; yet it is not drawn into the air by evaporation, nor does the salt diminish by the continual pouring in of fresh water from all the rivers flowing into it, yet not filling it; this saltness is necessary for certain purposes; it prevents the water from corrupting, and contributes to make it so heavy that the greatest ships may be transported from one place to another. The creatures of which the sea is full ought also to excite our wonder and admiration, as well as its depth, in some places as much as five miles.

Evil passions like the troubled sea in seven points:—

The quiet spirit of a good man is like the clear water of the fountain; but the restless mind of the wicked is like the dirty waves of the sea, when the mire of the bottom is stirred up by their motions. Such were *Samson* Judg. 16. 16, *Saul*, 1 Sam. 16. 14. The wicked are devoured by foolish lusts, 1 Tim. 6. 9. Our wicked passions, such as pride, wrath, and envy, disturb our hearts, like the winds which blow upon the sea, and nothing can quiet them but the word and grace of Jesus Christ, who spoke to the raging waves, and commanded them to be still; so can He now command our restless spirits, and restore them to peace; so that there shall be a calm within us.

The wicked and their passions are like the sea, (1) a collection of *many waters* (the sea in scripture sometimes means numerous armies); so the passions various, Jer. 51. 42.

2. Sometimes *roars* and *swells*, the waves rise in great storms 60 feet; such are persecutors swollen with pride, Ps. 65. 7.

3. *Bounds* set by God. The sea shut up by doors; hitherto shall thou come, Job 38. 8. God set the sand as the ocean's boundary, Jer. 5. 22, the clouds as its garment, Job 38. 9, and darkness as its swaddling bands, Job 38. 9. *Still at God's* commands; so God quiets the wicked. The winds and seas obeyed Jesus, Mat. 8. 26; so God stilleth the tumult of the people, Ps. 65, Jer. 5. 22.

4. *Monsters* in it, Job 41. 31, some are 80 feet in length; so Daniel's four beasts of the sea or monarchs, Dan. 7. 3: the Roman beast had great teeth; such was the emperor Nero, who killed his own mother.

5. *Restless* tides, currents, winds always agitate it

such was Haman against Mordecai—*i.e.*, the sea is always in motion even in a calm ; hence the peace of heaven is represented as there being no more sea, Rev. 21. 1—*i.e.*, no more trouble. The Bible compares the tranquillity of heaven to a sea of glass—*i.e.*, still without storms, no separation. Mud and dust are cast out, so from the wicked heart arise envy, malice, and the filthy waves of passion.

So men change from restlessness. Ahasuerus turns off Vashti his queen, and entertains Esther, a Jewish maiden. *Reuben* is unstable as water, Gen. 49. 4. *Pharaoh* now on the throne, anon in the bottom of the sea. *Hezekiah* healthy, now anon hears, set thy house in order for thou shalt die. *Jerusalem* besieged and freed in one night. In youth we are for pleasure, in manhood for fame, in age for riches, as if thick clay must be a provision for heaven. There is no constancy in health or wealth.

6. *Deceitful ;* the sea allures by its calmness, then heavy storms arise ; so the world promises content, but that cluster never grew on the world's thorns ; it gives an hour's pleasure and violent torture. *Dives*' dainties now bite like a serpent. *Achan's* wedge of gold purchased the stones that beat out his brains. *Judas's* thirty pieces bought the halter that hanged him. *Sechem's* lust brought the sword upon himself and the city; like a man in the sea with his pockets full of gold, which hastens his drowning. *Job* presented kindness to Amasa, but it is cruelty, he kissed and killed him, 2 Sam. 20. *Agag* is hewn in pieces, and *Jezebel* was eaten by dogs like a piece of carrion. *Jael* began with milk and butter, but ended with a hammer ; so *Adonijah*, 1 Kings 1. 50.

7. The *sea-water is unsatisfying.* A *Persian* proverb states : " He who covets this world's goods, is like one who drinks sea-water ; the more he drinks, the more he increases thirst, nor does he cease to drink until he dies."

We all have to pass over this worldly sea, but we have

the Bible as our chart. Christ is the Pilot, and the winds from heaven waft us on; hope is our anchor—we can thus escape the hidden rocks and whirlpools which abound in this sea.

Tamul.—Will the headache be cured by changing the pillow?

Lalita Vistara.—Men consumed by desire can gain as little repose as fire can be extracted from rubbing two pieces of green wood under the water.

Mahabharat.—Passions, when uncontrolled, are sufficient to destroy a man, as unbroken and unchecked horses can destroy an unskilful charioteer on the road.

Telugu.—Like flies that, longing for honey, approach it, enter, are intoxicated, and unable to extricate themselves,—so, plunged in a multitude of passions, a sinner perishes without escape.

Talmud.—Passions are like iron thrown into the furnace, as long as it is in the fire you can make no vessels out of it.

Telugu.—If thy heart become calm as the breezeless firmament and the unruffled waveless deep, changeless and unfluctuating—this is denominated freedom.

Persian.—What fear need he have of the waves of the sea who has Noah for his pilot? Mat. 8. 26.

Syriac.—Let not your beast run in a meadow without a wall—*i.e.*, passions without a bridle.

Syriac.—Be not as water which takes the tint of all colours.

China.—The water that bears the ship is the same that engulfs it.

Turk.—Trust not the promise of the great, the calm of the sea, the evening twilight, the word of a woman, or the courage of the horse.

Afghan.—Neither does a libertine's eye rest nor a thief's hand.

Veman.—Cupidity makes a man as restless as a dog. Mat. 21. 5.

Bhagavatgita.—As a lamp, standing in a windless place, moves not—that is the likeness of the devotee, whose mind is subdued, who is collected in self-devotion.

Hebrew.—Were there no passions no one would build a house, marry, bring up children, or drive any trade.

Buddhaghosa.—No fire like passion ; no spark like hatred ; no snare like folly ; and no tyrant like greed.

Bhagavatgita.—The heart which follows the dictates of the moving passions, carries away his reason, as the storm the bark in the raging ocean. Prov. 25. 28.

Conscience seared as with a Hot Iron.—1 TIM. 4. 2.

Men's conscience is compared to a *candle*, Prov. 20. 27, to lighten us in the darkness of this world, to a *judge*, John 3, 20 ; a *witness*, Rom. 9. 1 ; a *worm*, Mat. 10. 44.

The *Telegus*, referring to a conscience dead to all moral restraint, say "it is a tongue without nerves moving all ways." Reason is compared by Plato to a *charioteer* driving his two horses, concupiscence and anger.

Conscience called God's *vicegerent* ; named, Luke 11. 35, the *light* within, as a law also enlightens and directs ; a blind man sees not evil coming, neither do sinners good and evil, life and death. Sin blackens and darkens the light of conscience ; dirt obstructs the sun's rays ; so *David's* soul was darkened when his eye was dimmed by adultery. Nathan awoke him, 2 Sam. 12. 7. Holiness compared to white, shines as crystal, or is transparent, but only when the sun is on it.

Conscience is called by Christ the *eye* of the soul, which, if single, the body is full of light ; the affections are apt to go to excess ; like a balance when one side moves up, and the other moves down, so with the *flesh* and spirit, Gal. 5. 7; thus—(*a*) *Sensuality* blinded Samson and *Herod*. (*b*) *Intemperance* others, Hos. 4. 11; fumes of meat and drink obscure the upper regions, hence Paul's watching and fasting, 2 Cor. 11. 27 ; he who comes to make his belly his business will quickly come to have a conscience of as large a swallow as his throat; loads of meat and drink are fit for none but a beast of burthen to bear; and he is much the greater beast of the two, who comes with his burden in his belly than he who comes with it on his back, Prov. 23. 29; such as are *best at the barrel* are generally *weakest at the book*. (*c*) *Covetousness* buries the soul underground in darkness, while the body is above it, Deut. 16. 9, 1 Sam. 12. 3, Ecc. 7. 7. (*d*) *Ambition* looks high, and giddiness from it makes a mist before the eyes. Satan, like an expert wrestler, usually gives a man a lift before he gives him a throw. Sensuality, covetousness, pride are the devil's trident to strike men's hearts.

The conscience is seared when a man's wounds cease to *smart*, only because he has lost his *feeling;* they are nevertheless *mortal;* he does not see his need of a *surgeon;* *acquitment* before trial can be no security in this case. Great and strong *calms* usually portend and go before the most violent storms.

China.—A fleshy pupilless eye (a mind with conscience blind).
Talmud.—The flesh of the dead feels not the knife—*i.e.*, is past feeling.
Arab.—Reckon him with the beasts who does not distinguish good from evil.
Bengal.—He hides his head in the bushes—*i.e.*, fancying he is not exposed.
China.—Talent without virtue like silver without a master.

The Seed of God's Word.—Luke 8. 11.

The Word of God is compared in Scripture to a *key*, to open out the treasures of Divine Wisdom; as *milk*, to nourish the feeble-minded; as *fire*, to consume or enliven; and to *gold*, for its value and use: here it is compared to a seed on account of its hidden qualities, its power of spreading from a small beginning. There is a tree in New

Zealand, 400 feet high and 50 feet in circumference, yet this has sprung up from a small seed.

The Word of God like seed in seventeen points :—

1. *Seed is small, compared with its future produce ;* so faith is like a grain of mustard seed or leaven which leaveneth the whole lump ; the seeds of faith, in the 11th chapter of Hebrews, "yield plentiful fruit."

2. *Seed must be sown.* Industry and forethought are required, but bad seed springs up of itself, for God cursed the ground, so that it gave of itself thorns and thistles. The seeds of faith spring up as the gifts of God, as the radicle from the kernel; when God sows in the wilderness an oasis springs up.

3. *A good seed requires good soil.* The application of the plough is, however, necessary, as weeds grow anywhere ; Christ in his parable mentions three soils as unproductive. Our heart is the soil, and conviction the plough : we must be moistened by the tears of godly sorrow, saturated by the dews of God's grace, like the 3,000 pricked to the heart who were baptized, Acts 2. 40, 41.

4. *Seed must be buried.* Some seeds, though thrown on the surface, however, strike their roots deep, and require soil above them, Mat. 13. 6, but in other cases the root and stem soon wither; so Lydias's heart was opened, Acts 16. 14 ; believers are rooted and grounded in love, Eph. 3. 18.

5. *Seed lies for a time in the earth in darkness.* Sometimes a very short time—so the thief on the cross. Egyptian mummy seed, after being buried 3,000 years, springs up—so the *Prodigal son* came to himself after he had spent all in riotous living, and was feeding swine ; so *Manasseh,* after many years, sought in affliction his father's God, 2 Chron. 33. 13, "cast thy bread on the waters," Eccl. 11. 1 ; one soweth, another reapeth.

6. *Seed once sown makes steady progress.* Christ speaks of the blade, the ear and the full corn, Mark 4. 27, 28 ;

grow in grace. They shall bring forth fruit in old age, Ps. 92. 14. The righteous shall grow like a cedar of Lebanon, Ps. 92. 12.

7. *Seed depends on the influence of heavy rain, which waters the earth.* Light, soil, and moisture are necessary; we must wait for the latter rain; so Paul plants, Apollos waters, but God gives the increase, 1 Cor. 3. 6. God will pour floods on the dry ground, Is. 44. 3.

8. *Seed matured yields a rich return.* God's word is compared to rain that returns not again, Is. 55. 10. You shall reap if you faint not, Gal. 6. 9, and have a hundredfold more in this present time, Luke 18. 30.

9. *Produce is as the seed sown.* There is a great variety of seeds, but the generic distinction remains, as figs come not of thistles, Mat. 7. 16. He that sows to the flesh, reaps corruption, Gal. 6. 8.; he sowing the wind reaps the whirlwind, Hos. 6. 7. Haman sowed pride, reaped defeat; so the drunkard, Prov. 23. 29; so the rich man drowned in destruction, 1 Tim. 6. 9; so war from lust, Jas. 4. 1.

10. *Water is required;* hence the thorny ground allows none; early rain necessary after the seed is sown, and the latter rain when the corn is ripe, Jer. 5. 24: so the dews of the Spirit.

11. *The seed dies—i.e.,* the albumen dissolves; an emblem of the Resurrection, 1 Cor. 15. 36.

12. *If sown too deeply no air comes:* hence ploughing brings the seeds up: for malting barley, heat, moisture, and air are necessary, thereby the starch is changed into sugar: the seed to sow is reserved from the choicest grain by the husbandman.

13. *A skilful sower required.* Such was Christ.

14. Seeds must be *covered* from the birds, Mat. 13. 4.

15. The *sooner* the seed is sown the better the crop, 2 Tim. 3. 15.

16. *Diligence* needed; winds, storm, thunder hinder not the sower.

17. *Seeds must be widely scattered,* 1 Cor. 1. 16. Seed must be sent from land to land, and handed down to others; some seed bad, some not successful.

When the corn is fully ripe it bends down the ear; so the believer is to be clothed with humility, 1 Pet. 5. 5.

Tamul.—Those who are of inferior stature may accomplish great things.
Tamul.—The seed of the banyan is small, but the tree affords a large shade.
Persian.—Vegetables do not grow on a stone; what fault in the rain? Mat. 23. 37.
Tamul.—Though it may rain to the end of the world, a broken potsherd will not germinate, Mat. 13. 5.
Afghan.—When you fixed your hopes on the soil you lost your seed in it—*i.e.*, by neglecting to weed and water.

Self-conceit.—Prov. 26. 12.

Wise in one's own eye, Prov. 3. 7.

Afghan.—The fox thought his shadow very large—*i.e.*, a little man puffed up.
Syriac.—If the camel had seen his hunchback he would have fallen and broken his neck.
Oriental.—When the wolf is alone he is a lion.
China.—He who cannot sleep finds his bed badly made.
Japan.—To hide the head but not hide the tail—*i.e.*, as the ostrich.

Selfishness.

Afghan.—The one was dying and the other was asking his daughter of him.
Panjabi.—The goat was weeping for his life, the butcher for his fat.
Afghan.—What does the satiated man know of the hungry man's state.

The Righteous as Sheep.—MAT. 10. 16.

The righteous resemble sheep in ten points:—

1. *Cleanliness.* Not like swine, dogs, or wolves, the righteous come out of the wilderness of sin, yet, as subject to *filth*, need washing, 1 Cor. 6. 11, Ps. 51. 7: hence they love still water, Ps. 23. 2; 2 Sam. 24. 17.

2. *Harmless:* innocent as doves, but wise as serpents, Mat. 10. 16: not crafty as foxes, or devouring as a lion, 1 Cor. 14. 20.

3. *Meek.* So Christ was led as a lamb to the slaughter, Is. 53. 7; so Stephen and Job; so David, Ps. 39. 9; and Aaron when his sons were killed.

4. *Profitable;* in life by fleece, in death by their flesh. So the blood of the martyrs was the seed of the Church; so saints are lights. Ten saints would have saved Sodom, Gen. 18. 32; being dead they yet speak, Heb. 11. 4: so Jacob proved to Joseph, and Joseph to Potiphar.

5. *Obedient:* follow the shepherd; the shepherd knows their name; calling them they follow him, John 10. 4.

6. *Feeble,* Gen. 33. 13. They are apt to go astray, 1 Sam. 17. 20: they have many enemies—wolves, dogs, Rom. 8. 36; nourished for slaughter, Ps. 64. 22; subject to many diseases, Jer. 7. 28.

7. Love *union.* Saints are like David and Jonathan scattered by dogs they soon unite, Acts 4. 23.

8. *Live on little:* often on barren commons; so the righteous are content, 1 Tim. 6. 8.

9. *Need a shepherd,* Acts 10. 3, to select pasture, 1 Pet. 5. 1; to select shade, Ps. 23. 2; sheep may be lost, not so believers: pigs and cats find out their way, not so sheep. When one strays the others follow, 2 Sam. 20. 1, 2; Acts 5. 36, 37. Sheep may return of themselves, the spiritual sheep never.

10. Love green *pastures,* Cant. 1. 7.

China.—A sheep was never known to climb a tree.

The Shipwrecked Soul.—I TIM. I. 19.

The body has been compared to a casket, the soul to a jewel; in the text the soul is like a ship, launched at birth on the river of life, constructed with great skill, fitted up for a long and dangerous voyage over the ocean of life; exposed to the storms of temptation, the rocks of sin, the waves of passion, needs a good bottom of faith, so necessary to prevent a leak, the wind of God's Spirit to fill the sails of the affections, and the compass of God's word; Christ is the pilot.

Turk.—The soul is the ship, reason is the helm, the oars are the soul's thoughts, and truth is the port.

Malay.—The boat which is swamped at sea may be baled out, but a shipwreck of the affections is final.

Silence.—LUKE 21. 19.

Solomon states, "Where no wood is the fire goeth out; so where there is no talebearer, the strife ceases, or is silent."

Sanskrit.—Silence is the ornament of the ignorant.

Arab.—Silence is the remedy for anger.

Syrian.—Shut your door and you will not fear an enemy—*i.e.*, silence the remedy against calumny.

Sanskrit.—By silence there is no quarrel; by vigilance no fear.

Turk.—Two ears to one tongue, therefore hear twice as much as you speak.

Modern Greek.—The tongue has no bone, yet it breaks bones.

Arab.—Silence is the sweet medicine of the heart, Ps. 37. 7.

Sanskrit.—Where frogs are the croakers, there silence is becoming.

Turk.—A great river makes no noise.

Avyar.—Do not come near one in a passion.

Esthonian.—Time heals wounds.

Avyar.—A calumnious mouth is a fire in a wind.

Death a Sleep to the Righteous.—JOHN 11. 11.

Sleep called death's brother. Death is a departure, Phil. 1. 23, from a wilderness to the promised land; the wicked are driven away, Prov. 14. 32. Sleep in death is applied in Scripture only to the righteous, as to Lazarus, Solomon, Hezekiah, Jehoshaphat, Stephen.

Death is like natural sleep in four points:—

(1) *Calm* in its *commencement;* people know not when they are dropping off to sleep. We gradually become insensible to outward things; such was Moses' death. (2) *Rest* from labour; life is warfare; death is peace; the slave hears not the voice of the oppressor, Job 3. 18. (3) *Awakening* to vigour after sleep, Is. 26. 19; Isaiah calls the grave a bed. (4) *Mind active* even in dreams.

Conscience Asleep.—EPH. 5. 14.

An impenitent sinner is said both to be "asleep" and also to be "dead." He is "dead," because his soul is destitute of spiritual life; as, however, it has a capacity for receiving spiritual life, he is compared also to one who is "asleep," but who can wake again.

A man who is buried in sleep is unconscious of all that is going on around him. His mind is entertained, indeed, with dreams, which for the time he takes for realities, while the real and important business of life is totally unheeded and neglected by him. Matters which affect his interest, or even his life, may be transacted around him, he is dreaming on; and when he awakes, he will find how material it would have been to him to have resisted the drowsiness in which his faculties for the time were lost. The building may be in flames, or the thief may have broken through the house, but the owner sleeps on in total ignorance of his danger or his loss, until it is too late to escape the one, or to prevent the other. The ship was on the point of being engulfed in the raging waves, when *Jonah* was fast asleep!

In sleeping we are disturbed by vain hopes and fears; on awakening they are all gone, Job 20. 8. In dreams we run away when there is no danger, and are delighted with that which is nothing but a shadow. We think we are flying through the air, while we are motionless in our bed; we think we have found great treasures, but we awake and are as poor as ever. Of that which is real we have no knowledge, while our mind is thus filled with shadows: but, perhaps, we dream that we are sailing on the water, while the chamber in which we sleep has taken fire; and we know it not till the flames reach our body and awaken us; then we start up, but it is too late to escape.

Shánti Shatak.—The careless sinner is a moth, unaware of approaching evil, hovering over a lighted lamp until consumed by it, or a fish falling into the hands of the angler.

Telugu.—What matters it whether we drink milk in a dream out of bell-metal or gold? Is. 14. 20.

Arab.—To sleep on the mountain peaks.

Malay.—To fight in a dream—*i.e.*, labour in vain.

Tamul.—The wealth seen in a dream, the water observed in a mirage.

Veman.—They live like a silkworm in a cocoon, seemingly secure, but in reality helpless, Prov. 7. 22.

Mahabharat.—Seeing thy spirit abides like a bird in a body, which resembles mere foam, why sleepest thou in this dear abode, which is so transitory?

The Smoke of God's Anger.—Is. 65. 2–5.

Nothing is more offensive to the nostrils than smoke, Prov. 10. 20. The expression, "There went up a smoke out of his nostrils," signifies God's wrath against those who did what was offensive to him. When Sodom and Gomorrah were destroyed by brimstone and lightning, a dense smoke arose from the ruins indicating the terrible fire that was there, Gen. 19. 28; so God is said to be to the wicked a consuming fire, Heb. 12. 29; as fire he appeared in the burning bush, Ex. 3. 2; on Sinai, Ex. 19. 18, to Isaiah, 6. 4, Ezekiel, 1. 4, John, Rev. 1. 14, and as a flaming fire will he appear at the Judgment Day, 2 Tim. 1. 8; then all will be *confusion*, as when fire breaks out, Rev. 6. 10; it will be sudden, like at Belshazzar's feast, Dan. 5. 5; it will destroy everything; while the wicked will be only stubble, Nah. 1. 10, the righteous will be as the burning bush on which fire had no effect, Ex. 3. 2. God's anger is described in Job, 37th chapter.

Smoke quickly disappears, not so the smoke of God's anger, Rev. 14. 11. In Rev. 9. 2, the smoke which rose from the bottomless pit refers to gross errors which darken the understanding.

The Righteous a Soldier.—2 Tim. 2. 3, 4.

A soldier is one employed in military affairs, bearing arms under military command, Mat. 8. 9. Every true believer is a soldier to fight the good fight of faith against the world, the flesh, and the devil, Is. 51. 9, Col. 2. 15, 2 Tim. 4. 7.

The righteous is like a soldier in twelve points:

1. *Under a captain.* Christ is the Captain of our salvation, Heb. 2. 10; there is a covenant in Baptism.

2. *Leaves all other worldly affairs,* 2 Tim. 2. 4. The righteous forsake all, as did the apostles; their heart was set on things above, they minded not the things of the flesh, Rom. 8. 5; they were crucified with Christ, Col. 3. 1—*i.e.*, a painful separation from the world like crucifying.

3. *When enlisted is armed,* so the believer has armour, Eph. 6. 10, 12, but only one offensive weapon, the sword.

4. *Uniform worn to distinguish him,* so the garment of love and humility, 1 Pet. 5. 5.

5. *Clad at the King's expense.* The believer's white raiment, an emblem of purity, was purchased with Christ's blood, Rev. 7. 14.

6. *Enemies fixed for him.* The world, the flesh, and the devil. Paul writes, that the believer is more than a conqueror, Rom. 8. 37.

7. *Obedience in everything,* Mat. 8. 9; so Paul, Acts 26. 19.

8. *Order and discipline,* 1 Cor. 14. 33.

9. *Acquainted* with devices of the enemy; wise as serpents, 2 Cor. 2. 11.

10. *Courage* necessary, no turning back, Heb. 11. 38, the cause good, Is. 41. 10, a good conscience, 1 Pet. 3. 16, sure of victory, Rev. 12, 11.

11. *Endures hardships,* Mat. 10, 22, Heb. 11. 38, David watered his couch with his tears.

12. *The righteous soldier is sure of victory,* more than conqueror, Rom. 8. 37.

Tamul.—Of what use is a moustache to a sneaking soldier?
China.—To hide the head and leave the back exposed, Eph. 6. 13.
Breton.—A cat in gloves is no use to catch mice.
Telugu.—Even a sheep will bite a man without a stick.
Tamul.—Those who regard relationship are not fit for military service, 2 Tim. 2. 4.
Tamul.—The handle of the axe is the enemy of its kind.
China.—Armies are kept 1,000 days to be used on one.
Niti Shatak.—Fortune conquers the wise no more than a straw; the elephant, whose cheeks are streaked with the marks of passion, is not fastened by the filaments of the lotus.

The Righteous shall shine as the Stars.—DAN. 12. 3.

The bodies of the righteous after the resurrection will be bright and dazzling, like Christ's body on the mount of transfiguration, Mat. 17. 1; Paul, on his way to

Damascus, saw a light brighter than the sun, the effulgence of which blinded him for three days, Acts 11.

The righteous will be like the stars in five points :—

(1) A great *ornament* to the Heavens; (2) they *differ* in brightness, 1 Cor. 15. 40; (3) guide mariners on the ocean and travellers at night, so believers on the dark ocean of life; (4) though *distant*, they exercise an influence, as a cloud of witnesses, Heb. 12. 1; but many do not, as there are stars so far from this world that their light has not reached the earth from the time of Adam's creation, though travelling like the sun's light at the rate of 12,000,000 miles in a minute; many of them are bigger than the earth, though they seem so small, and are so remote that a cannon ball would take 700,000 years to reach the nearest of them; (5) their *number* is immense; the redeemed in Heaven are a great multitude which no man can number.

Tamul.—Though astrological calculations prove false, the stars will not.

The Rich are only Stewards.—1 Cor. 4. 2.

Parable of the Steward.—Luke 19. 11–27.

In this place, as in many others, God compares himself to a *master*, and we are placed on earth not to do our own will, but the will of him who placed us here; we have nothing which is properly *our own*, but whatever we seem to have is *entrusted* to us by another, who has left us in charge for a season, and will call us to account when he shall return, Luke 16. We are not our own, but are bought with a price; and it is therefore our great duty to glorify God in our body and in our spirit, which are his, 1 Cor. 6. 20.

The various faculties of our soul and body; the opportunities afforded by having our days lengthened; the gifts of station, education, friends, and worldly substance; the knowledge of religious truth and all the means of grace; the various occasions for doing or receiving good; these and numberless advantages and blessings, which are daily and hourly extended to us, must all be accounted for.

The rich are stewards, having a great *master*, the King of Heaven; a great *charge*, their souls; and much *entrusted* to them; they must *improve* their property (see parable of the *Talents,* of the *Barren Fig Tree,* and of the Rich Fool, who thought he was absolute proprietor; hence Christ said it was easier for a camel to go through a needle's eye than for those trusting in riches to enter heaven—*i.e.,* an impossibility in human sight—as the Bengalis say, "A horse's eggs, or putting an elephant into a narrow dish."

Tamul.—Money is a man-stealer.

Talmud.—Riches without wisdom is food without salt.

China.—Fortune is the good man's prize, but the bad man's bane.

Tiravellavar.—When the good man gets riches it is like fruit falling in the midst of a village—*i.e.*, all partake of it.

Canara.—The riches of the good are like water turned off into a rice field. Prov. 19. 17 and 11. 25.

China.—Wealth among men is like dew among plants;
Foam on the waves is the fame which earth grants.

Raghuvansa.—The good, like clouds, receive only to give away.

Sanskrit.—The rivers themselves drink not their water; nor do the trees eat their own sweet fruit. The clouds eat not the crops; the riches of the good are employed for the benefit of others.

China.—Wealth is but dung—*i.e.*, useful only in being spread.

The Stronghold, Faith in God.—Is. 26. 1.

In times of plunder and war in India property and people were insecure, hence they were taken to strongholds for protection. Oude, in the days of the king, had many of these.

Faith is like a stronghold in three points :—

(1) Built on a *rock* to prevent its being undermined; such were the fortresses of Gwalior, Chunar, Dowlatabad; the believer dwells in the munition of rocks, Is. 33. 16; Christ is the rock of ages, 1 Cor. 10. 4. (2) Strongly *defended;* yet Babylon, with its walls 300 feet high and gates of brass, was taken. Tyre like Calcutta, a great trading-place, is now only a rock for fishermen to dry their nets, though it was once a stronghold. Jerusalem had three walls round it, yet it was ploughed up; not so the heavenly Jerusalem, God is to it a wall of fire. (3) Fully *supplied* with provisions and arms, not like Jerusalem where the women eat their own children, or Carthage where the women cut off their hair to make bow-strings; in the believer's weakness is God's strength made perfect, 2 Cor. 12. 9. Elijah was surrounded by a strong army, but he saw the mountain full of Angels under the form of horses and chariots of fire, 2 Kings 6. 17.

Arab.—The strength of the heart is from the soundness of the faith. Mat. 17. 20, Heb. 11. 33-38.

The Death of the Righteous an unsetting Sun.
Is. 60. 19, 20.

The righteous dying sets like the sun in one part of creation, but it is only to rise amid glowing clouds and a clear blue sky in another region; but even when setting his light lingers, and the western clouds are bright with his beams. The heat of the day has gone, and man ceases from labour. Even the twilight is beautiful—at eventide it shall be light, Zech. 14. 7. The Hindu writings state that old age "is like a dried-up stream, fallen as a tree levelled by thunder, dreaded as a house in ruin; it takes away vigour, as if a man were placed in a marsh." Very different is the English proverb, "Nothing old but shoes and hats." Solomon compares the path of the just to the light shining more and more to the perfect day, though the morning might be cloudy and stormy; such as was that of Simeon's, Luke 2. 28–32, Peter's, 2 Pet. 1. 3, 11–16; they were not like the wicked, *driven away* in his wickedness.

As the *Aloe* is green and well liking, till the last best summer of its age,
And then hangeth out its golden bells to mingle glory with corruption;
As the *Meteor* travelleth in splendour, but bursteth in dazzling light;
Such is the end of the righteous; their death is the sun at its setting.

Modern Greek.—The more a good tree grows the more shade does it afford.

Japan.—The heart is the same at sixty as at three.

China.—By length of journey he knew the horse's strength. So length of days shows a man's heart.

Earthen Vessels hold the Soul's Treasures.

2 Cor. 4. 7.

The body is compared to an earthen vessel as being brittle, leaky, mean, of little value. The unsearchable riches of Christ are the soul's treasures.

Bengal.—In a coarse torn bag to put fine rice.

Arab.—Good honey in a dirty vessel.

Arab.—Though the bow be crooked the arrow reaches its mark.

Persian.—The ignorant is in the midst of riches like an earthen vessel covered with gold; the learned man in the midst of poverty like a precious stone encased in a vile metal.

Veman.—When one has learned to speak prudently, why should we think of his youth or age? May not a lamp burn bright though held in the hand of an infant?

Badaga.—So busy in saving a grain of salt he lost the salt vessel.

Tamul.—The vessel may be crooked: what matters it if bakes the bread?

Persian.—The diamond fallen into the dunghill is not the less precious. The dust which the wind raises to the sky is not the less vile.

Christ the Lily among Thorns.—CANT. 2. 2.

The wicked compared to thorns in nine points:—

1. *Little use or value* except for hedges or fuel, Prov. 10. 20; so Antiochus, Dan. 11. 21; men gather not grapes from thorns, Mat. 7. 16.

2. *Change not their nature,* the same in the garden as in the jungle, so Pharaoh was not changed by miracles nor Saul by being made king, so Jeroboam worshipped a calf notwithstanding God's promises.

3. *Encumber the earth;* draw away its moisture, so the Canaanites, Num. 33. 55; Josh. 23. 13; Abimelech called the bramble was made king, killed his seventy brethren, plagued the Shechemites, Judges 9. 1; so the barren fig-tree, Luke 13. 7; when the wicked perish there is shouting, Prov. 11. 10.

4. *Low things;* mount not as the cedar; they overrun fields.

5. *Annoy by their pricking;* so the Canaanites were thorns in the Jews' sides, Num. 33. 55, Josh. 23. 13; so the Samaritans to the Jews, Neh. 6. 6; scoffing at the Jewish sabbaths and sacrifices, Neh. 4. 2, 3; so the priests threatened the apostles, Acts 4. 17; so Saul breathed out slaughter, Acts 9. 1; Christ was called a wine-bibber, a Samaritan or devil; Paul was called a pestilent fellow, Acts 24. 5. Ahab said to Elijah, Are thou the troubler of Israel? 1 Kings 18. 17; Lot's righteous soul was vexed in Sodom, 2 Pet. 2. 7, 8; Delilah vexed Samson, Judges 16. 16.

6. *Care needful in walking among them,* otherwise one gets entangled and scratched; Christ warned us to be wise as serpents, Mat. 10. 16; Paul was scratched by the Jews who were thorns; thorns hindered the growth of good seed, Mat. 13. 7.

7. *Sometimes useful* as hedges, so the earth helped the woman, Rev. 12. 16.

8. *Hard and knotty*, 2 Sam. 23. 6.

9. *Thorns thrown into the fire*, Is. 10. 17; Ps. 9. 17; Is. 30. 33; so Saul and his family, the Jews.

Telugu.—A jackal's rage—*i.e.*, a contemptible thing.
Italian.—A thorn is small, but he who has felt it does not forget it.

Treasures laid up in Heaven.—Mat. 6. 20.

Veman observes: "If you consider your possessions as your own fools alone will agree with you; that alone is yours which you have bestowed on others."

Earthly treasures can be destroyed by fire, floods, the Hindus could be secured against Mahrattas and thieves, white ants, rust, Job 20. 5–29. No treasures of Moguls. The earth itself, with its treasures, is kept in store reserved unto fire, 2 Pet. 3. 7; Solomon calls ill-got riches treasures of wickedness, Prov. 10. 2, as Rehoboam found, so did Nebuchadnezzar, Dan. 4. 31.

See the parable of the hid treasure, Mat. 13. 44, and of the rich fool.

Telugu.—Worldly possessions are like a drop of water on a *lotus* leaf.

Death's Shadowy Valley.—Ps. 23. 4.

Life is a journey through a waste howling wilderness, the dark valley of the mountain of death forms its close, bounded by the river of death.

Death is like some valleys in seven points:—

1. *Dark;* the sunbeams enter not, so no natural light illumines the grave's path; it is like a dark tunnel. The apostles feared when they entered the cloud, Mat. 17. 5. Satan wraps the valley often in clouds of doubt and dark-

ness—a darkness that may be felt; so the Jews, when entering the dark cleft of the Red Sea, found it "a land of darkness," Job 18. 5–21; the righteous in death, however, have no sting, 1 Cor. 15. 57; the Sun of Righteousness illumines the gloom.

2. *Lonely;* mountain passes are solitary—all pass through this, but none meet even though they die together. Angels, however, are present, but as a matter of faith more than of consciousness. Jacob said of the desert, "How dreadful is this place?" Gen. 28. 17. Moses, entering the cloud, exclaimed, "I exceedingly quake," Heb. 12. 21. The Jews crossed the Red Sea at night when quite dark.

3. Sometimes *Painful;* thorns, stones, and briers abound; so death is the wrenching of soul and body; even Christ prayed that the cup might pass from him, Mat. 26. 39.

4. *Dangerous;* robbers, wild beasts in the dark possess the valley; the domain of death, the king of terrors. Some have passed through this valley amid showers of stones, others wrapped in flames, others knee-deep in blood.

5. *Leads to a strange land.* Separates temporal and seen from eternal things; no correspondence with friends; in a moment, millions of miles distant from earth.

6. *A route never retraced;* the great *gulf* between; this tree sprouts not again, Job 14. 7; no work, no device in the grave, Ecc. 9. 10.

7. *Has two terminations;* the gate of life, the gate of death, the land of rest, and that where the worm never dies, like Pharaoh's butler and baker, who looked forward to the third day, but with very different feelings, Gen. 40.

All have to pass this valley; it is the house appointed for all living, Job 30. 23; the righteous walk in the valley implying calmness, Prov. 14. 32; as to them the shadow of death is like the shadow of a sword harmless. Death is even counted a treasure, Phil. 1. 21.

Tamul.—**Is it kind to abandon one in the middle of a river?**

Tamul.—I rest my foot on a branch breaking, and my hand on one about to break.

The Spiritual Warfare.—2 Cor. 10. 3.

Life is compared in the Bible to a dream, an eagle hastening to its prey, a hand-breadth, a swift ship, a tale told; in the text to a war. The *Niti Shatak* states "time no more conquers the wise than a straw the elephant; he, whose cheeks are streaked with the marks of passion, is not fastened by the filaments of the *lotus*."

What a strange thing is war, yet it is everywhere, and vile as it is and very destructive to life and comfort, we ourselves are engaged in it, whether we will or not; there is war in the natural creation; the hawk is always in arms for the seizing of his prey; the tiger and the wolf are at war with cattle; birds and beasts are persecuting one another; and the innocent birds are destroyed by the cruel and rapacious. Even in seas and rivers, there are sharks, alligators, and pike which devour other kinds. Among mankind, nation rises in arms against nation, and kingdoms are divided against themselves. The invisible world is also at war; *there was war in heaven*, Rev. 12. 7, when Satan and millions of Angels rose in rebellion against God, prompted by pride and jealousy. God himself has his enemies among Angels that excel in strength; principalities and powers are confederate against all the great and merciful designs of heaven; and the war, which they began there, is carried on upon earth against us (men) and our salvation. We are, therefore, born to a state of war, and are accordingly enlisted as soldiers at our baptism under Jesus Christ the *captain of our salvation*, under whose banner we are to fight against His and our enemies. Our Christian profession is called *a fight of faith*, 1 Tim. 6. 12, because it is subject to all the dangers, losses, fears, and miscarriages of war; and the same rules are to be observed, the same measures followed, in the one case as in the other; with this difference, that *spiritual* dangers are a thousand times worse than *bodily,* and call for more valour and more vigilance.

Being, therefore, soldiers, we are to do as soldiers do. To put on the whole armour of God; the helmet to save the head in natural war; and there is the protection of God, the *helmet of salvation* in spiritual war. The *shield of faith,* which we are to hold up against the fiery darts of the enemy. The *sword of the spirit,* the word of God, *sharper than any two-edged sword,* which, when skilfully used, will give mortal wounds to the adversaries of our faith. We must practise the *prudence* which is necessary in earthly war, considering that we are here in an *enemy's country,* in continual danger of being surprised by evil spirits, who are always upon the watch, and, therefore, we must be *sober* and *vigilant.* A drunken soldier, in a time of war, is in danger of death—a drunken Christian is in danger of damnation. All levity, dissipation, and foolish jesting are to be avoided, as tending to make the mind effeminate and careless, and insensible of its dangerous situation in this life; in consideration of which we are to *pass the time of our sojourning here in fear,* as they do who are encompassed with enemies. We are to study the interests of the two parties at war. The last enemy is death, our worst the enemy within. The grand enemy of man, which is the devil, has his allies who assist him in his warfare against us; these are the world and the flesh. The *world* receives his principles, and works with him by the great force of custom, fashion, and example; the *flesh* wars against the spirit, and is to be denied and mortified as we stop and seize the supplies of provision when they are upon the road to the camp of an enemy. As the mind of a soldier is intent upon victory, and he runs at all hazards to obtain it, so has the Christian the same object in view; sin and death are to fall before him, and the kingdom of heaven is to be the prize.

In war soldiers must submit to hardships from want of clothes, houses, food, sleep; but they look forward with joy to the expiry of their time of enlistment, Job 7. 2. So believers wish like the dove to flee away and be at peace, Ps. 55. 6.

Malabar.—We lie straight only in our coffin, Rom. 1. 24.
Urdu.—A snake in the sleeve.
Arab.—The best fighting is against yourself.
Bhagavatgita.—The soul floats like the lotus on the lake, unmoved, unruffled by the tide, Acts 20.24; 16.25.
Bengal.—The crocodile in the water and the tiger on shore, both strive to break my neck.
Telugu.—Like fish going against the stream.
Basque.—The wolf and the dog agree at the expense of the goat which they eat together.
Turk.—The world is a mill: sometimes it grinds flour; one day it will grind us.

The Righteous are Watchmen.—Mat. 26. 42, 43.

The *Shánti Shatak* compares man to "one in a ferry-boat crossing the whirling gulf of this world, which he must do with watchfulness so as not to be drowned in the abyss." David says, his soul watched for the Lord more than they that wait for the dawn, Ps. 130. 6; an allusion to the watchmen on the city wall or the watchers of the temple who passed the night there in devotional exercises, anxious to catch the first beams of the morning sun on the hallowed day of atonement.

Watchmen were set on high towers to give notice of fire, or the invasion of an enemy's approach, hence called seers, 1 Sam. 9. 9; Is. 21. 11; watchman, what of the night, Is. 21. 11; the night is far spent, Rom. 13. 12.

The righteous are watchmen in seven points:—

1. Must have *sharp* eyes to be overseers, see to a distance, Ez. 33. 6; if the blind lead the blind both fall into the ditch, Mat. 15. 14.

2. Must be *active*, not drowsy, look for the morning, Ps. 130. 6, otherwise wolves come in, Acts 20. 29; while men slept the enemy sowed tares, Mat. 13. 25.

3. Must endure *hardship*, the heat of the day, cold of night; sentinels are out in all weathers, so Paul, 2 Cor. 11. 23–30; the Apostles were beat, Acts 16. 22.

4. Consult not their own *interest*, Paul sought not theirs but them, 2 Cor. 12. 14, Is. 58. 1.

5. Charged with the *care* of others, Heb. 13. 17; death the punishment of sleeping on their post.

6. *Appointed* to the duty, Ez. 33. 7.

7. Prevent evils of fire by *forewarning*, so angels were watchmen to Lot in Sodom, Gen. 19.

Angels called watchers, Dan. 4. 17; hence represented full of eyes, Ez. 1. 18; said to have wings to move about, Zech. 1. 11; 1 Kings 22. 19; 2 Kings 6. 17; gave warning to Lot, observant. All men have to set a watch on the door of their lips, Ps. 141. 3.

Malay.—The crow knows the instant we look at it, and the bison will perceive the approach of the hunter.

Kurd.—Think of the wolf, but keep a rod in readiness for him.

Basques.—When you have the wolf in your company, you ought to have the dog at your side.

Modern Greek.—When the fox is hungry he pretends that he is asleep—*i.e.*, in order to catch the chickens.

Arab.—"The mouse fell from the roof. Take some refreshment," said the cat. "Stand thou off," was the reply—*i.e.*, trust not an enemy.

Arab.—They trusted the key of the pigeon-house to the cat.

Welsh.—The fence of a bad farmer is full of gaps.

Tamul.—Like a cat on a wall watching his position.

Bengal.—The fowl knows the serpent's sneezing.

Talmud.—Repent a day before your death.

Afghan.—Though the cock crows not, morning will come.

Servian.—When you go as a guest to the wolf, see that you have a hound with you.

Russian.—Thieves are not abroad every night, yet every night make fast.

Turk.—The day dawns late in the house where the cocks are numerous.

Menu.—Women, if confined at home by faithful guardians, are not really guarded; but those women, who guard themselves by their own will, are well guarded.

Turk.—He is a fool who falls twice into the same hole.

What six proverbs illustrate the need of watchfulness?

The Waterer Watered or Fatness for the Liberal.

PROV. 11. 25.

Liberality is called a sowing, 2 Cor. 9. 6; a lending, Prov. 19. 7. *Abraham* was no loser by his liberality to Lot Gen. 13. 9, 14, 15), nor by his hospitality to the three men Gen. 13. 2). He thereby entertained angels unawares; in the care he took of the religious instruction of his servants, he was rewarded by their fidelity to him, as appears from the conduct of his eldest servant, Gen. 24. The widow's oil increased not in the vessel, but by pouring it out, 2 Kings 4. 1, 7. The *barley bread* in the Gospel multiplied by breaking and distributing it; the grain brings increase not by the lying in a heap in the garner, but by scattering it upon the land, so with the graces of faith, hope, and love; the talent gathereth nothing in the napkin but canker and rust.

China.—As the rivers pour their waters back again into the sea, so what a man has lent is returned to him again.

Arab.—The garment in which you clothe another will last longer than that in which you clothe yourself.

Bengal.—A giver is like a cocoa-nut, hard without, good within; a miser is like a bambu, hard without, but hollow within.

Persian.—A closed fist (miser) is the lock of heaven; an open hand (liberal) is the key of mercy.

Arab.—A rich miser is a summer cloud without rain.

Arab.—Spend that which will not remain with you; purchase that which will remain.

Arab.—Purchase the next world with this, so shalt thou gain both.

China.—Wealth is but manure—*i.e.*, useful only in being spread.

Telugu.—Doing with this hand, receiving the reward with the other.*

Turk.—You will not carry away with you but those things which you have given.

Turk.—Who gives alms sows one and reaps one thousand.

The Wedding Garment, or Meetness for Heaven.

MAT. 18. 3.

Urdu.—The deaf man is fit for heaven—*i.e.*, he hears no evil.

Russian.—The cat wishes for fish, but fears the water.

Telugu.—If you put a crow in a cage will it talk like a parrot?

Tamul.—Though the little bird soar high, will it become a kite?

Talmud.—This world is the antechamber of the next, a preparation before entering the palace.

Afghan.—Asses cannot be tethered in heaven—*i.e.*, though there be room, it is only for men.

Telegu.—They seated the dog in the palankin, on seeing filth it jumped down and ran after it.

China.—The pig who has been fed on dirt nauseates rice boiled in milk.

Veman.—A thief, if he goes to a holy place, will only pick the pockets of the comers; he has no leisure to draw near and bow to the God. If a dog enters a house, will he tend the hearth? 2 Peter 2. 22.

Persian.—The ass of Jesus does not go to Mecca.

The Wilderness World.—CANT. 8. 5.

The *Shánti Shatak* states " our mortal bodies are liable to decay—our earthly friends are like passengers on a

* The *Germans* say, Many will swallow an egg and give away the shell in alms.

journey whom we meet casually and from whom we soon separate." In the wilderness the sun smites by day and the cold by night, serpents infest the rocks, while sand-storms often overwhelm the traveller, or the simoom destroys thousands of men and camels, sometimes they perish by thirst; like this is the world which Solomon, the wisest and richest of men, called vanity of vanities, Ecc. 1. 2, and Paul called dross and dung, Phil. 3. 8. Man is born to trouble as the sparks that fly upwards, Job 5. 6. People hasten through a desert looking for rest at the end, Heb. 4. 1, like Lot, they must not linger in Sodom; all creation is groaning under the curse, Rom 8. 22.

In reading of the journey of the Hebrews from Egypt to Canaan by the way of the wilderness, we see a pattern of our own life, and of all the trials we are to undergo in our progress through this world to the kingdom of heaven. The Jews' journey began with baptism in the Red Sea, a deliverance from Pharaoh and his host, so our baptism, with which our Christian life begins, is an escape from the Spiritual Pharaoh. As they were *supported* by manna, and the waters of the rock, so must we live by bread from heaven, and our thirst must be satisfied by the waters of life. The *end* of this our pilgrimage upon earth is the possession of the heavenly land, which God hath promised to us, but in the way to it, we must undergo trials and temptations of every sort, and die in this wilderness, as Moses and his people did, before we can obtain it. As they proceeded by encampments, and wandered many years in the wilderness, so is our life a pilgrimage, and their example assures us that we have here no abiding place, no fixed habitation; like them we have the pillar of cloud by day and of fire by night.

The world a wilderness in fifteen points :—

1. A *waste* wild place, little planting; so the earth in spiritual matters.

2. Abounds in *thorns;* the wicked are briars destined to be burnt, Heb. 6. 8.

3. *Dangerous;* wild beasts numerous, the wicked are compared to wolves, bears, lions, dogs, Deut. 8. 15; Jer. 2. 6; Mat. 12. 43; hence is God a wall of fire to keep off beasts, Zech. 2. 5; *thieves* abound, Acts 21. 38; Job was robbed in Arabia; people travel in caravans composed of persons of different countries, this keeps off robbers, so is the communion of saints necessary.

4. *No path,* liable to wander, hence a guide necessary through the sands, Is. 35. 8. *Lonely.*

5. *Storms* frequent; the simoom buries thousands of men and animals. So passions.

6. *The sand is burning;* the sky is as brass; water and shade wanting.

7. Though *barren,* oases are found—*i.e.,* cultivated spots for a short rest, so for the Christian are ordinances.

8. *Foggy and misty,* so Satan raises heresies to hide sin (misleads travellers).

9. *Food* little, so the husks of this world, Luke 15. 16; the believer gets manna from heaven.

12. *Lightly equipped* to travel easier, Heb. 12. 1; the covetous man loads himself with thick clay, Hab. 2. 6.

13. A *varied route*—mud, good roads, desert, green fields, slough of despond, valley of humiliation, mountains of opposition, the rock of ages.

14. A *strange* country passed through, Heb. 11. 13; Ps. 39. 12; stay only a day or two in each place, Heb. 13. 14.

15. Congenial *companions* and fellow-travellers divide griefs and double joys, Ps. 119. 74, Ecc. 4. 9–10; relieve the tedium of the way.

Turk.—A traveller amid the discomforts of a bad khan (inn), reflects he has only to pass the night there.

China.—To meet an old friend in a distant country is like the delight of rain after a long drought.

Afghan.—The world is a traveller's serai (inn).

Tamul.—Conversation on a journey is equal to a conveyance.

Turk.—Though the ass goes to Mecca he becomes not a pilgrim for this.

Ramayane.—As two logs of wood meet on the wide ocean and soon part, so wives, relatives, riches, having come into contact with men, hasten away again.

The Wicked are Wolves and Locusts.—MAT. 10. 16.

Stephen, surrounded by the fierce Council, when they gnashed upon him with their teeth, stopped their ears, and ran upon him with one accord, although they had just before seen his face, as though it had been the face of an angel, Acts 7. 57; Stephen was like him who is brought as a lamb to the slaughter, and as a sheep before her shearers is dumb, so he opened not his mouth.

Wolves are fierce and cowardly; they often carry off children and devour them; they love to hunt in packs, are particularly fierce against sheep, fond of darkness, hence bad judges were compared to evening wolves, Zeph. 3. 3. The wicked are also called slaves of sin, John 8. 34, dry bones, Ez. 37. 3.

The wicked are compared to *locusts*, Rev. 9. 3, as being cunning, Prov. 30. 24–27, voracious, rapid in movement, carried about by every wind, very numerous.

Modern Greek.—Nourish a wolf in winter that he might devour you in summer.

The Words of the Wise Goads and Nails.—ECC. 12. 10, 11.

As the elephant, when sluggish and disobedient, must be quickened and corrected by the goad, which has a stinging, correctly aiming, and deeply penetrating effect, so does our sleeping conscience need the continual pricks and admonitions of a faithful expounder of Scripture, both for correction and instruction in righteousness, 2 Tim. 3. 16. And as it is the use of "nails" to fasten what is loose, or what would otherwise drop to pieces, so the exhortation of a wise preacher should fix in our treacherous memory what we might otherwise "let slip."

God's word is compared to a *hammer* breaking the rock in pieces, but the hand of God is required; according to the strength and skill of the holder is the blow; this hammer fastens the nails of conscience and of promise; it pierces even a stone.

Fit words are apples of gold in pictures of silver, Prov. 25. 11; this is a definition of a parable or a proverb which sets off grave sentiments by elegant language, as the appearance or imitation of finely-coloured fruit is improved by its shining as through a veil, through the network of a silver vessel finely carved, or like oranges in baskets of silver. The beauty of truth is heightened by the veil of imagery. Christ, without a parable, spoke not unto the people.

Arab.—Proverbs are the lamps to words.

Persian.—A word and a stone thrown away do not return.

Persian.—Great talkers are like broken pitchers, everything runs out of them.

Tamul.—The force of an elephant is subdued by a goad.

Tamul.—An elephant requires a goad, and boiled rice a chilli (a spice).

Hebrew.—What flowers are to gardens, spices to food, gems to a garment, and stars to heaven, such are proverbs interwoven in speech.

Sanskrit.—Chewing the chewed—*i.e.*, repeating idle words.

China.—Good words are a string of pearls.

Telugu.—Sweet as a cuckoo warbling in a garden are the charming words of the wise; but the words of sinners are vile as the cawing of a crow.

Arab.—Truth is a cutting sword.

PART III.

Who is the Altar for Believers?—HEB. 13. 10.

Christ's sacrifice like an altar in six points:—

1. All, even the most polluted, might *approach* it. Christ was also the brazen serpent on high, John 3. 14; (2) Its horns or four corners a place of *refuge* for the guilty, 1 Kings 2. 28; (3) The altar the only place for sacrifice, so prayer can be offered only through Christ's mediation, Heb. 9. 28; (4) The *incense* for it was beaten and prepared, so prayers must be from an humble spirit; no strange incense allowed to be offered; incense to be offered morning and evening, so special prayer then; (5) The altar was sprinkled with *blood* once a year, so Christ was once offered; (6) *Fire* was necessary to kindle the incense on it, so the Holy Spirit's influence is requisite.

Who has the Everlasting Arms?—DEUT. 33. 27.

God's strength is denoted by his arms. A stretched-out arm attributed to Him, Jer. 27. 5.

1. *The arm an essential part of man,* man's strength in labour and fighting is shown by it, Ex. 15. 16; so is the power of God to protect us from three enemies, the flesh, the devil, and the world; God lays bare His holy arm, Is. 52. 10—*i.e.,* as servants strip up their sleeves and make their arms ready for service.

2. *Holds things;* so God led the Jews through the wilderness by his glorious arm, Is. 63. 12.

3. Sign of *love*; young lambs carried in arms, Is. 40. 11; outstretched by father to call back his child. Thus Laban embraced Jacob, Gen. 29. 13; and on meeting them Jacob embraced Joseph's sons, Gen. 48. 10; so Esau embraced Jacob at meeting, Gen. 33. 4.

4. Sign of *strength*, so Sampson broke with his arm the cords like flax, and slew many men with the jawbone of an ass, Judg. 15. 15, and overthrew the house of the Philistines, so God's arm brought salvation, Is. 63. 12.

Man's arm is of flesh, and cursed is he that makes flesh his arm, Jer. 17. 5; God's of spirit, Job 11. 9; man's arm short, God's long, Jer. 60. 1; man's arm for a time, God's always; no king saved by the multitude of an host, Ps. 33. 16.

Persian.—God, who gives teeth, also gives bread. Is. 49. 15.
Bengal.—If a man's destiny be crooked, even in a jungle of dark grass, a tiger attacks him.
China.—To catch a man with his teeth.
Mahabharat.—Long are the arms of a clever man.

What Bags wax not Old?—Luke 12. 33.

Men count up their money, put it into bags, seal them up that they may be safe, and reserved for a long time.

God seals up the sins of his people in His bag, Job 14. 17; thus *Israel's defection* was remembered after 390 years, Ps. 25. 7; his *bones* are full of the sins of his youth, Job 20. 11; *Saul* was dead, but his sin was alive, there was a triennial famine on account of Saul having slain the Gibeonites. God brought the sin of *Joseph's brethren*, committed twenty years before to their mind, Gen. 42. 21; old sins will be old serpents, and sting unto death, Num. 32. 23.

Canarese.—Alms are food prepared for a journey, Rev. 14. 13.

Rabbinical.—The pious need no memorial; their deeds are their memorial.

How Born again?—John 3. 3.

A Brahmin is called *dvija,* twice-born—*i.e.,* first by nature, and second by dedication to his religion. A Christian is twice-born in regeneration, which is compared to an old tree grafted, through which its nature is changed and improved, and the old stock is made to bear good fruit. A child when new born is a perfect man as to limbs, though not yet at their full growth and size; similar is God's grace in the new birth. Christ, in his conversation with Nicodemus, showed the need of the new birth.

The new birth of a Christian is expressed by the emblems of a *resurrection,* Col. 3. 1; a *transformation,* Rom. 12, 2, having a *heart of flesh,* Ez. 36. 26; a *new creation,* 2 Cor. 5. 17; *putting off the old man,* Eph. 4. 22; metal figures cast in a *mould,* Rom. 4. 17; *adoption,* Rom. 8. 15.

Believers are called by the world its *offscouring,* but by God His jewels, yet though by nature children of wrath, by the new birth they become sons of God; like the angels, they have access to their Father, Rom. 8. 14; their petitions are heard, Mat. 7. 7–11, and they become heirs of God, 4. 7.

Sakontala.—How could a mortal to such charms give birth?
The lightning's radiance flashes not from earth.

African.—The daughter of a crab does not give birth to a bird.

Who is the Bread of Heaven?—John 6. 51.

Man has a soul as well as a body, and as the body cannot live without food, so neither can the soul. The soul can never die like the body; the death of the soul is when it has no life to love and serve God; like a dead body it can serve no one; is displeasing to God, as a dead body is offensive to us. Our Lord Jesus is called "bread" because all our spiritual life must come from him. Bread, to do us good, must be eaten; and, by faith, we feed on Jesus Christ. Faith, then, is the mouth of the soul, or the way by which this spiritual nourishment is received into the soul. Jesus is called the "Bread of Life" and the "Living Bread" to those who believe or trust in him; he gives this spiritual life to serve God here, and this is but the beginning of a life which shall never end, for he who eats of this bread "shall live for ever."

The hungry know the value of bread, Prov. 27. 7; gold is no use in a starving city, and all need bread, for hunger will eat through a stone wall.

Who are Buried with Christ?—Rom. 6. 4.

The *old man*—*i.e.*, our corrupt nature, derived from the first man, dies by the *painful lingering* death of spiritual crucifixion to the world; it becomes dead to sin but alive to righteousness, Rom. 6. 11, and is buried *with Christ*, a great honour, not like Jehoiakim, said to have had the burial of an ass, Jer. 22. 19.

Satan in Everlasting Chains of Darkness.—Jude 6.

Chains signify the degradation of the devils; they are —(1) marks of *bondage*, as Paul wore them before Felix, Acts 26. 29; pride compassed the wicked as a chain, Ps. 73. 6, while love is to the good, the bond of perfectness, Col. 3. 14; (2) *heavy*, 1 Kings 12. 10; Peter was fastened with two chains to prevent his escape, Acts 12. 6; (3) a subject of *reproach*, 2 Tim. 1. 6. The devils are banished from the presence of God, the light of heaven, and now in their dungeon, lead a severer captivity than the Jews endured in Egypt.

The City in Heaven.—Heb. 12. 22.

An earthly city differs from the heavenly in five points—

Earthly cities were often founded by blood and rapine, Mic. 3. 10, or like Babel to perpetuate a name, Gen. 11. 4; built of stone or wood surrounded with walls, infested by dogs, often burnt or sown with salt, Judg. 9. 45; the city of the heavenly Jerusalem has God as its architect; nothing evil in it. A city, from its numerous inhabitants, is called a mother, 2 Sam. 20. 19; while Babylon was called a widow as desolate, Isa. 47. 9. The city in heaven is—(1) well situated far above earth; (2) surrounded by walls of salvation, Job 1. 10, its walls of gold and streets of pearl; no enemy can approach it; the palace and court of the king; guarded by holy angels, Ps. 34. 7, Dan. 4. 23; (3) various nations in it, a great multitude of which no men can number, Rev. 7. 9; (4) enriched by the best of earth and creation; (5) its *citizens* are all first-born—*i.e.*, the choicest, the first-born, thus had a double portion, and were superior in rank, Gen. 49. 3. The term first-born is applied also to inferior things, Job calls worms the first-born of death, 18. 13, as death is called by the Arabs the mother of vultures.

Content.—1 Tim. 6. 8.

Arab.—Content lies in three things—satisfied with what is given—no reliance on what is in men's hands—acquiescing in God's decrees.

Hebrew.—Who is rich? He who is content with what he has.

Tamul.—Though the river is full to overflowing, a dog laps—*i.e.*, amid the greatest abundance one enjoys only what is required.

Takeram.—Trees are carried away by the flood, while rushes remain.

Christ drank a Bitter Cup.—MAT. 26. 39.

The master of a feast appointed to each of his guests his particular cup, Jer. 25. 15. This cup denoted Christ's intense sufferings, Mat. 20. 22, he sweat blood; wine mixed with bitter ingredients was given to malefactors before being put to death, to render them insensible to the acute pain of hanging on a cross. Christ refused to drink the latter cup. Babylon is represented, Jer. 51. 7, as a golden cup in the hands of Jehovah—*i.e.*, to give pain; the cup of salvation, Ps. 16. 13, denoted the joy from the river of God's pleasure, Ps. 36. 8; the cup of the wine of God's wrath, Rev. 14. 10, was the vengeance of God apportioned to each.

Joseph's cup was that out of which he drank, and which was taken from Benjamin's sack, Gen. 44. 12; and the cup which our Lord gave to his disciples at the Last Supper was one out of which they drank the wine. "The cup of salvation," is an expression taken from the custom of the Jews of making a feast after presenting their thank-offerings, when the priests and offerers ate and drank together. Among other rites, the master of the feast took a cup of wine in his hand, and solemnly blessed God for it, and for the mercy which was at that time acknowledged, and then gave it to all the guests, of which every one drank in his turn. Christ, suffering on behalf of sinners, in the hour of his agony, prayed, "O! my Father, if it be possible, let this cup pass from Me," Mat. 26. 39. When afflictions are the result of God's vindictive justice, then "cup" has a more awful sense, and the wicked are often threatened with the dregs, which is the most unpleasant part of the liquor, Isa. 51. 17.

Japan.—A good medicine tastes bitter.
Telugu.—Are there sweet diseases and delicious medicines?

Hell is the Blackness of Darkness.—MAT. 22. 13.

Heaven is compared to a *banquet* in which, amid blazing lights, chosen guests sit down; no night there; but hell is the cellar outside all in darkness; this implies *terror* as in Egypt, Ex. 10. 21; *separation* from good people, they stumble and wander; evil deeds in secret are called chambers of imagery, Ez. 8. 12.

Some fires have light but are dark. Hell is the blackness of darkness, Jude 13; in earth there is some light; in hell none natural, artificial, or spiritual; in earth some comfort, in hell none. The Egyptian darkness might be felt, Ex. 2. 22, but was only for a time.

Death-bed Repentance, or making Swords when the War comes.—LUKE 12. 20.

Persian.—Barley at the foot of a steep ascent is useless—*i.e.*, You have starved your horse, so that he has become thin and weak, it will be to no purpose to feed him when you come to a steep ascent—*i.e.*, Preparation for an enterprise should be made beforehand.

Russian.—When he was drowning he promised an axe; when he was rescued he gave only the handle.

Oriental.—The wise know how to quit the world before the world quits them.

Turk.—He who at eighty begins to learn music can hear himself at the judgment day.

Arab.—While the antidote is coming the snake-bitten man dies.

Kurd.—When the hen dies her eyes are fixed on the dung-hill.

Gujerati.—When thirsty to dig for water.

Telugu.—Three causes of transient repentance—viz., the pains of travel, the effects of preaching, and the sight of death.

China.—It is too late to pull the rein when the horse is on the edge of the precipice. It is too late to stop the leak when the vessel is in the midst of the river.

Turk.—We die as we live.

Sin as a Debt Blotted out.—Acts 3. 19.

Chanak writes, "to extinguish fire, remove disease, and pay debts are of use as they increase if they remain." Sinners are debtors, the money duty to God, Gal. 5. 3; Rom. 8. 12, 15, 27.

The wicked are bad debtors in six points:—

1. *Unconcerned* about the debt, so Cain who slew his brother, Gen. 4. 7; Mat. 18. 24; Luke 16. 1.

2. *Wasteful* about saving up; so the prodigal son.

3. Love not to *see the creditor* or settle accounts; who is God, say the wicked.

4. Afraid of the *bailiff*, so Cain afraid of every one he met, Gen. 4. 13, 14; Adam hid himself, Gen. 3. 8; so Felix, Acts 24. 25.

5. *Dilatory*, so the *debtor* who *asks* a suspense, Mat. 18. 29; so excuses for the supper, Luke 14. 18.

6. Unable to *pay*, Rom. 3. 19; hence punishment, 2 Kings 4. 1. *Death* will arrest, Eccl. 8. 8.

God forgives the Debt, now by

1. Staying the process, Job 33. 19, 21, 24.

2. Cancelling the bond, Col. 2. 14; the handwriting against us, he abolishes the old covenant, Heb. 8. 13; sins cast into the depths of the sea, Mic. 7. 19.

3. Acquittance written on the conscience, Rom. 8. 6.

The Dew of God's Providence.—Hos. 14. 5.

The dew arising from the moisture evaporated by the sun in the day, and falling by night, refreshes the parched earth, and often supplies the want of rain. The short-lived character of the form of godliness, without the power, is compared to early dew exhaled soon by the sun, Hos. 6. 4. The love of brethren is compared to the dew, Ps. 133. 3. God's Word is said to drop as rain, and distil as dew, Deut. 32. 2. God's influences are likened to a cloud of dew in the heat of harvest, Isa. 18. 4. The refreshing, vivifying influence of God's spirit is in this text compared to the silent but powerful dew as the dew of herbs, Isa. 26. 19.

Providence like the dew in seven points:—

1. *Dew comes from above,* from the air, not from the clouds; "drops down;" so Christ promised to send from above the Comforter, John 14. 16. Every good gift is from above, Jas. 1. 17.

2. *Dew is the result of the sun's influence.* The sun evaporates the water which the cold makes to descend, hence the brighter the sky the more dewy the night; so Christ shed down the Spirit. The sun must withdraw for the dew to fall; so Christ said he must go, but the Spirit will abide, John 14. 16.

3. *Dew falls from a calm unclouded sky.* Wind or a cloud will dissipate it; Christ, the Sun of Righteousness, dispels the clouds of unbelief. If we walk in the light we have fellowship with God; when the mind is so clouded by passion, the dew of the Holy Spirit does not fall.

4. *The dew's descent* is silent and *imperceptible;* rain falls in torrents. Dew is seen only by its crystal drops, Job 38. 28; 2 Sam. 17. 12. The dew like gravitation is known by its effects. The Kingdom of God cometh not by observation. The still small voice alone is heard, 1 Kings 19. 11, 12. Conversion is a change taking place in the mind; hence the Spirit's influence is compared to the wind, John 3. 2; we cannot see it or tell whence it comes, but we know it by its effects.

5. *The dew's influence is all pervading.* Where dashing rain will not enter dew will; it rests on blades of grass; the traveller's head is filled with dew; so under Christ's influence. All partake, it pervades each. All things are become new; the dry bones live, Ezek. 37. 3.

6. Dew often *copious,* always seasonable. In Israel once for 3½ years there were no dews—how lamentable were things, 2 Sam. 1. 21. The Spirit in the latter day is to be poured on young and old. When the weather is hottest, the dew is heaviest; so Stephen, when stoned, saw heaven opened, Acts 7. 55; so John, banished to Patmos, was in the Spirit and saw wonderful visions, Rev. 1. 10. Innumerable are the drops of dew; such are God's graces.

7. *The dew's effects are most obvious and salutary.* Egypt would be almost uninhabitable, were it not for the dews; the dew of heaven was promised to Ishmael. When the ground is parched the dew gives new life; so the letter killeth, but the Spirit gives life, 2 Cor. 3. 6. The sun hardens the soil. The growth of plants from the dew is often wonderful; so the believer strikes his roots deep in the Rock of Ages, and in humility bends towards the dust, but the refreshing, sheltering branches shoot up in beauty, the flowers and leaves from the dew-drops look as pearls, so beautiful are they—so the robes of righteousness. A fragrant *smell* arises in the morning from the dew on flowers; so Christ is the savour of sweet ointment, "Awake, O north wind;" dead souls are nauseous. Fruitfulness and moisture are necessary to the growth of plants, the dew of heaven, and fatness of the earth are conjoined to the fruits of the Spirit; the righteous bring forth fruit in old age; are we withered, God is no niggard with gifts. God will open the windows of heaven, Mal. 3. 11.

The Spiritual Life mounting on Eagle's Wings.

Is. 40. 30, 31.

Spiritual life like the eagle in eight points:—

1. The eagle is the *king* of birds as the lion is of beasts, so the saints are the excellent in the earth, Ps. 16. 2, 3, more excellent than their neighbours, of whom the world was not worthy, Heb. 11. 38. Believers are sons of God and of royal blood, Rev. 1. 6; while the wicked feed on the wind, or husks, Hos. 12. 1, the righteous have spiritual manna and angels as attendants.

2. *Long and quick sighted,* Job 39. 29, hence a man is called eagle-eyed. The eagle can look at the sun, or see from above fish in the water, so believers behold the glory of God with open face, 2 Cor. 3. 18; and as the secrets of the Lord are with them that fear him, Ps. 25. 14, Gen. 18. 17, they see the end of the wicked, 2 Sam. 14. 20.

3. *Swift,* they have long wings; hence *Solomon* says, "Riches make themselves wings, and fly away like an eagle," Ps. 23. 5. *David,* lamenting the death of Saul and Jonathan, says, "They, as friends, were stronger than lions and swifter than eagles," 2 Sam. 1. 23. *Nebuchadnezzar* came as an eagle against the temple. Job compares life to an eagle, 9. 26, Ez. 17. 2–10, Rev. 14. 6; hence, Nebuchadnezzar is represented as a great eagle, with great wings and long feathers—*i.e.,* having various nations in his empire, and took the highest branch of a cedar. The Romans are called eagles, Deut. 28. 49. The prayer of the righteous swiftly reaches heaven.

4. *Mount high,* out of sight; lost in the clouds, above the tempest and lightning, trees appear as shrubs, a city as a village; worldlings are moles or worms which grovel in the earth, but believers have their conversation in heaven, Phil. 3. 20, mounting up on the wings of faith and prayer, Col. 3. 3, not like *Nebuchadnezzar,* who built his nest on high for purposes of pride, Dan. 4. 30.

5. *Not tired* in their flight. Believers do not faint, Is. 40. 31; though the flight to heaven be long, yet the wings of faith and love bear them up.

6. *Aim at high things,* not at flies or worms. A Russian proverb says, "Eagles catch no flies," Ph. 3. 8; not like the crow, who goes out early for this purpose, Job 39. 27, 28.

7. *Nestle on high,* Ez. 17. 37, amid lofty rocks above the clouds, where no enemy can come.

8. *Lively in old age,* by moulting the eagle's youth is renewed, Ps. 103. 5. On getting new feathers his power of flight is renewed. The eagle is so strong as to be able to carry away a lamb or a child. Believers put on the new man, the old is cast off. Angels have immortal youth.

The young are borne on the mother's wings, Deut. 32. 11–14, so the Jews, Ex. 19. 4.

Aitareya Veda.—Though a hundred bodies like iron chains hold me down, yet like a falcon I quickly rise.
Persian.—The lion does not eat the dog's leavings.

The Earnest of the Spirit.—2 Cor. i. 22.

In various parts of India at the ceremony of betrothal the bride's father offers to the bridegroom's father, as an earnest, betel-nut, turmeric, and flowers; betel-nut, clothes and flowers are offered on a similar occasion.

An earnest is something of *value* which one person gives to another to *bind* a bargain. If one has a house to sell, and any one is disposed to buy it, it might not be quite the proper time for the seller to give him immediate possession, or for him to settle all the terms; but to make sure of the house, the buyer would give a part of the payment, and this would show that he was in earnest, and engaged to have it, and that the seller was quite in earnest, and engaged to sell it. Then, to have the Spirit of God in us, is to have God's earnest that he will give us heaven. And how shall we know that God's Spirit is acting *in* us? Why, when he is acting *by* us. If we are "led by the Spirit" we shall "walk in the Spirit," Rom. 8. 14. We cannot have the Holy Spirit if we lead unholy lives.

The Angelic Encampment.—Ps. 34. 7.

Angels are said to be full of eyes, before and behind, Rev. 4. 6, to denote their knowledge of the past and future, 1 Pet. 1. 12. Angels are called a *host*, Gen. 32. 1; commanded by Christ, the Captain of Salvation; they protect the saints; they slumber not like some watchmen, are called holy watchers, Dan. 4. 13; the figure of Cherubim, an order of angels, had four faces—that of a *man*, representing their majesty, prudence, and beauty; that of a *lion*, their strength and courage; that of an *ox*, their patience and diligence; and that of an *eagle*, their quick vision and continued vigour.

The great Mogul at Agra used to have an encampment several miles in circumference, accommodating many thousand soldiers; it was soon broken up, and removed to another place. The angels' encampment has many millions of troops in number, Dan. 7. 5–14. Christ on the Cross said he could call to his aid twelve legions of angels, or 80,000. Those angels are encamped, and are powerful; they broke the iron gates, Acts 12. 10; caused earthquakes, Mat. 28. 2; destroyed 185,000 Assyrians in one night; killed all the first-born in Egypt in one night; they are orderly; Michael and his angels fought with the devil, Rev. 12. 7–9. They smote Herod for his pride, Acts 12. 23, Balaam for his covetousness, Sodom for its sin, Gen. 19. 11.

Example.—1 Pet. 2. 21.

China.—The best cure for drunkenness is when sober to observe the drunken man.

Arab.—The mistakes of a learned man are like a shipwreck, which wrecks many others with it.

Basque.—Corruption begins from the head—*i.e.*, from the chiefs.

The Great Family of Believers.—EPH. 3. 14.

God is our father, the Church our mother; all the faithful are our brethren. The many millions of angels in heaven are comprehended within this family as well as the saints upon earth. As faithful people are our brethren, it must be our duty to love them, and to bear in mind that wise advice of *Joseph* to his brethren, *see that ye fall not out by the way,* Gen. 45. 24. In our journey through life, we are under so many trials and afflictions, that it is both foolish and wicked for the faithful to add to one another's troubles by strife and envying, by quarrellings and disputings. Proud people are ashamed of their poor relations; but we must not be ashamed to own the poorest child in the family of God, who, perhaps after a laborious life of faith and patience, will be our superior in the kingdom of heaven.

A family is a resting-place from worldly cares, so is the family whose father is God; Christ the elder brother or head, Col. 1. 17; the Holy Spirit the guide; and all true believers members.

Russian.—Away from our native country even a crow is dear.

Basque.—Blood boils without fire—*i.e.*, injury done to one's relations.

China.—A powerful man regards no burden; a tradesman no distance; to a learned man no country is foreign, and a fine speaker finds no enemy, Eph. 2. 19.

Malay.—Will a man put out his salt in the rain?—*i.e.*, a man exposing the faults of his family.

Basque.—The big fish lives on the little ones.

Spanish.—The wrath of brothers is the wrath of devils.

Satan the Father of Lies.—JOHN 8. 44.

Jesus Christ is the true *light;* but the devil is the prince of *darkness,* the god of this world, who blinds men's eyes that they may not see the truth, 2 Cor. 4. 4. The

Saviour is a *shepherd* who gives his life for the sheep; but the devil is a *lion* who goes about seeking what he may devour, 1 Pet. 5. 5. The one is a *lamb*, meek and harmless; the other a *serpent*, full of devices and more subtle than any beast of the field. The one raises men to *life;* the other was a *murderer* from the beginning. The one is our *advocate* with the Father, suffering and pleading for the pardon of our sins; the other is the *accuser* of the brethren; first tempting them to fall into sin, and then accusing them that they may fall under the judgment of God. Jesus Christ is the truth and the devil is the father of lies. And lastly, Jesus Christ is the true God worshipped by all believers, and the devil is the false god worshipped under a variety of names. The children of the devil are like the devil, as the young viper is like the old one.

Judas, the traitor, was hence called a devil, John 6. 70, as God is called the father of mercies, so is the devil of lies; he was first an angel of light, and then by his lies induced one-third of the angels to rebel against God; he told lies to Eve in the garden, Gen. 3. 6, and to Christ in the desert. The devils are also compared to *birds of prey* for their piercing eye, sudden pouncing, residence in the air, Eph. 2. 2, yet Satan was once called the son of the morning, Is. 14. 12. The Danes call lies the devil's daughters.

Spanish.—When the devil says his prayers he is about to cheat—*i.e.*, an angel of light.
Afghan.—She herself commits the sin and curses Satan for it.
Arab.—He gives advice such as the cat gave to the mouse or the devil to men.

Keep the Feet in God's House.—Ecc. 5. 1.

This text means take heed to your ways in God's house. See that ye walk circumspectly. As in walking we take as much *care* as we can to keep our *feet* from stumbling; so, in going to the house of God, we must take care about the state of our minds. When Moses saw the Angel of the Lord in the burning-bush, the voice of God said to him, "Put off thy shoes from off thy feet, for the place whereon thou standest is holy ground," Ex. 3. 5; and when Joshua saw the same Angel, he said, "Loose thy shoe from off thy foot, for the place whereon thou standest is holy," Josh. 5. 15. In both these instances it is believed that the Lord Jesus Christ took human form in appearance, before he really took our nature, and died to redeem us, and, by commanding the removal of the shoe from the foot, he showed that nothing which was defiled could acceptably appear in his presence. So Jacob in the desert, Gen. 28. 17.

Look before you leap. He that hastens with his feet sinneth, Prov. 19. 2; John 18. 10. *Chanak* says, "A prudent man moves with one foot, but does not move the other till he considers where he goes to." The *Philistines* were punished for touching the ark, 1 Sam. 6. 19; a beast that touched Sinai was to be killed, Heb. 12. 20; *Nebuchadnezzar* was chastised for using at a feast the vessels of the temple, Dan. 5. 23. The sacrifice of fools is an offering without obedience. Christ flogged those that bought and sold in the temple, John 2. 15.

Chinese.—Destroy all passion when you light Buddha's lamp.
Malabar.—Sport not with a king, nor with fire, water and elephants.
Veman.—Observances void of purity of heart! to what end are they? to what is the preparation of food without cleansing the vessel? Mat. 15. 8.
Malabar.—Elephants will fall down if the feet slide.
Russian.—Set a fool to worship and he will break his neck.
Persian.—What has a dog to do in a temple?
Tamul.—A cat that lives in the temple fears not the gods —*i.e.*, familiarity breeds contempt.

God's Name on the Believer's Forehead.—Rev. 22. 4, 5.

The *Vishnuvites* have the *tiluk*, or forehead mark, a longitudinal line marked in vermilion; the *Sivites* a parallel line of a turmeric colour. The *Athenians* marked an owl on their captives' forehead; *idolaters* put on such the mark of their god as Jupiter's thunderbolt, Neptune's trident. The *forehead* is the most *conspicuous* part; the countenance being the index of the mind, and implies an *open* confession, as Paul was a chosen vessel to bear Christ's *name* before the Gentiles, Acts 9. 15, 16. It was a custom of ancient date in Asia to mark *servants* on the forehead; hence in Ezek. 9. 4, the Angel sets a mark on the foreheads of the men who cry for the abominations of the time. The Jews were forbidden to *brand the forehead*, Lev. 19. 28. Only the *High Priest* bore on it a plate of gold, on which the name of God was written.

Paul said, I bear on my body the *marks* of the Lord Jesus—*i.e.*, the scars of the stripes he received, Gal. 6. 17. Believers have God's mark in regeneration, and sanctification impressed on them, 1 Pet. 2. 9; the *name* is Jehovah, Zech. 14. 20; written not with *ink*, but with the Spirit of the Living God, 2 Cor. 3. 3.

Christ the sure Foundation.—Is. 28. 16; 1 Pet. 2. 6–8.

God's Church is compared to a building, as the temple was the visible residence of God. "Ye are the temple of God," 1 Cor. 3. 16.

A good building must—

1. Be erected on a *solid foundation*: all rests on the foundation. Christ is the "*rock* of ages," "the foundation of *Apostles and prophets*, Christ being the chief *corner-stone*," Eph. 2. 20, as well as the foundation. Some build on the *sand* of self-righteousness, but "God lays in Sion a tried stone, a precious corner-stone," Is. 28. 16. The

foundation is out of sight, so Christ must be *strong* to bear the superstructure; earthquakes cannot destroy it.

2. Have a regular and *orderly erection*, the rule of *architecture* applied to its building, so Israel's Church was "according to the *pattern* shown in the mount," Heb. 8. 5. Sin breaks up the harmony of society, grace *unites* in a church, "God is not the author of confusion." "That he *might gather together* in one all things." On the *regularity* of a building depends much of its strength, so "the unity of the spirit in the bond of peace," how symmetrical was *Solomon's temple*, so the spiritual one, "the *whole building* fitly framed."

3. Be composed of many *stones.* Every stone has *its place*, though there be many; some are polished, as James, Cephas, John "pillars," some of these are hidden, some form the *coping*, yet all are on the foundation. Some houses are of turf, or layers of brick, or sandstone, or marble, but God's houses are of *lively stone*, 1 Pet. 2. 4; *pictures, statues*, sometimes seem *alive*, but here the stones are *living*—*i.e.*, active.

4. Undergo *a great transformation.* Polished statuary and fine buildings are originally from the *quarry*, so believers were *encrusted* with fleshly lusts, sunk in the *mire* of spiritual corruption; so *Paul* the blasphemer preached the faith he once destroyed, "Look unto *the rock* whence ye were hewn."

5. Have *a skilful architect* in their transformation, Christ is such, Heb. 3. 4. Stones are *inactive* to raise themselves from the quarry; *scaffolding* and *masons* are required; so in *Solomon's* temple, Jews, Canaanites, Tyrians, were employed; *Cyrus* was subsequently God's servant for its rebuilding, Ez. 5. 13; in the scaffolding of Solomon's temple no noise of axe or hammer was heard.

6. Be *cemented in the strongest* way. Their *position* unites stones, but the best union is *cement*, the whole body composed of that which every joint supplieth, Eph. 4. 6; love is the *bond* of perfectness, Col. 3. 14. Earthquakes may

split the building without breaking the cement, "who shall separate," Rom. 8. 35.

7. Be *formed into a complete habitation, vast* in extent, and *ornamental,* "a *fount* for cleansing, *illuminated* by the seven spirits of God;" it has a *throne* of grace.Heb. 4. 6.

Malabar.—The foundation for a thatched and for a tiled house will be laid the same way.

Persian.—A little water is sufficient for clay already moistened—*i.e.*, little instruction will suffice for him who has got a *foundation* by previous study.

God the Fountain of Living Waters.—Jer. 2. 13.

Water is essential for life as well as for health, it is continually applied in Holy Scripture to represent the necessity of divine *grace;* and thus a *well* or *spring* of water becomes an emblem of the eternal source of all spiritual blessings, and of salvation itself. The blood of our blessed Saviour, by which his people are washed from the defilements of sin, is called a fountain opened to the house of David, and to all the inhabitants of Jerusalem, for sin and for uncleanness, Zech. 13. 1. The quickening and refreshening *influences* of the Holy Spirit, are in like manner compared by our Lord Himself to rivers of living water, John 7. 38; God declaring Himself "a fountain of living waters," sets Himself forth as the source of all temporal and spiritual good.

With what eager longing must the pilgrims crossing the desert look forward to their repose on the favoured spot, where a perpetual spring creates a little island of verdure or oasis in the midst of the burning plain!

God is called "The Fountain of *Living* Waters,"—*i.e.*, waters always moving, flowing, and in action; the constant supply of all the comfort and relief we can possibly need; in contrast to dead or stagnant waters, which constantly send forth a noisome smell.

The sun has not the less light for filling the air with light. A fountain has not the less for filling the lesser vessels. There is in Christ the fulness of a fountain. The overflowing fountain pours out water abundantly, and yet remains full. God is such an overflowing fountain; he fills all, and yet remains full. As the worth and value of many pieces of silver is in one piece of gold, so all the petty excellences scattered abroad in the creature are united in God.

God is like a fountain in eight points:—

(1) The *source* of rivers, so God of life, natural and spiritual, Rev. 21. 6; (2) yields *abundantly:* God is an ocean of goodness; (3) *pours* freely into low places, Jas. 4. 6; so the founts of the Ganges, rising in the snows of Gangotri, flow into the Ganges valley; (4) *free* to all, Is. 54. 1; (5) *clear:* rivers have sediment in them; (6) *pleasant:* refreshes the garden of the Church; water makes vegetation spring up, even in the sandy deserts; (7) *constant:* tanks dry up often in hot weather. Abraham's servants dried up the well; but this is a fountain sealed against filth, Cant. 4. 12; (8) often *hidden:* yet known by its waters. Christ's fountain was opened on the cross when his side was pierced, and when he sweat blood; the dying thief was a monument of its efficiency.

Raghuvansa.—The roads leading to perfection, which vary according to the different revealed systems, all end in Thee (God), as the waves of the Ganges flow to the ocean.

Bhagavat Gita.—On God all this universe is woven, as gems on a string.

The Fowler of Souls.—Eph. 6. 11.

We sometimes see a fluttering of wings among the grass on a bank, which shows that some poor bird is taken in the snare, and is vainly struggling to be free, but the snare was set so skilfully that the bird could see nothing of its danger, but flew into it unawares.

There is an enemy who is ever setting snares in our path—Satan; and the snares are those many false reasonings and vain seductions by which he misleads to their ruin such as are unwary and unstable. To one he says, "Stolen waters are sweet, and bread eaten in secret is pleasant," Pr. 9. 17. Satan tried to sift Peter like wheat, Luke 22. 31; against some he sends fiery darts, Eph. 6. 16, with others he wrestles, Eph. 6. 11. Satan as a fowler is crafty, appears in disguise as an angel of light, 2 Cor. 11. 14; cruel, hunts and persecutes God's people, who are like the dove before the hawk. He is also for his destructiveness called the great Dragon, Rev. 20. 2.

Persian.—He is put into a sack with a bear—*i.e.*, in the hands of one too strong for him.

Persian.—The devil does not spoil his own house, Mat. 12. 26.

Christ a Friend.—John 15. 15.

Christ's friendship differs from earthly friendship in five points:—

True friendship implies *sympathy:* such Job's friends showed not, but Christ is touched with a feeling of our infirmities, Heb. 4. 15. *Union:* can two walk together unless they be agreed? Saul and Jonathan had their hearts knit, 1 Sam. 18. 1, so Christ to his people, Eph. 2. 14–16, Prov. 27. 17. *Love:* the offspring of desire; Christ loves to the end, and has peculiar knowledge, the fuel for this love, John 10. 27; but the love of Christ passes knowledge. *Intercourse:* absence regretted: Christ was a great friend to Lazarus and the Bethany family. Christ is said to sup with the believer, Rev. 3. 20. John lay on Christ's bosom, John 13. 23. *Secrets* are made known, so Abraham, the friend of God, found, Gen. 18. 17, Prov. 27. 6; faithful are the *wounds* of a friend.

Christ's friendship is never broken up—formed with mean persons—Christ forsakes not in adversity, and even lays down his life—no king a friend to a beggar; Christ the companion of publicans and sinners—no time or circumstances change it—always able as well as willing; as shown in Dorcas and Lazarus's case, Acts 9. 38–41, John 11.

> *Persian.*—Those false friends whom you see are like flies around the sweetmeats.
>
> *Naladayur.*—Friendship with the mean, like the shadow of morning, will continually decrease.

Christ the first Fruits of them that Slept.—1 Cor. 15. 20.

The first fruits of the harvest were the *pledge* of the whole, such was Christ's resurrection of ours, or as the swallow and budding of flowers are of spring; when the body which called the worm its sister shall shine as the sun. The first fruits, like the first born, were esteemed the most *valuable*, hence the Canaanites caused their first-born to pass through the fire, in order to appease the anger of their deities; one of the *kings of Moab*, when in danger from enemies, offered up his eldest son, 2 Kings 3. 27. *Cain* brought to God the first fruits of the ground, as Abel did the firstlings of the flock, Gen. 4. 4; the Jews always did so, Num. 18. 12.

Affliction's Furnace.—Is. 48. 10.

There are two furnaces, one of sanctified affliction, as Egypt was to the Jews, Deut. 4. 20, 1 Pet. 1. 6, 7; the fiery furnace injured not the three Hebrew children, Dan. 3. 25; the other of unsanctified like Nebuchadnezzar's fiery furnace which consumed the evil, Dan. 3. 22; the former is like a pruning-knife which improves the plant, the latter like a chopper that cuts it off, Mat. 13. 42–50.

God's afflicted people are compared to silver. The precious metals are first taken out of the earth. They are then *impure*—mixed with other substances, and in this state they are called ores. In order to refine them they are put into a *furnace*, and exposed to great heat. But this does not *injure* them; it only takes from them what is impure, and leaves the gold or the silver bright, beautiful, and clear. The refiner watches the metals all the time they are in the fire; and when he finds that they are so clear and pure that he can see his own face reflected in them, he takes them out of the furnace and uses them for the purposes he intended.

Afflictions of righteous and wicked differ in four points:—

In Malachi 3. 3, God compares the afflictions with which he tries his people, to the furnace into which the gold and silver are cast to be refined and purified. God loves and values his people. He calls them his "treasure," his "jewels." But, like the gold and silver, they have that in them which is impure—sin. And this sin must be taken away. God's people must be made pure and holy before he can have pleasure in them and use them for his service, or take them to adorn his glorious home in heaven. And how does God purify them? Sin must be taken away by Christ, and the heart must be made clean by the Holy Spirit. God has many ways of working all this in his people, and one way is by affliction. Like the refiner, he puts his precious gold and silver into the furnace—the furnace of affliction. He sends sorrow and pain and sickness upon them. And why? Not to hurt them: no; but just for the same reason that the refiner puts his metals into the fire, to melt, to soften, to purify them. And then, like the refiner, God watches over them. He does not let them suffer more or longer than is right; and when he has made them what he intended by putting them into the furnace, he takes them from it. What God desires is to see his own image, his own likeness, reflected in his people.

A silver coin or medal is generally stamped with the image of the sovereign; this can be done only when the metal is soft, and it is made soft by the heat of the fire. So, God's people should bear the likeness of Christ, their King, stamped upon them in their conduct; and God sends affliction to soften their hearts, that they may more easily receive that holy impression, and so become more and more like Jesus.

Sanskrit.—A bad man, gold, a drum, a woman, a bad horse, stalks of sugar-cane, sesamum seed, and Sudras, should be beaten to improve their qualities.

Atmabodh.—After mortifying the body, the pure spirit is discerned by reason, as rice is separated from the husk by beating it.

Bengal.—The crocodile on the water and the tiger on land both strive to break my neck.

Tamul.—Though worn by attrition, the sandal-wood loses not its savour.

China.—Clouds pass, but the rains remain.

Sanskrit.—A crane's meditation—*i.e.*, seem to be meditating, when they are ready to pounce on the fish.

Sanskrit.—He who is wise is strong; the foolish have no strength.

Sanskrit.—Fools learn by the past—*i.e.*, experience a dear school.

The Church a Garden enclosed.—Cant. 4. 12.

The Church like a garden in seven points:—

Paradise means a beautiful garden, to which Christ refers, Luke 23. 43; Babylon had hanging gardens on the roofs of the houses.

As the waste wilderness is the emblem of the world, so a choice garden is set forth as an image of God's Church, as is also a vineyard, Mat. 20. 1–16. A garden is a place *enclosed* out of the common *waste* ground, and set apart for special culture and fruitfulness. Its site is *chosen* for advantage of soil and shelter; as well as for that abundant supply of *water*, which is so needful for the health and produce of its plants. Care is ever taken to *screen* it from every rude *blast*, to maintain or improve the natural goodness of the ground, and to make the water flow in such channels as may conduct it most easily to the several plots and borders. In laying out a garden, it is divided and arranged according to some well-ordered pattern; and he, who is set "to dress it and to keep it," is ever careful both to remove whatever is common and unsightly, and to fill every nook and angle with the choicest flowers, and the most useful and delicious fruits. The owner of the garden delights to come into it when the tender shoots are first showing themselves above the ground, or when it is in all the pride of summer beauty or autumnal fruitfulness, Rev. 1. 13. Its sunny *stillness* and repose invite to peaceful meditation. Its exact order, its smooth lawns, its many-coloured borders, cool shades, and clear waters are soothing to the eye that is wearied with the glare and confusion of the crowded marts; while the soft breeze that whispers among the fruits and flowers is laden with the most grateful fragrance.

It is thus that God has chosen out of the world a Church, or "peculiar people," to be his own portion and inheritance. He *fences* and protects it from the enemies that seek its ruin; he is a wall of fire, and sets in it the choicest plants, to bear those fruits and flowers which are of price in his sight. So Abraham gave the flower of faith, Moses of meekness, Peter of boldness, Paul of zeal, Gal. 5. 22. It is the Paradise of his beloved Son, who is the second Adam, and whose care it is to remove from it the *weeds* of sin and selfishness, and to preserve it in that godly order, and that blessed unity, which makes it the image upon earth, not only of the heavenly peace, but even of the Divine Unity itself. His Holy Spirit is the *fountain* in the midst of the garden which nourishes and refreshes the plants; and is also the gentle *breath* which bears the fragrance of its flowers to Him who is pleased to receive graciously what in itself is unworthy of being offered to Him. He sets His *servants* to tend and cherish the various plants on which He is pleased to set such store, and to see, when He shall come into His garden, that there be nothing there to offend those eyes which are too pure to behold iniquity. Whatever resembles the fruits of the evil world must be rooted out; whatever is useful and lovely must be planted and fostered.

Faith more Precious than Gold.—1 PET. 1. 7.

In Rev. 3. 18, Divine Grace, which stands the fiery trial, is called gold, faith in the text is not mere knowledge.

Faith like gold in ten points:—

1. *Scarce,* so the grace of God.

2. *Searched after,* men go to deep mines for gold, or to California; so search the Scriptures, John 5. 39.

3. *Tried in fire,* to distinguish it from false metal, sometimes a touchstone used, so God's word like faith is tried by fire, so Abraham three times, Job six times.

4. *Precious* in its nature, hence faith called lively, effectual, 1 Thess. 1. 3; faith precious as bought with Christ's blood, wrought by God's Spirit, object of is Christ; unites to God, eye of the soul; unfeigned working by love, Gal. 5. 6; holy, procured by Christ's blood, Col. 2. 12; its fruits, Heb. 11; faith made a river go back, caused a man to give half of his goods to the poor, Luke 19. 8; and people to burn bad books, Acts 19. 19.

5. *The Chief Metal.* Babylon called the golden city, Is. 14. 4; the skull called the golden bowl, Ecc. 12. 6.

6. *Much in little,* compared with brass, so with faith.

7. *Weighty* and firm, so faith in adversity, Heb. 11.

8. *Splendid,* used in crowns; Babylon had a golden cup, Rev. 17. 4.

9. *Forms fine vessels,* as the vessels in Solomon's temple; so saints are golden candlesticks, Rev. 1. 20.

10. *Durable*, wastes not in fire, so the three Hebrew children, Dan. 3.

Chinese.—True gold fears not the fire.

The Righteous Groan in their Bodily Tabernacle.

2 Cor. 5. 4.

The righteous groan from six causes :—

Creation itself groans, being under a curse for sin, Rom. 8. 22. The soul dwells in the body as in a tent which is easily taken down, being made of *frail* materials that flood or fire soon destroys ; the body soon returns to dust.

The soul's dark cottage battered and decayed
Lets in new light through chinks which time has made.

Few care to ornament a tent, as they are but a short time in it ; it is crazy and leaky in bad weather, so disease makes the body.

It is better to groan for a while in this tabernacle than for ever under God's vengeance ; the tears from groaning God puts in his bottle, Ps. 56. 8. This groaning arises from the burthen of the *body*, which hinders the soul rising on eagle's wings ; from *Satan's* temptations, 1 Pet. 1. 6 ; bad *company*, 2 Pet. 2. 7 ; *afflictions*, Ps. 42. 7 ; *indwelling* sin, Rom. 7. 24.

Naladiyar.—The soul carries the skin bag—the body.

The Right Hand of God dashes in Pieces his Enemies.

Ex. 15. 6.

His *right hand* in the text imports a signal display of his Almighty power, his love, mercy, or wrath in relation to the exalted station of Christ. It imports the highest power, authority, glory, and dignity. Elymas the sorcerer was struck blind by God's hand, Acts 13. 11. Hand denotes strength, thus Ishmael's hand as an Arab robber was against every man, Gen. 16. 12. Christ sits at the Father's right hand—*i.e.*, the seat of power, Mark 14. 62. The *hollow of his hand* denotes his easy comprehension, protection, and support of all things. God's *arms*, hands, fingers, denote Almighty power manifested in acts of sovereignty, justice, and grace. God is called the *head* of Christ, to him, as man and mediator, he is the undoubted superior, and it is his to support, rule, and direct him, as such. His *countenance* and face, when represented as set against any, denote the manifestation of his indignation and wrath; in other circumstances, they signify the discovery of his glory and grace. God's *eyes* import his knowledge, his care, and regard; but sometimes the display of his wrath. His *ears* denote his perfect knowledge, his exact observation and favourable regard. His *nostrils* and nose signify his anger, his approbation, and his exact judgment. His *mouth* and lips denote his will, authority, and wrath. His *back* imports his anger and disregard. His *bowels* are his most ardent love, his tender mercy, and unbounded compassion. His *bosom* imports secrecy, safety, eminent nearness, amazing intimacy, and endeared love. His *feet* are the less glorious manifestations of his presence; the exercise of his power and providence, for the relief of his people and overthrow of his enemies.

Pilate washed his hands in Christ's case to denote that his power was used innocently, Mat. 27. 24. Persons were consecrated by the imposition of hands to denote spiritual power imparted, Gen. 48. 14.

Russian.—God is an old worker of miracles.

Svetasvatare Upanished.—Without hands or feet, God grasps and moves; without eyes he sees; without ears he hears; he knows whatever is knowable, but no one knows him.

The Soul thirsts for God like a Hart.—Ps. 42. 1.

Prayer compared to the *importunate friend* at midnight, Luke 11. 5–8; the *importunate widow*, Luke 18. 5; *wrestling* Jacob, Gen. 32. 21–32; called *pouring out* of the heart, Ps. 62. 8; *drawing* near to God, Heb. 10. 22; *looking* up, Ps. 5. 3; *waiting* as a servant.

The deer are accustomed to gather themselves at noon to the cool solitude and refreshing brook, and are often seen reclining in groups upon the mossy bank, or quenching their thirst in the shallow stream. Sometimes the hunters scare them from their nook, and chase them over the open brow above the woods under the sultry sun. Panting with the heat and exertion, they make for their favourite haunt and the quiet brook. From some change of purpose, the pursuers discontinued the chase; and the frightened and exhausted creatures are suffered to plunge into the copses, and find their way to the shades for which they longed. How eager must have been their draught, when they reached the brook!—how grateful and refreshing the plunge into the flood, and the rest amidst the moss and fern! Such is the soul in the desert of this world thirsting for the true *amrita*, or waters of life, flowing from God's throne.

Urdu.—The thirsty person goes to the well, not the well to him. The thirsty is most eager for water.

Persian.—When one is thirsty, one thousand pearls are not worth one drop of water.

Turk.—It is the squalling child that gets the milk.

Badaga.—Do we give milk to the cat that cries, or to the cat that does not cry?

China.—Even the ripest fruit does not drop into one's mouth. We must knock that it might be opened.

Russian.—Pray to God, but continue to row to the shore. We must watch, as well as pray.

Talmud.—Should man not go after wisdom? wisdom will not come to him.

Sanskrit.—The king is the strength of the weak, crying is the strength of children.

What six proverbs illustrate the thirst of prayer?

Urdu.—Hunger is the best sauce and fatigue the best pillow.

The Heavenly Home.—JOHN 14. 2.

Heaven unlike a good earthly home in three points:—

Heaven is represented under the emblems of "a better *country,*" "*a paradise*" without any serpent, "*a city*" paved with gold, "a *palace;*" but "home" is an emblem familiar to all—all can understand the "*father's house.*"

Allusion in the text to the *temple of Jerusalem* where God dwelt, 1 Kings 8. 10, 11, with many chambers for priests and Levites. Kings' palaces have many rooms. The *Vatican,* the Pope's residence, has 4,000 chambers.

In this world we are only *pilgrims;* heaven is our home.

Heaven like a good earthly home in six points:—

1. *Place of birth—earliest recollections:* early recollections, like the *tamarind roots* are not easily pulled up, cling to the memory, so *heaven* to the believer; he is "*born* from above." The heavenly *Jerusalem* is the mother of us all, "light from heaven first illumined him," hence he seeks the things above; his religious affections fixed on an unseen world.

2. *Residence of our best friends,* our family, and the old servants attract us to it, so heaven the residence of the Father of mercies, of "Christ, our eldest brother," the spirits of just men made perfect, "our younger brethren," besides ministering spirits. No family contentions there; the Father of lights there without variableness, Jas. 1. 17.

3. *Source of sweetest comforts:* the child found in clothes and education, the prodigal son thought of his father's house, Luke 15. 17; so the Christian has *bread* from heaven and the *water* of life, they shall go no more out; "the lamb shall feed them."

4. *Security:* a father's house a sure refuge; "no plague comes nigh our dwelling," Ps. 91; "no lion shall be there." "Under the shadow of the wings of the Almighty."

5. *Habitation* to which a *right is claimed;* the child considers the father's things "ours," my father, your father. Though here we may not have where to lay our head, *there* is heaven, "a building of God."

6. *Free of care:* children have no anxiety to provide for the family; "they shall enter into peace." They shall sit down with Abraham, Isaac, and Jacob, Mat. 8. 11.

The earthly father's house often *desolate* after years, but Christ the "same yesterday and for ever." Earthly abode a shifting one, small in tents; heaven has *many* mansions, the "palace of the great king," "if children, then heirs." David said, "Though father or mother forsake me," believers, though here they may wander in dens and caves, Heb. 11., "shall sit with Christ on his throne," "as one whom his mother comforted, so will God." "Forget thy father's house"—*i.e.*, the earthly.

The Righteous are God's Husbandry.—1 COR. 3. 9.

The righteous God's husbandry in twelve points:—

The relation of Christ to his Church is pointed out in the Bible under a variety of pleasing images, such as of a *building, jewels, friends* (see Parable of Vineyard, Mat. 21. 33); here it is under that of a well-managed farm.

1. *Believers are God's special property.* Ground in commonage is not well cultivated, it must become the property of some person to be attended to; so the Lord's portion is his people, purchased from the waste of this world, of a price, if not according to the intrinsic value, yet according to the interest taken by the purchaser.

2. *Meted out, separated.* Boundaries for farms are necessary, so the boundaries of the visible and invisible

church, of the church and the world—"I have chosen you out of the world."

3. *Fenced and protected.* A stone may be a landmark, or a furrow may be a line of division; but a fence is necessary to prevent trespass. "My beloved had a garden, he fenced it." Church discipline and laws are a fence; so is God's providence. "Hast thou not set a fence around Job?" "A garden enclosed is my sister." Come out from among them and be separate.

4. *Subject to a spiritual cultivation.* The fruits of righteousness are the great object. Many improvements of late have been made in agriculture; so it is necessary to improve in spiritual husbandry. God says, "What could I have done more for my vineyard than I have done?"

5. *An adequate band of labourers is provided.* Labourers are necessary for a farm; among the Jews, a whole tribe was set apart for this spiritual work; God gave some apostles and some prophets; he finds labourers idle in the market; sees and thrusts them out; "he that puts his hand to the plough and looks back is not fit for the kingdom of God."

6. *Suitable instruments are furnished.* Man's hand could do little without the spade and plough. God's word is the plough to root out weeds. The fallow ground of the heart must be ploughed up. Weeds must be destroyed, and the light must enter; "the word of God is sharper than a two-edged sword;" the ploughshare of conviction breaks up the fallow soil; such were those who were pricked to the heart when Peter preached, Acts 2. 37. "The peaceable fruits of righteousness," rending the heart, not the garment. The mattock of the law from Sinai will break very hard soil, Is. 7. 25; so the hammer of God's word, Jer. 23. 29. Affliction destroys the weeds of corruption.

7. *The soil is improved and enriched.* Drainage for some, manure for other, soils is necessary; as the field

becomes fertile from blood and bones, so the blood of atonement purges the conscience from dead works. God gives a heart of flesh.

8. *The soil must be sown with heavenly seed.* Without this seed vice will spring up; sowing requires good seed, good soil, and a good season; no good seed of itself, John 3. 6.

9. *The crop must be watched and dressed.* Seed must be pressed into the soil, and protected from vermin and cattle; the crop is sometimes over-luxuriant.

10. *The soil must be watered.* Egypt was watered by the foot to convey water in rivulets. Blessed are they that sow beside all waters "floods on the dry ground."

11. *Fruit is expected:* hence the waiting for the latter rain. "The harvest of the earth will be gathered" in by God, then the joy of harvest home, Is. 9. 3.

12. *Low lands are more fertile than high.* Rain descends on the valley and remains, Jer. 17. 8.

Fruit was sought on the fig-tree three years, Luke 13. 7, hence Christ cursed it. The husbandmen that would not cultivate were destroyed, Mark 12. 9. The seven Churches of Asia had their hedges broken down. God is the sole proprietor, and cannot be dispossessed. He is never weary, and never grows old, Is. 40. 28; he can make bad trees good and sends rain.

The Incense of Prayer.—Rev. 5. 8.

Prayer like incense in five points:—

Incense was made from the gum extracted from the bark of a tree; being used in sacrifices, it was brought as a present to the Infant Saviour, Mat. 2. 11. It was a symbol of prayer as it *ascended,* so did Cornelius's prayer, Acts 10. 4, Ps. 141. 2; was made *pure* from the gum of a tree in Arabia; was *purifying,* removing the smell from the burning flesh and blood of the sacrifices;

was *fragrant,* Ex. 30. 34; *pleasant,* so when Hannah prayed she was no more sad, 1 Sam. 1. 18.

The 24 elders are represented, Rev. 5. 8, 8. 3, 4, as having an harp and a cup full of incense, which is the prayers of the saints. Daniel hazarded his life to offer this incense, Dan. 6. 10.

Prayer is compared to knocking, Luke 11. 5–8; to wrestling, Gen. 32. 24; to an importunate widow, Luke 18. 1–8.

Arabic.—Prayer is the pillar of religion. Acts 10. 4.
Arabic.—Prayer comes not in answer to the cat's prayer.
Afghan.—To say bismillah (in God's name) brings a blessing, but not in jackal hunting.

Begotten to an Unfading Inheritance.—1 Pet. 1. 4.

Heaven is the inheritance of those who, by the new birth, belong to the Church of the *first born,* who get the blessing of the spiritual birthright. In an inheritance the heirs are (1) *heads* of the house, the prop of the family; believers are joint heirs with Christ, who is the heir of all things. 2. The heir must be *qualified* to manage the estate properly, so believers are made partakers of the divine nature, 2 Pet. 1. 4; the proud God knoweth afar off, Ps. 138. 6. (3) The *estate* is in proportion to the wealth of the donor. God is Lord of all. (4) An inheritance is *future,* but this is kept in heaven, and as certain as money in a good bank; here the heirs have little, but are like the Jews in the wilderness who had no house,. yet called God their dwelling place, Ps. 90. 1. God's promises are a heritage, Ps. 119. 11.

The Inheritance of the righteous differs from an earthly inheritance in five points:—

Earthly inheritances are *small,* subject to *law suits,* limited in *duration, unsatisfying, common* to the wicked and good, *often* pillaged or *wasted* as the prodigal son did his.

Justice.

Pushtu.—The mouth eats the food, and the eyes bear the shame.

Pushtu.—She commits the sin, and blames Satan for it.

Pushtu.—The oxen eat up the crops, and they cut off the ear of the donkey.

Christ has the Keys of Death and Hell.—Rev. i. 18.

When a person is put into office, he is often intrusted with keys; thus a jailor has the keys of a prison. Ancient keys were often made of wood; and, to be strong, they were made very large, so that they were carried on the shoulder; and, in the east, the carrying of a key on any great occasion was a mark of a person's holding some office of rank and power. Thus it is said of Jesus, "And the government shall be upon his shoulder," Is. 9. 6; that is, he shall have power as one that carries the key to mark his authority.

Silence was represented by the Greeks as a golden key on the tongue. Authority to explain the law and the prophets was given among the Jews by the delivery of a key; in the case of one rabbi after his death they put his key and his tablets into his coffin, because he did not deserve to have a son to whom he might leave the ensigns of his office.

Christ said to Peter *I will give unto thee the Keys of the Kingdom of Heaven,* Mat. 16. 19, as stewards of a great family, especially of the royal household, bore a key, probably a golden one, in token of their office; the phrase of giving a person the key naturally grew into an expression of raising him to great power, Is. 22. 22, Rev. 3. 7. This was with peculiar propriety applicable to ministers, the stewards of the mysteries of God, 1 Cor. 4. 1. The Bible is the key of knowledge, Luke 11. 52. Peter's opening the kingdom of heaven, as being the first that preached it both to the Jews and to the Gentiles, may be considered as an illustration of this promise; as also the power given of binding and loosing.

Jesus Christ declares he who believes on him shall never see death—*i.e.*, Spiritual death. The Danes say "A golden key opens every door except that of heaven."

Talmud.—A man knowing law, but without God's fear, is a man having the key of the inner, but not of the outer chamber.

Arabic.—Patience is the key to joy; penitence to pardon; modesty to tranquility.

Atmabodh Prakasika.—Without knowledge resembling fire for cooking, no liberation.

The Righteous are Kings.

The righteous like kings in six points:—

Death is called in the Bible the king of terrors, Job 18. 14, as the alligator is called a king, Job 41. 34.

Believers are like kings occupied with *high* things, Ph. 3. 20; shall *rule* the kingdoms of this world, when they become the kingdom of God, Rev. 11. 15; Dan. 9. 27, highly *honoured;* high *born,* Christians born from above, 1 John 3. 1; well *attended,* angels their servants, Heb. 1. 14; *crowned,* 2 Tim. 3. 8.

Chanak says "a learned man and a king are not on an equality; the king is honoured only in his own country, the learned everywhere."

Christ is called King of kings, while the church is styled his daughter all glorious within, Ps. 45. 13. Christ is the only begotten son; the treasures of wisdom are hid in him, 1 Cor. 1. 24; he was proclaimed by a star, and by the angels singing to the shepherds; his palace was the heaven of heavens; angels his attendants and ambassadors; all are his subjects, even the winds obey him, while rulers like Cyrus and Nebuchadnezzar, work out his will.

Christ's Kingdom Immovable.—HEB. 12. 28.

Parable of Marriage Feast, Mat. 22. 1–14; *Parable of the Great Supper, Luke* 14. 16–21.

Christ's friends are heirs of a kingdom, but not of this *world,* where everything is so uncertain. Christ said his kingdom was not of this world, John 18. 36.

Christ's kingdom differs from earthly kingdoms in five points:—

1. Its *throne is stable:* a throne is a great object of human ambition, yet like a *high tree* yields soonest to the storm, Job 12. 21, such are earthly kingdoms, but in heaven "the Lord reigneth." Christ once took the form of a servant, "but he is now highly exalted," ruling with the *ancient of days* God the Father; he has an everlasting dominion, Dan. 4. 34.

2. Its *constitution unalterable—i.e.,* these fundamental ordinances which determine the form of government. Christ's is an absolute monarchy, but it is the rule of absolute wisdom, goodness, and truth; a change of earthly government upsets men's minds, but Christ's kingdom is stable.

3. Its *privileges inviolable* "life that never ends," *property* secure, "an inheritance incorruptible," *liberty* "from the bondage of corruption," "the son makes free." Every Englishman's *house is his castle,* but the believer's abode is more so; he dwells under the shadow of the Almighty. Every Englishman has a right to be tried by his peers; Christians have a divine advocate; "who shall lay anything to the charge of God's elect," Rom. 8. 33. All in this kingdom are *brethren;* all

things are yours—the true *equality*—all raised to be *kings* and *priests.*

4. Its *prosperity imperishable ; wealth* takes wings; all the old empires have perished; weather and disease blast the best expectations; but to the believer *all things* shall work together for good; the *poor* of this world are rich in faith.

5. Its *duration eternal:* Dan. 7. 14; *Egypt, Babylon, Greece, Rome,* all perished. *David's stem* buried in the rubbish of a carpenter's shop, but *Christ's kingdom* is eternal, not supported by human ambition or an arm of flesh. "The kingdom of this world will become the kingdom of our God." Christ will be "King of kings," Ps. 146. 10.

Who knocks at the Door of the Heart?

REV. 3. 20.

The Prodigal Son, Luke 15. 17–19.—*The Marriage Supper, Luke* 14. 16.

God's ways are not as our ways; with man the inferior waits on the superior, in the text the great God waits on the lukewarm Laodiceans. The *door* is the heart; this is barred by nature against Christ through vile lusts and passions, and by unbelief.

Christ continues to *knock* by his *word,* Heb. 4. 12, by his Spirit, by his *Providence.*

China.—Men will be no more virtuous without exhortation than a bell sound without being struck.

Telugu.—Unless the child cries, even the mother will not give it suck.

Christ the Lamb of God.—JOHN 1. 29.

Christ was like a lamb in four points:

(1) *Harmless,* Heb. 7. 26, John 21. 15, he was surrounded by wolves, by Satan a roaring lion, and by Herod

a fox; (2) *meek,* bore the wrongs of spitting on and scourging when led to the slaughter, Heb. 12. 3; (3) *contented,* Christ had not where to lay his head, Mat. 8. 2; (4) *used in sacrifice,* Rev. 12. 11; Christ like the scapegoat bore our sins away into the wilderness, so the *Asvamedh,* or horse-sacrifice of the Hindus, was designed to typify a sacrificial purpose. An hypocritical power is compared to a lamb with two horns, but speaking as a dragon, Rev. 13. 11. In the millennium the lamb is to dwell with the wolf, Is. 11. 6, 65. 25.

The Spiritual Legacy.—LUKE 22. 29.

These words were spoken by Christ previous to his Crucifixion, giving to his disciples high honour in the next world: his legacy. A legacy is a proof of friendship, a sign that death does not dissolve it, so Christ, eighteen hundred years ago, in an upper-room, eating his Last Supper gave this proof; the next day he was to hang on a Cross; he sealed this legacy by breaking bread, and drinking wine.

Christ's legacy differs from a common legacy in six points:—

This Legacy is—(1) in the *Bible;* we are to search the Scriptures as the miner searches for gold, or as people examine a will immediately after the death of the testator; (2) *Eternal;* some are left things acquired by fraud or force, and therefore disputed; this property does not corrupt the possessor, 1 Pet. 1. 4; (3) The legatees are *ruined* sinners; blessed are the poor in spirit, Mat. 5.; (4) *Ratified* by a seal; baptism and the Lord's Supper; the Sunday is the memorial of it; (5) *Unconditional;* no debt or mortgages entailed; Boaz's kinsman wished Naomi's property, but not without the condition of marrying Ruth: so Moses rejected the treasures of Egypt, when the condition implied forfeiting the reproach of Christ; (6)

Enough for all; when the division is small, quarrels are apt to arise, as in Abraham's, Isaac's, and David's families, but this kingdom is boundless; many mansions in the Father's House.

Who comes as the Lightning?—Mat. 24. 27.

Christ's second coming compared to a *bridegroom,* Mat. 25. 1–13, a *supper,* Rev. 19. 6–9, a *restitution,* Acts 3. 21. We are to *wait* for it, Rom. 8. 19–22, to *hasten* to it, 2 Pet. 3. 12. The Virgin's cry was at midnight, Mat. 25. 6: at midnight the first-born of Egypt died, Ex. 12. 29: at midnight 185,000 Assyrians were smitten.

The *sudden* flash, which brings so near to us the thought of an awful power that might consume us in a moment, *should* remind us of Christ's coming. He came at first in great humility, and many years passed by before he manifested forth his glory, that his disciples should believe on him. But when he shall come again, he will be seen "in the clouds of heaven." "Every eye shall see him, and they also who pierced him." From one end of heaven to the other, his presence like lightning will be made manifest: and his coming will be as sudden as it will be terrible to the wicked. The heavens shall pass away, 2 Pet. 3. 9.

At Christ's first coming: He was a babe; a servant, his forerunner, John a fakir in the desert; fishermen his attendants; acted as a mediator; spat on, derided.

At His second coming: He will be King of kings; the trump of the archangel shall sound; angels, archangels, his attendants; Judge and Lord of all.

Christ's coming is also compared, Rev. 3. 3, to a thief in the night. The thief comes to *destroy,* so in the day of the Lord, the wicked shall be cut asunder, Mat. 24. 37. The thief comes with *weapons,* so Christ comes in flames of fire, 2 Thes. 5. 7–8; and he comes *unexpectedly* when men are at ease and asleep, like as in the days of Noah,

Mat. 24. 37; all will be fright and confusion; they will call on the rocks to cover them, Rev. 6. 16, 17. The thief comes with *wicked intent*, Christ, on the other hand, to punish injustice, and deliver his people; the thief's coming may be prevented, but the day of the Lord *will* come, 2 Pet. 3. 10. The thief injures a few; Christ executes judgment on all.

Telugu.—If the thief said beforehand that he was coming, I would have secured witnesses.

Talmud.—The owl and the hen waited together for the morning: "The light is of use to me," said the hen, "but of what use to you?"

Russian.—Prepare for death, but neglect not to sow.

Christ the Lily of the Valley.—CANT. 2. 1.

Christ is compared to a lily among thorns; like a lily he is *fragrant*, Gen. 8. 21, *white and pure*, Rev. 19. 8, *fruitful*, not destroyed by the snow of persecution, *beautiful*, like a lily among thorns. Sadi compares an amiable youth to a white lily in a bed of narcissuses.

The simple beauty of the lilies drew on them their Creator's approving notice, when, in the days of his flesh, he went in and out among men, and was himself capable of being soothed by the works which he made so fair and pleasant for the children of men. Those sweet and lovely flowers were then as unreprovable in his sight as in the day when he first "saw that they were good." Man, for whose delight and solace they were made, was now sinful and fallen; but the handiwork of God in these his humbler creatures, was still such as he could behold with complacency. "They toil not, neither do they spin;" the bright clothing, which it is so pleasant to behold, is furnished for them without any task imposed on them of painful labour; and they close their flowers at night without any anxious care, lest the kindly shower or the genial sun should fail them on the morrow, Mat. 6. 28.

Our Saviour does not mean to discourage the toils of honest industry and wise foresight, or obedience to the law which is laid on all of us, "Six days shalt thou labour;" but he means, that in these innocent "flowers of the field," we should see an emblem of those who are "without carefulness;" and who, having diligently done whatever their hands find to do," are enabled to trust God for the result.

Buddhagosha.—The righteous shines amongst the ignorant as the lilies in a heap of rubbish.

Looking to Jesus.—Heb. 12. 2.

As the weary traveller at night looks for the morning star, so is Christ's advent regarded. The wicked have to look for a fearful judgment day, believers for Christ's coming in the clouds, Phil. 3. 20.

A man's looks often indicate his frame of mind; the eye is a mirror of the passions of the soul; it expresses like the tongue, joy, and grief, thus the look of a *dying husband* on his surviving wife or of a *drowning* man wishing aid.

Looking to Jesus implies—(1) *distinct knowledge,* Hos. 4. 5; (2) *eagerness for relief,* Ps. 123. 2, Jonah 2. 4; (3) *humble dependence;* (4) *affection.*

This looking implies likeness, 2 Cor. 3. 18. A cat may look at a king, but the looking does not change her. In this looking we are to look *off* from other things, we are not to let the plough stand to catch a mouse.

Panchatantra.—The lost, the dead, and the past the wise mourn not over.

Persian.—One's eyes are more delighted at seeing the faces of friends, than by beholding a garden or a parterre.

Meekness.

Tamul.—Are there any snakes who will not bite those who tread on them?

Arabic.—Mild speech enchains the heart.

Syriac.—He who gives not wood to the fire prevents burning.

Tamul.—A loving disposition is a river without a ripple.

Probodh Chandroday.—The *equanimity* of rational men is steady as the clear unruffled ocean, so that they bear with reproach from persons whose eyebrows, gathered up in black anger, present a fearful appearance, and whose eyes are red as the setting sun.

Turk.—Have the sweetness of the lamb, the force of the lion, and the sagacity of the elephant.

China.—Stir not a fire with a sword—*i.e.*, provoke not a fool.

Syriac.—Shut your doors, and ye will not fear enemies—*i.e.*, be silent, no fear of calumny.

Turk.—Tread not on a sleeping snake.

Church Membership.—Rom. 12. 4, 5.

The text refers to the different offices and qualifications of Christians. See the Fable of the Belly and Members.

The Church is called the body of Christ, and He is the *head*, Eph. 1. 22, which implies *superiority* and *sympathy*, 1 Cor. 11. 3; when the head is cut off the body, in one minute life ceases.

Christ, the Head who is in heaven, is also dwelling by his Spirit in all his members, so as to make them one with him and with each other by an union which is closer than that of parent and child. If we are "the body of Christ," then we have the comfort of knowing that Christ is our life. He is to our souls what the living principle is to our bodies. Being our "Head," he is our counsellor and guide in all difficulties and anxieties. Being our "life," he is our strength in all assaults of Satan, in all trials and temptations. So that it is not our own strength nor our own wisdom that we depend upon; but the strength and wisdom of Christ. As "the members of Christ," we shall regard both our souls and bodies with a more solemn and reverential feeling, and shall fear above all things to defile by any wilful sin what is his and not our own.

The Church like the body in four points:—

That is scarcely to be called a member of our body which is of no *use* to the body, nor can he be called a true member of Christ who is of no use to the Church (which is Christ's body) according to the calling in life which God has appointed for him. The apostle says, "There are many members in one body, and all have not the same office." All have some office, but all have not the same office. And thus in Christ's body, every member is appointed to some useful office, some work of faith and labour of love, in the daily duties of his various callings. No two members are appointed to the *same* office, but all have some service or other assigned to them. The services of some are more *honourable* than the occupations of the other; but there is no member of Christ that is not called to serve God in some course of useful and dutiful obedience. The eye cannot say to the hand, "I have no need of thee," nor again the head to the feet, "I have no need of you." If any member could sever itself from the rest in a proud independence it would utterly perish. The members have the same *care* one of another. The little brook, which waters a few fields, fulfils the office assigned to it by Providence as truly as the mighty river which bears on its bosom the commerce of a nation.

Japan.—The back and the belly are not interchangeable.

Tamul.—Who would wish to cut off the hand because by mistake it struck the eye?

Persian.—The hands do not perform the business of the heart, but the heart performs that of the hands.

Bengal.—Are the five fingers equal in length?

Tamul.—The head is the chief member of the body, though the others may be larger.

Malay.—If the right thigh be pinched, pain will also be felt in the left.

Hebrew.—All the fingers are not equal.

Turk.—Two hands are made for the service of a single head.

Urdu.—Sometimes a boat on a waggon (carrying on shore), and sometimes a waggon on a boat (in crossing a river). Individuals of different rank can help each other.

Urdu.—Is the flesh separate from the nail?

Persian.—One roof and two winds—*i.e.*, persons of opposite tempers living together.

Persian.—The knife does not cut off its own handle.

Who are Spiritual Merchants.—Prov. 3. 13, 14.

The righteous as spiritual merchants in seven points:—

Some supposed in Paul's time that gain was godliness; this is not true, yet godliness with contentment is great gain, 1 Tim. 4. 8.

The *righteous* is a good *merchant*, Mat. 13. 45. Must be *diligent*, Heb. 6. 11, *punctual*, Ecc. 9. 10, *regular* in correspondence like the importunate widow, Luke 18. 1; *useful*, Christians are the salt of the earth, but losses at times occur from storms, robbers. His *articles of trade* are the gold of God's love, Rev. 3. 18; the pearls of Christ's blessings, Mat. 13. 45; the oil and wine of God's spirit, Ps. 23. 5; the spices of graces, Cant. 3. 6. His *capital* is Christ's offices, as prophet, priest, and king; the *port he trades* to is a distant one, Is. 33. 17; a rich one, a royal one, all made kings and priests there; a heavenly, Ph. 3. 20; his *profits* are satisfying, enduring, Jas. 4. 13. The spiritual merchant deals not in adulterated articles; is sure of his profit; he has arms of defence, Eph. 6. 11.

Mahabharat.—Amass that wealth which has nothing to fear from kings or thieves, and which does not desert thee in death.

The Church compared to the Moon.—Cant. 6. 10.

The Church is called a pillar, 1 Tim. 3. 15, illustrated by the parables of the Tares and Wheat, the Net, the Mustard Seed.

The moon receives her brightness from the sun. She is dark herself, and reflects his light. One-half of her orb is always illuminated therewith—a circle of beautiful splendour; but the whole of that circle is not always visible, sometimes but a thread-like portion thereof, and sometimes it is entirely hidden from the eyes. The moon is not in darkness, when we see not her light; her face still looks towards the sun, and is bright with his brightness; but we are so placed not to have the full view thereof.

Such is the Church; it is dark itself, but reflects the light of its Lord. For the graces of Christ beheld by faith produce like graces in the soul.

The Church like the moon in seven points :—

(1) *Receives light* from the sun; Christ is the Sun of Righteousness, Mal. 4. 2; (2) *Dispenses* and reflects what she receives, Mat. 5. 14; (3) Gives light at *night,* so Christians in this dark world; (4) Though fair has *spots,* Jud. 12; (5) Sometimes full, sometimes *waning;* the Church now in prosperity, again persecuted, but the wicked have reserved for them the blackness of darkness, 2 Pet. 2. 17; (6) *Above* the earth, so Christians, Ph. 3. 20; (7) Acts by *unseen* influence, like the moon on the tides and weather.

Rabbins.—Be rather the tail of a lion than the head of a fox, Ps. 84. 10.

Bengal.—The moon mocks the thieves.

Cinghalese.—Like the moon shining in the desert.
Polish.—Life is like the moon—now dark, now full.

The Holy Spirit's Influence like Oil.—Ps. 23. 5.

The Holy Spirit like oil in five points :—

High priests and kings were appointed to office by anointing with oil; in this way Saul was made king, 1 Sam. 10. 1. Christ was anointed to heal the broken-hearted, Luke 4. 18, hence his name. Cyrus, though a heathen, was called God's anointed, Is. 45. 1.

The Holy Spirit's influence is like oil in its effects; in —*softening,* hard tumours are mollified, so the swellings of pride; *healing,* draws the bad humours out, so the wounded traveller had oil poured into his wounds, Luke 10. 34; the sick were anointed with oil, Jas. 5. 14; *refreshing,* used in banquets, and called the oil of joy; made a person *active,* hence wrestlers and warriors used it for their limbs; makes the face to *shine,* Stephen's face shone like that of an *angel,* Acts 6. 15.

Christ's name is compared to ointment poured forth in its *prciousncss,* Mat. 26. 7, *fragrance. Brotherly love is* compared, Ps. 123. 2, to oil in its qualities of softening, making supple, fragrant, healing, precious, poured forth.

Phariseeism or Straining at a Gnat while Swallowing a Camel.—Mat. 23. 24.

The Pharisees urged the murder of Christ, yet refused to take the money as the price of blood, Mat. 26. 65. The Budhists strain water to prevent their swallowing insects. Christ called their pride and hypocrisy leaven, as being sour and penetrating.

Tamul.—A terrible ascetic, an atrocious cheat.
Bengal.—Scented oil on the head, the body, so filthy as to drive away sleep.
China.—Water under the grass.

China.—The mouth of a Buddha, the heart of a snake.
Badaga.—If he is in the wilderness, he is a robber. If he comes to the village, he wishes to be a guru—*i.e.*, a religious teacher, Mat. 23. 4–7, 14.
Veman.—His forehead is that of a worshipper; his mouth that of a wolf; and his heart that of a roaming demon: is he so shameless as to say he has learnt of the divinity?
Japan.—To clothe a wolf in priest's clothes.
Tamul.—He tells lies by thousands, and builds a temple.

Who is the Great Physician?—Mat. 9. 12.

Christ went about healing all manner of diseases and spiritual maladies; he said the whole have no need of a physician, but those who are sick.

Christ a good physician in ten points:—

1. *Good natural qualifications:* Christ has infinite *intelligence;* "all things are naked to his eyes," Heb. 4. 13; he has infinite *power;* we are his workmanship. His heart is *tender;* a High Priest touched with a feeling of our infirmities. A merry and feeling heart does good like a medicine, particularly so with a physician; but Christ has sympathy, as he suffered being tempted.

2, *Training*: A doctor must know the structure of the body, the symptoms of disorders, and the properties of medicines. Christ partook of flesh and blood, Heb. 2. 14.

3. *Authorized* by competent authority; Christ called of God as was Aaron, lifted up as a serpent in the wilderness. The Lord anointed him to bind up the broken-hearted, Luke 4. 18; his miracles were his diploma, John 5. 36, 37.

4. Efficient *medicines* provided: he sent his word, and healed them, Ps. 107. 20, to be spiritually minded is life and peace. These medicines are not dear or

difficult to procure; the word can be received into the heart by simple faith; all can come to his dispensary, he varies his medicine according to the disease.

5. *Experience:* Christ has had 6,000 years' practice ever since it was said the seed of the woman shall bruise the serpent's head. Age does not impair his skill; he saves to the uttermost, even in Heaven the song is worthy the lamb; cholera baffles doctors, but Christ searches the reins, and checks all diseases; he can make Paul's thorn in the flesh contribute to his humility,

6. *Attentive:* Comes at all times without being asked, and watches the crisis.

7. *Generous to the poor:* Christ takes no fees; says buy without money or price, Is. 55. 1; Christ is the poor man's doctor; he healed the woman who had spent all her money on doctors, Luke 8. 43.

8. *Perseveres:* Christ makes the dry bones live, Ez. 37. 4; he has the brand plucked from the burning.

9. *Successful:* Christ said come all that labour. Adam's rebellion, Noah's drunkenness, Manasseh's tyranny were cured; even death is cured, Is. 25. 8. The Persians say of ordinary physicians—when fate arrives the physician is a fool.

10. *Accessible:* Christ is always so; he never sleeps.

Christ differs from earthly physicians in nine points:—

(1) Sometimes *deceived,* kill sometimes instead of curing; (2) require to be *sent* for, Luke 19. 10; (3) *charge* for services, Is. 55. 1; (4) make few sacrifices for their patients. Christ gave his blood; (5) cannot raise the *dead;* (6) sometimes *impatient;* (7) visit only *one patient* at a time; (8) subject to *disease* themselves, Heb. 2. 17; (9) their *medicines* lose their virtue by long keeping.

Talmud.—A doctor at a distance is blind.

Bengali.—He who has had the ringworm knows what it really is.

Tamul.—Faith in medicine makes it effectual.

Japan.—No medicine for lovesickness and a fool.

Tamul.—Is there any medicine for a bad temper?
Russian.—A golden bed cannot cure the sick.
Tamul.—The friendship of the doctor ends at the threshold.
Telugu.—Are you to ask the bullock before you put on the pack-saddle?
Urdu.—The barber washes everyone's feet, but thinks it beneath him to wash his own.
Tamul.—He who has killed 1,000 persons is half a doctor.
Urdu.—There is no physic for false ideas.

Who are Pilgrims on Earth?—Heb. 11. 11, 13.

Moses gave his son the name of Gershom (the stranger), to signify he was not in his own land, though it gave him shelter when treated with neglect by his own countrymen, and driven away from a royal court, Ex. 2. 22.

The Jews' journey in the desert—a type of the Christian pilgrimage in ten points:—

1. A journey *from* a house of *bondage;* the Jews worked in hot weather in Egypt, a land like a furnace, and were deprived of their children; so the righteous were slaves to Satan, and their offspring were heirs to misery, serving divers lusts, 1 Pet. 2. 11. God says to them, as the angel did to Lot, "Escape for thy life, look not back," Gen. 19. 17.

2. A journey *through* a dangerous desolate *wilderness,* hunger, fiery serpents, burning sand, flinty rock, a land of drought, of the shadow of death, Deut. 8. 15; so is this world; no food for the soul, temptations for the trial of faith, storms, quicksands of affliction, the enemies of the Christian are fear, Prov. 22. 13; unbelief; sloth, 1 Tim. 5. 13; covetousness, Mat. 16. 24; presumption.

3. A journey *to* a land of *Promise:* the Jews in the wilderness saw this not, yet they had God's word for it;

the stones were iron; a land of fountains flowing with milk and honey, Deut. 8. 8; so the Patriarchs were not mindful of that country from whence they came out, Heb. 11. 15.

4. A *long* and roundabout *journey.* The Jews might have reached Canaan in one month instead of forty years, but thereby their trial and punishment were intended, Deut. 8. 2; so Christians have a variety of experience, joy, and sorrow; rest will be therefore more sweet.

5. Rely on a heavenly *guide* coming up from the wilderness leaning on the beloved, Cant. 3. 8; underneath are the everlasting arms, Deut. 33. 27. A journey under *Divine Government;* the Jews were few in Egypt, yet kings were reproved for their sake; they multiplied in slavery; in Babylon God was with the Jews, but in the desert there was the pillar of cloud by day, of fire by night; they had angels' food; their garments and shoes waxed not old; so Christ is with his Church to the end of the world, Mat. 28. 20; as an eagle over her young ones, Deut. 32. 11; they mount up with wings as eagles, Is. 40. 31; there are various pretended ways, but Christ is the true one.

6. A journey with a *happy termination;* Jordan crossed, each sat under his vine and fig-tree, so a rest for God's people, Is. 35. 10; all journeys in this world not certain of success.

7. Enter by the *straight* way—of religious conviction, their foot on the flesh, their eye on the cross.

8. Their *Provision* on the way, bread from heaven.

9. *Perseverance*—of all that came out of Egypt few entered Canaan, so Lot's wife with regard to Sodom, like man putting his hand to the plough and looking back, Luke 9. 62.

10. In *motion* always, but towards home, Gen. 47. 9.

Afghan.—To every one his home is kashmir—*i.e.*, very good.

Badaga.—A single coal burns not well, a single traveller finds the way heavy.

Ramayan.—As a man going to another village stays outside, and next day leaving that abode proceeds on his journey, so home and property are only men's resting places.

Providence Rescues from a Horrible Pit.—Ps. 40. 2.

This text alludes to the custom of digging pits to catch wild beasts, and covering them with straw or dust, or such like things, that they might not be discerned. The Psalmist in this, as in some other passages of his writings, means by digging a pit to express the mischievous designs of the wicked, who, in trying to do him harm by their subtlety, treated him as men did wild beasts which they endeavoured to catch. Joseph was cast into a pit by his envious brethren, where they would have left him to perish, if Judah had not interposed on his behalf, Gen. 37. 26.

"Pit" also signifies the *grave*, and the Psalmist expresses the despair he should be in if God slighted him. He should become as a dead man, lost and undone. Nothing is so painful to a gracious soul as the want of God's favour and the sense of his displeasure. His frowns are worse than death and the grave. "Pit" also means *trouble.* Despondency of spirit under the sense of God's withdrawings, and prevailing doubts and fears about our eternal state, are like unto a horrible pit and miry clay. David found himself sinking more and more into inward disquiet and perplexity of spirit, out of which he could not work himself.

Atonement a Propitiation through Faith in Christ.
Rom. 3. 25.

Christ's death as an atonement was typified by the *Paschal Lamb,* Ex. 12; the *smiting the rock,* Ex. 17. 6;

our sins are imputed to Christ, as Adam's were to us, Rom. 5. 12–21; in England, when a woman is married, her husband is responsible for her debts; the Church is Christ's bride, and he pays her debts, so David was kind to the house of Saul for Jonathan's sake.

The atonement was also typified by sacrificing the firstlings of the flock, Gen. 4. 4; by Isaac, about to be offered, Gen. 22. 2; by the mercy-seat not approached without blood, the scapegoat was type, Lev. 16. 21. The atonement is a *washing out* stains, Ps. 51. 2; a *passing by*, Mic. 7. 18; scattering a cloud that hides the sun; removing sin far away, Ps. 103. 12; healing, Ps. 30. 2. The brazen serpent which cured the Jews bitten by the snakes on their looking at it typified the eye of faith looking on Christ, curing the soul bitten by the serpent—sin.

If the mercies of God be not loadstones to draw us to heaven, they will be millstones to sink us to perdition; the wicked are no better for mercies, as the Dead Sea or ocean is no sweeter from the rivers of fresh water that flow in.

Death Rest to the Righteous.—Job 7. 3; 3. 17–19.

Rest spiritual differs from worldly rest in four points:—

The saints are weary of battling with their three great enemies—the world, the flesh, and the devil, like Job, 2 Pet. 2. 8. Paul wished to depart and be with Christ. On Jewish monuments is this inscription: "Rest in peace in Eden." This rest is not the rest of a stone, but is a change to a better state, not like the rest of Jonah in the whale's belly. How strong was Job's wish for rest when he had to clean his burning boils with a potsherd, 2. 8; his flesh was clad with worms, 7. 4, 5; his breath was corrupt; his bones cleaved to his skin; his friends knew him not, 19. 14.

The righteous ought not to be in death like a child compelled by the rod to give up play; but like one who, tired of play, wishes to go to bed, or like a seaman who only waits for a favourable wind to raise his anchor, 2 Thess. 1. 6, 7.

How faithfully does the labourer exert his strength, that he may honestly earn the hire for which he has undertaken to bear the burden and heat of the day! Now and then he looks wistfully at the lengthening shadows, and notices how far the sun has gone down in the heavens, Job 7. 2. Most welcome to him will be the hour of rest and payment; but he does not suffer himself to suspend his work until the time agreed upon is come. The time for rest will come when the time for work is over. Thus is man set upon the earth to work the work of God for an appointed season; and thus faithfully should he spend himself, and be spent in the service of his gracious Maker. He owes to his Maker every faculty of soul and body; and that gracious Being has promised to all who serve him truly a rich reward when the day of life is over. The reward, indeed, will be of grace and not of debt, for at best we are unprofitable servants, who have done only what it was our duty to do. And which of us has done even so much?

On the other hand, the grave to the *wicked* is a slaughter-house; death like a wolf feeds on them; like sheep they are laid in the grave where their beauty consumes, while the upright shall have dominion over them in the morning of the Resurrection, Ps. 49. 14, Prov. 7. 22.

Telugu.—The man who has crossed a river and reached the shore, cares no longer for the hide-sewn boat; why should the man who has attained *happiness* trouble himself about the body? 2 Cor. 5. 1, Phil. 3. 13.

Urdu.—When I die, I shall get a good nap.

Atmabodha.—Having crossed the sea of Fascination, and having killed the giants, Inclination, Aversion, the wise shall, married to Peace, enjoy repose of soul.

He sparing the Rod hates his Son.—PR. 13. 24.

The bee sucks sweet honey out of the bitterest herb! So God will by afflictions teach his children to suck sweet knowledge, sweet obedience, out of all the bitter afflictions and trials he exercises them with; that scouring and rubbing which frets others, shall make them shine the brighter; that weight which crushes and keeps others under, shall but make them, like the palm-tree, grow better and higher. Stars shine brightest in the darkest night; torches give the best light when beaten; grapes yield most wine when most pressed; spices smell sweetest when pounded; vines are the better for bleeding; gold looks the brighter for scouring; the juniper smells sweetest in the fire.

Joseph's advancement might have been fatal to him, had he not been previously prepared for it by a long course of suffering. We should have looked upon him with concern, had we seen him in bonds and known his innocence. But God, who had a far more indulgent and tender compassion for him, left him in a condition from which we would have delivered him, Gen. 37. 23–36, 39. 20, 21. 23. So with the Israelites in the wilderness, and God's love in subjecting them to such trials in it, Deut. 8. 3–6, 15, 19.

Proud Nebuchadnezzar became humble after his awful punishment, Dan. 4. 34–37. So with Jehoshaphat—God destroyed his fleet to disengage him from his connexion with wicked Ahaziah, 2 Chron. 20. 35–37, and it seems to have had this effect, 1 Kings 22. 49. It is a mercy to have that taken from us that takes us from God. The people of Judah were sent into captivity to Babylon for their good, Jer. 24. 5–7; and in this, as appears from Ezra, Ezra 9. 10, and from Nehemiah, Neh. 9, the effect was good. *Paul's thorn* in the flesh was sent to preserve him from pride, 2 Cor. 12. 7; these examples show that the gem cannot be polished without friction, nor man perfected without adversity, that affliction is an angel of mercy sent to lead us out of Sodom; that the way of the Cross is the royal way to the Crown; and that the waters, which drowned the world, only lifted up the ark.

Who shall see God?—Mat. 5. 2.

Our knowledge of God in heaven is expressed by seeing in four points:—

The Hindus express by *darshan* the privilege after a long pilgrimage of seeing the idol. Knowing God is explained by the emblem of seeing, because sight is (1) the *clearest* of the other senses, as light is given, so our knowledge comes from God; (2) the sense most *universally* exercised; (3) *pleasant*, Ecc. 11. 7, seeing a friend is very different from hearing about him, the eye is the window of the soul; (4) the most *comprehensive* the eye is never satisfied with seeing.

Dirt loves not a sunbeam, nor the impure to see God, Gen. 3. 8, 4. 14. Moses saw God through Christ, Num. 22. 8, so did Jacob, Gen. 32. 30. Believers while pure walk in the light of God's countenance; like the moon dark when away from the sun; bright when facing it.

Sins like Scarlet made White as Snow.—Is. 1. 18.

Scarlet is obtained from the eggs of an insect found on the leaves of the oak in Spain; being bright is used for clothing, *Saul's* daughters wore it, 2 Sam. 1. 24. Neither dew, rain, washing, nor long wear can remove the scarlet die, it is the fastest colour, so with sin the stain is not removed by ordinary means; a scarlet thread was fastened to the scapegoat on the day of atonement; white, on the other hand, was the emblem of purity, Rev. 1. 14; hence the Nazarenes, a sect of the Jews, were said to be purer than snow, Lam. 4. 7.

Who are the Sealed Ones?—2 Tim. 2. 19.

The Holy Spirit like a seal in three points:—

The ancient Hebrews wore seals in rings on their fingers, and in bracelets on their arms. The wicked queen Jezebel wrote the condemnation of Naboth, whose death she plotted to get his vineyard for her husband Ahab, and sent it to the elders of Israel, signed with his seal, 1 Kings 21. 8.

So the ambitious Haman sealed the decree of king Ahasuerus against the Jews with the king's seal, Esth. 3. 12, 8. 8; it is afterwards stated that the king took off his ring, which he had taken from Haman, and gave it to Mordecai. The seal was a *mark* to prove that things were genuine, as in the above cases it showed that the royal *authority* was granted for the purposes named within; at other times, it was a *pledge* for fulfilling terms agreed on between two parties, and also to secure anything by closing it up. So God, when he seals us by his Holy Spirit, marks his image upon us. God is holy; and we cannot be marked with his seal unless we are made holy too. When the Holy Spirit so seals us, he also secures us to the day of redemption, as a thing is shut up from harm by being sealed up; in this way men seal up their writings and treasures, marking them with their own seal, that none may break in and steal them.

The Jews used to write on the head of a corpse with ink, "May he be in the bundle of life, Jehovah the Lord;" this was called sealing the dead. The *seal* makes impressions like itself, so the believer is changed into the same image, 2 Cor. 3. 18; the *wax* must be soft to receive the impression, Heb. 10. 16; so the heart; the wicked have stony hearts; the things are secured, so believers sealed on their forehead, Rev. 7. 3; they are a fountain sealed—*i.e.*, secured against weather, sand, beasts, Cant. 4. 12; the sins of the wicked are sealed up in a bag—*i.e.*, not forgotten, but the seal of the Holy Spirit on the believer is God's image.

The Woman's Seed bruises the Serpent's Head.
GEN. 3. 15.

In the Iceland Mythology the Deity is said to have bruised the Serpent's head, so among the Hindus Krishna tramples on the Serpent's head, who bites his heel.

Jesus Christ was the seed of the woman—*i.e.*, born of the Virgin Mary; he destroyed the Serpent's—*i.e.*, Satan's head, or power; the head of the Serpent is the seat of life. Satan is the old Serpent, Rev. 12. 9.

Satan is like a serpent in five points:—

1. *Subtle*, lies in wait in holes to catch his prey, so the Egyptians behaved to the Babylonians.
2. *Poisonous*, Deut. 32. 24, yet Paul by Divine aid shook off a viper, Acts 28. 8.
3. *Watches opportunity* to sting; so Ahab could not sleep on account of Naboth's vineyard.
4. *Feeds* on dust; Satan's food, sin.
5. *Fair* in appearance, 2 Cor. 11. 14.

Self-respect.

Arabic.—He who makes himself bran is pecked by hens.
Syriac.—Cut your vine with your own hand, not with the hand of others.

Who are Servants of Christ?—2 TIM. 2. 24.

The Jews had a class of house servants, as the Hindus had, who were slaves sold for debt or by their parents; but among the Jews they were set free on the seventh year, unless they had with their own consent their ears bored with an awl, and fastened to the doorposts.

The devil's children are like them—bond *slaves* of sin. Believers were slaves to the world, the flesh, and the devil, but are redeemed by Christ, who freed them from hereditary bondage. Christians, though servants, as the sons of a king by regeneration, have a high dignity in the court of heaven; such a servant was Joshua to Moses, Elisha to Elijah. Moses was the servant of the Lord, Jos. 1. 2.

Christians are like good servants of Christ being *appointed,* Is. 40. 10; *obedient,* Luke 22. 27; *trusted,* Gen. 41. 42; *delight* in work; act according to *orders,* Ex. 25. 40; expect *wages;* render an *account,* Mat. 18. 23.

Angels, though far higher in rank, power, and intellect than any kings of earth, yet act as servants. They took charge of a beggar's soul, when only the dogs attended to his body; these angels are called servants, Heb. 1. 14; they proclaimed their Master's will to Lot, Gen. 18; to Elijah, 2 Kings 1. 3; to Daniel, 9. 21; opposed God's enemies, so Michael fought with the dragon, Rev. 12. 9; executed God's judgments in Egypt, Ex. 12. 23; blinded the Sodomites, Gen. 19. 11; and smote a king, Acts 12. 23; defending the godly, they hold the four winds, Rev. 7. 1–3; they protected Elisha, 2 Kings 6. 17; were guides, and carried Lazarus into Abraham's bosom; will be the reapers in the day of judgment, Mat. 24. 31.

The Shield of Faith.—Eph. 6. 16.

As the soul is the life of the body, faith is the life of the soul, and Christ the life of faith. Faith is the master-wheel that sets the other wheels in motion. Faith is also compared to gold tried in the fire, 1 Pet. 1. 7.

A shield was made of hides, or even gold, so as to be proof against fiery darts; it was large, so as to defend the vital parts, and movable, to protect the head, arms, and chest.

A shield made of iron warded off darts and sword cuts, so faith, spiritual assaults, 2 Kings 6. 15. Abraham's servant committed himself in trust, Gen. 24; so Moses, Ex. 33. 15; Ruth 1. 16; Paul in prison, Acts 16. 25.

Telugu.—Like a gadfly on a tiger's side.

Affliction refines as the Fire does Silver.—MAL. 3. 2.

Affliction like refining silver in eleven points:—

This simile is taken from the refiners, who in their crucible separate by fire the dross from the ore; so believers have the fiery trial of trouble, 1 Cor. 3. 13.

1. *A refiner's work is to try and refine metals;* so affliction tries people's graces, Is. 48. 10.

2. The metal *before refinement* is full of dross, Mat. 15. 19, Job 25. 4, so we are by nature sinners.

3. *The metal is not pliable before refinement,* so our will is stubborn; Job said, God makes my heart soft, Job 23. 16, Jer. 9. 7.

4. *More fire required to hasten the work;* so in heaviness through manifold temptation, 1 Pet. 4. 12.

5. The dross removed makes the metal, though less in quantity, yet of more value, Is. 13. 12.

6. Refining required *several times;* so silver seven times refined. God has many modes of refining—fires, floods, storm, disease, Ps. 37. 20.

7. The fire is not for *wasting* the metal, but for purifying it, chastened for our profit, Heb. 12. 2.

8. Fine vessels made by this process, 2 Tim. 2. 20.

9. The refiner refines but *a little at a time;* God, however, refines a kingdom. Alloy is put in to make metal pliable; but the Holy Spirit is the hammer of God's word.

10. The metal is not left in the fire after purifying.

11. The refiner uses *fuel;* so the wicked are God's

fuel to refine the good; such were Pharaoh, Babylon made a burnt mountain, Jer. 51. 25, the great captains, Rev. 6. 17.

Tamul.—Though gold be put into the fire to be refined, its hue is not lost.

Canarese.—Sandal wood in burning gives off perfumes; so the afflictions of the good, Heb. 12. 11.

Tamul.—Rape-seed and sugar-cane are profitable when crushed.

Raghuvansa.—Iron by rust becomes soft; why not the soul by grief? 2 Cor. 7. 10.

Polish.—He who does not understand how to pray, learns it when he goes to sea.

Chinese.—Though the screen be torn, its form is still preserved. Though the good man be in want, his virtue still remains.

Afghan.—Though the cloud be black, white water falls from it—*sic*, " a silver lining to the cloud."

What are the Dead sown for?—1 Cor. 15. 42.

The Resurrection is called a morning, Ps. 49. 14, after the night of life, it makes things manifest, its sun comes out and joy arises. Wonderful is the progress of the seed from its first to its second life; for it has two lives. During its first life, it grows, and ripens in the plant which bears it, and then falls away to the earth out of which it grew. But it has a second life after its resurrection from the earth; from whence it springs up with a life of its own, and with a new body. From every seed grows a plant of the same kind with that which bore the seed. *God giveth to every seed its own body.*

The Word of God teaches us to expect two lives. The one is our present earthly life which we have of our parents; the other is the life which we shall have after we have been buried. Our body will be a spiritual one, not an animal one, as now, having carnal appetites and desires. For as the seed *is not quickened except it die*, so we cannot obtain eternal life, but by the way of death. The grave is as the *furrow* of the field in which the seed is sown; and as the sunshine of the spring raises the seed to life, so shall the Sun of Righteousness return to raise all those who are buried in the earth. The time is coming when they that are in their graves shall hear his voice, and come forth, as Lazarus came forth from the tomb when Jesus called him. The good seed of wheat and other grain is gathered for use, and laid up in the barn, as the righteous, when they die, are gathered to their fathers; but the evil seeds of the thistle are blown about by the winds, and scattered over the face of the earth.

Our bodies every seven years change every particle; so the seed in the darkness of the ground decomposes, drawing its new body from earth, water, and air, until it becomes like the banyan or cotton tree; so the body in the grave may be like a worm, but it will become like a butterfly. Seeds in Egyptian mummies have germinated after a thousand years. We cast our rice seed into muddy waters, it sinks, but soon a plentiful rice harvest appears.

Katha Upanishad.—Like corn a mortal ripens, like corn he is produced again.

Who is the Morning Star?—Rev. 22. 16.

Angels are called morning stars, as being made in the morning of creation, Job 38. 7. The dawn said in the *Vedas* "to be born in the eastern quarter of the firmament, displaying a banner of light bringing health to human habitations, many tinted;" angels as the morning star beautiful, so Stephen's face when dying like an angel's, Acts 6. 15; Satan was called Lucifer—*i.e.*, an angel of light.

The morning star, called the day star, arising in the hearts, 2 Pet. 1. 9; the King of Assyria is so called, Is. 14. 12, as Babylon was the first of kingdoms.

Christ like the Morning Star in nine points :—

1. *Solid light*, twinkles not, fixed in its orb, so no intermission in Christ, his spiritual light the same yesterday, to-day, and for ever, Heb. 13. 8; so Christ will never leave, Heb. 13. 5; Mat. 28. 20.

2. *Harbinger of the sun*, so when the day-spring came, people that sat in darkness saw the light, Mat. 4. 16; forerunner of the morning of the resurrection, Ps. 49. 14; the night of life is far spent, the day of resurrection is at hand, Rom. 13. 11, 12.

3. *Ornaments the heavens*, beautiful to see, so is Christ above Moses, Ps. 47. 1; David in his day said I shall be satisfied when I awake after his likeness, Ps. 17. 15; Paul said I have a desire to depart, Ph. 1. 23.

4. *Guides mariners*, when they have lost the polar star, so Christ, the light of life, warns against the rocks and shoals of the world, the flesh, and the devil, in the ocean of life.

5. *Most useful in wintry darkness*; so are Christ's offices, now of prophet, priest and king in this dark world.

6. *A star of the first magnitude*; John, Peter, James were stars, but Christ, though the offspring of David, was the brightness of the Father's glory, Heb. 1. 3.

7. *Terrible to thieves*, indicating the departure of darkness, so Satan, at the dawn of redemption, attempted Christ's destruction in the temple, Mat. 4. 5; Jews said, let us kill the heir, Mat. 21. 38; the Jews led Christ to the brow of the hill, Luke 4. 29; so the devils thought he was come to torment them before the time, Mat. 8. 29.

8. *The same as the evening star*, so Christ is the Alpha and Omega, the author and finisher of our salvation, Rev. 1. 8; Heb. 12. 2.

9. *Clouds hinder not its course*; so Christ will come and will not tarry, Heb. 10. 37; *Galileo* said, men may imprison me for believing the earth moves, but it moves.

It is hard to kick against the pricks, Acts 9. 5; the blood of the martyrs was the seed of the Church.

The morning star is created; Christ made the heavens, Ps. 102. 25; is of a fiery red colour. Christ is meek, a mild light; the morning star and sun are different; Christ is both. The morning star gives light only by *night*, Christ is an everlasting light, Is. 60. 20; the morning star enlightens only this world; Christ both worlds. The morning star shall be dissolved; Christ never, Heb. 13. 8.

The Storm of God's Wrath.—Is. 25. 4.

The wrath of God wreaks itself by various agencies, Deut. 28. 22; heaven is represented as our Father's house, a marriage feast, the household of God, while earth is stormy, but Christ is a hiding-place from the wind. Earthquakes have destroyed cities, as Lisbon; so the blast of the Prince of the Power of the Air blew down Eden, hence David wished for the wings of a dove, when assailed by storm of calumny, Ps. 55. 6; so many make shipwreck of faith.

God's wrath compared to a winepress, Rev. 14. 19; to wiping out as a dish as God did Jerusalem, 2 Kings 21. 13.

God's storm is of *God's sending*, as in Jonah's case, Jonah 1. 4; *hail showers* destroyed the Amorites, *wind* buried the Egyptians like lead in the sea, Ex. 15. 10; *brimstone* was rained on Sodom, Gen. 19. 24; so Tophet was ordained of old, Is. 30. 33.

The *sinner first raised it*, Is. 17. 15.

Storms are *of fearful violence*, Ps. 107. 27; in a storm ships mount up to heaven and stagger like a drunken man, so the great day of wrath is come, and who will be able to stand? Rev. 6. 17,

Aerial storms are fierce, but short.

Who are Strangers on Earth?

HEB. 11. 9.

The righteous like strangers on earth in five points:—

A traveller sat by a well in a wilderness; he had been expelled from his country because he took the part of slaves against their royal oppressors. He quenched his thirst, and showed his politeness to several maidens, and procuring drink for their flocks; invited to their house, he spent forty years there in seclusion as a shepherd. A son was born to him, named Gershom or the stranger; the father's name was Moses.

David, though a king, acknowledged he was a stranger on earth, 1 Chron. 29. 15; saints are citizens of the New Jerusalem, Heb. 12. 22, being born from above, they have a new fatherland; they therefore rejoice as though they rejoiced not, 1 Cor. 7. 30; they abstain from fleshly lusts, 1 Pet. 2. 11; take joyfully the spoiling of their goods, 2 Cor. 4. 8, 9; fall not out with their companions on the way, Gen. 45. 24. Abraham left his country because it was idolatrous, Josh. 21. 2, 3. The patriarchs lived in tents to show they were strangers.

The righteous are strangers on earth as to—(1) *place*, heaven is their home, as they are born anew; the earth to them is like a wilderness with its brackish water, burning sands, fierce storms, such as are in Central Asia; (2) the *people*, worldly people have the devil as their father, believers in God bear the image of the heavenly; (3) *employment*, while one does the works of the flesh, the other does those of the Spirit; minding the one thing needful; their God is not their belly; (4) *manners*, believers are clothed with humility, roll not sin as a sweet morsel under their tongue; they have put off the old man; (5) *language*, believers talk of subjects which are sealed to the world, &c., they have little intercourse with worldly people.

Believers as pilgrims or travellers, finding no rest for

their soul on earth, carefully consider the cost, the difficulty, the danger, of their journey to Heaven; wisely they put on the light, the new, the defensive, and never worn out garments of salvation, and take to them the whole armour of God, for their safety against foes. Wisely they receive Jesus and his fulness as their gold, their treasure, to bear their *expenses* on the way. They receive his father for their *companion;* his Spirit to be their *guide*; his word to be their director and *compass;* his love, his power, and promises for their supporting *staff.* Carefully they ask for the good well-beaten *old way* of holiness, and continue walking therein; sweetly they drink out of its *wells* of salvation, and *refresh* themselves, but do not tarry in the inns of ordinances built close at hand! Now their duty is pleasant and easy; anon it is rugged and difficult. Now, they enjoy the *fine weather* of peace and prosperity; *clear views* of Jesus and his countenance, wide prospects of his loveliness and love; clear *discoveries* of the vanity of this world, of the happiness of their present, and of the glory of their future state; anon they are distressed with cold winters of trouble, storms of temptation, dark nights of sin and disorder, that they know not what to do, or whither to go. How oft fearfully pinched for provision! How oft the wells of promises seem dry, and inns of ordinances are found empty! How oft exposed to the gazing, ridicule, and malice of carnal men! How oft by Satan and their lusts harassed and robbed of their grace, or its evidence! How oft tempted like Lot's wife to turn back! But, through every tribulation they push forward to the city, the celestial kingdom of God, and with so much more cheerfulness, if they enjoy the company of eminent saints; they go from strength to strength till they appear before God in Zion. They are called strangers and sojourners with God on earth. How strange to carnal men is their state of union and communion with Christ! How strange their birth from above! Their having God their father! Christ their husband! Glorified saints their principal people! In what strange, what celestial country, are their portion, their inheritance, their hopes, their affections, their thoughts, their desires! With what strange robe of divine righteousness, implanted grace, and Gospel holiness are they decked! What strange armour of God they have put on! How strangely they speak the spiritual language of prayer and praise! Pour out their hearts, behave as becomes the high calling of God! Walk with Father, Son, and Holy Ghost whom the world see and know not! Feed on the strange provision of Jesus' person, righteousness, and benefits! How employed in the unknown labour of numbering their days; of considering their latter end; of ploughing up the fallow ground of their heart; of sowing to themselves in righteousness; of buying without money and without price; of denying and loathing themselves; of warring with principalities, powers, and spiritual wickedness; of renouncing the profit, pleasure, and honour of this world; of extracting good from evil and sweet out of bitter; of loving their enemies, and rendering them blessing for cursing.

The Sun of Righteousness with Healing on his Wings.

MAL. 4. 2.

In the *Vedas* the sun is called "ray-diffuser, deep-quivering, life-bestowing, golden-handed, the eye of the universe, the soul of all that moves."

In Judea every morning about sunrise a fresh breeze blows from the sea across the land; from its utility in purifying the infected air, it is called the doctor; this salubrious breeze, which attends the rising of the sun, may be considered the *wings* of the sun. So Christ is the one mediator, the sun of our system; he is the eye of the world, gives light to all, drives away gloom; like the sun he operates differently, hardens clay, and softens wax, eclipses the light of the stars by his own. Flowers, as the tulip and marigold, open to the solar, so do believers' hearts to Christ's, beams.

Sick or delicate people generally feel worse during night, when the sun ceases to shine; the morning dawn often revives them after a bad night. All the candles in the world put together could not give a light equal to that of day; which can come only from the sun; so with human intelligence compared to Christ.

The sun shines on all, penetrates deeply, exhales the noxious vapours from the earth, cheers by its light: veiled sometimes by clouds, it soon disperses them, and the light of the stars grows pale before it.

The sun is the source of light and beauty; without it all is gloom and dulness. David calls it God's tabernacle; in Chaldea they worshipped the sun; we are to use it, however, to lead us unto God as our rock, as an emblem of God's unchangeableness, and of his being the foundation of inexhaustible, overflowing benevolence. As the sun is a type of God's effulgence and energy, so the term Sun of Righteousness is peculiarly applicable to Christ.

Christ is like the sun in four points:—

1. *The sun is the centre of the planets,* his attraction is an adamantine chain which, hanging on nothing, keeps the planets in their place, so Christ is the head of the Church, Eph. 5. 23. Look not to yourselves, but to Christ. Thirty planets, with orbits millions of miles in diameter, some performing their revolution in a century, move round this sun; so Christ is the head of all principalities and of angels, Eph. 1. 21.

2. *The sun shines by its own light, not so the planets;* the light, though 95 millions of miles distant, comes in eight minutes. David compares the sun's rising to a bridegroom, Ps. 19. 5; so is Christ the brightness of the Father's glory, his eyes penetrate like the sun's rays, his light is

the same yesterday, to-day, and for ever; but the sun has spots, in the Spiritual Sun there is no darkness, 1 John 1. 5. The sun, however, shall wax old as a garment, not so Christ, Heb. 1. 12. The sun was stopped by Joshua, not so the Sun of Righteousness; various rays from the sun concentrate in the rainbow, so God's attributes blended in Christ's—righteousness and peace have kissed each other, Ps. 135. 10. Christ seen of angels, received into glory the gaze of Intelligences in other regions of creation.

3. *The sun is the source of light, heat, beauty:* in Christ is the true light, John 1. 7; the day-spring from on high. Light reveals things as a ray does particles of dust, so the publican found, Luke 18. 13. The sun's light awakens life in the spring, so in Ezekiel's valley of dry bones the breath of life, Ez. 37.

4. *The sun's rising is gradual but punctual,* so Christ illuminated first the Jews, then the heathen.

Atmaboda Prakasika.—Knowledge overcomes ignorance as sunlight darkness.

Rig Veda.—The dawn, the breath and life of all that breathes and lives, awaking day by day myriads of prostrate sleepers as from death, causing the birds to flutter from their nests, and rousing men to ply with busy feet their daily duties.

Kathá Upanishad.—As the sun, the eye of the whole world, is not sullied by the defects of external objects, so the inner soul of all beings is not sullied by the misery of the world.

The Sword of the Spirit.—Eph. 6. 17; Heb. 4. 12.

There are two words of God, one written on paper—the Bible, the other written by the Spirit on the heart. Christ is also called the word of God as being the Eternal Son.

God's revelation is compared to—a *letter* from the father

of mercies to his children at school—a *banquet* where all are invited—a *prism* which only glistens when in the light—a *portrait* of an absent friend—a *storehouse* of spiritual weapons—a *telescope* revealing the glories of the upper world. David compares it to silver tried in a furnace of earth seven times refined, Ps. 12. 6.

Heavenly Treasures in Earthen Vessels.—2 Cor. 4. 7.

The body is compared to an earthen vessel, as being brittle, leaky, mean, of little value, yet it has the souls treasure in it; as the *Bengalis* say—" like fine rice in a torn bag."

Treasure in earthen vessels may refer to the lamps which were concealed in Gideon's pitchers till they were broken, when he alarmed the army of the Midianites while asleep in their camp, Judg. 7. 16. So the Gospel is put into earthen vessels, and proves a glorious light to some, while it is hidden to others. Christ says lay not up treasures on earth, Mat. 6. 19, or in an earthen house easily dug through by robbers.

The Gospel is a treasure, for the reception of it into our hearts makes us " rich in faith;" presents to us " the unsearchable riches of Christ;" and teaches us to lay up for ourselves " durable riches and righteousness." The dying believer, though ever so rich in this world, loses everything at last which he has in it; but, if he has Christ for his portion, he is richer than all the world he leaves behind him; for everything belonging to the world must perish—moth and rust consume them—but nothing can deprive us of this treasure, " for who shall separate us from the love of Christ?"

Bengal.—Even in sweet mangoes worms breed.
Bengal.—Families and water descend—*i.e.*, decay.
Tamul.—A crooked pot will hold sugar.
Kurd.—The camel carries sugar, eats thorns.

Sanskrit.—A diamond is trodden under foot, and glass is worn on the head; even in that stage glass is glass and a gem a gem.

Mahabharat.—Neither mother, nor children, nor kinsmen, nor dear familiar friends follow a man in death; he departs alone. The deeds alone which he has done are his fellow-travellers.

Man revives not as a Tree.—Job 14. 7, 12.

The *Romans* made trees a symbol of death, planted those in burial-places, from whose roots no germs arise, such as the pine, cyprus. Man does not revive to return from death to the scenes of his earthly occupations; not so a tree. Night comes, but so does the *morning*, with fresh fragrance glittering with dew. *Winter* ravages, but the embryo blossom survives and spring comes. When the *trunk* of the tree is cut down, it dies not altogether, life remains within; but man cut down does not spring up again.

China.—Withered trees in spring burst forth afresh; but man cannot be twice young.

Japan.—Flowers on a dead tree.

Japan.—The flower returns not to the branch.

Who walks with God?—Gen. 5. 22.

Spiritual like material walking in five points:—

Communion with God is represented by going up through the wilderness, leaning on the Beloved, Cant. 8. 5, with hope and earnest desire to obtain the better country.

Walking refers to religious conduct. Thus *Enoch* walked with God, and he was not, Gen. 5. 24; *Noah* walked before God, Gen. 6. 9; *Josiah* after the Lord, 2 Kings 23. 3; *believers* walk in the spirit, Gal. 5. 25; the *Churches*, after Paul's conversion, walked in the comforts of the Holy Ghost, Acts 9. 31; *Nebuchadnezzar* condemned those that walked in pride, Dan. 4. 37.

Walking implies—(1) *Life*, the believer has a resurrection from the death of sin, Gal. 5. 24; (2) *Light*, to see the road; (3) *Motion*, not mere knowing, but doing, 1 Kings 11. 38; (4) *Progress*, steady, like an elephant, not by jerks as a goat goes; Paul forgot the things behind in pressing on, Phil. 3. 13; (5) *Perseverance*, so Hezekiah on his death-bed, 2 Kings, 20. 3; (6) a *Road*, the old path trodden by Abel, and marked out by sacrifices; (7) an *Object*, through the wilderness to the heavenly Canaan; circumspectly, "like a cat on a wall covered with bottles."

Walking in noble company is a great privilege for an inferior; Christians were slaves to Satan; converted, they walk with God as their Father. Thus did Enoch walk with God, and he was not, for God took him, Gen. 5. 22.

The Holy Spirit like Water.—Rev. 22. 1.

The Gospel is the ministration of the Spirit; hence the Spirit with his gifts is often compared to water, as Christ said to the woman of Samaria, John 4. 14.

The Holy Spirit like water in nine points:—

1. *Water comes from the ocean and clouds* and returns to them; so the Holy Spirit the Comforter comes from the Father the Ocean of Being, John 15. 26.

2. *Cleanses* the soul from sin, 1 Cor. 6. 11, John 15. 3; so Christ's blood through the Eternal Spirit, Heb. 13. 14, 1 Pet. 1. 22.

3. *Cools;* so evil desires cooled by the Holy Spirit, 1 John 1. 7; Saul's lust of blood was cooled, Acts 9. 20; but Dives begged for water to cool his tongue, Luke 16. 24.

4. *Fructifies;* man naturally is as the wild heath in the desert from drought, not like grass kept green. Zaccheus

the publican on his conversion, cried out, "The half of my goods I give to the poor," Luke 19. 8; so those who laid their money at the Apostles' feet, Acts 4. 37.

5. *Softens*, Ps. 65. 10. Water softens and prepares the earth for the plough. Saul so fierce, cried out, "What wilt thou have me to do," Acts 9. 6. Three thousand were pricked to the heart, Acts 2. 37.

6. *Quenches* thirst. The desires of the soul are only satisfied by the Holy Spirit.

7. *Accessible to all*, cheap, Is. 55. 1. Ho! every one athirst come to the river of water of life, Rev. 22. 7.

8. *Extinguishes* fire; so the fire of passion and of pride is extinguished. Too much earthy water may surfeit; it may become muddy. The Romans symbolized diseases by muddy waters. One of their punishments was to throw a criminal into a lake of muddy water. Many go long distances to get good water, but the Spiritual Water is in the reach of all. The water of purification among the Jews was mingled with the ashes of the red heifer being sprinkled by a branch of hyssop on the unclean party and he was purified, Ex. 12. 22. God will sprinkle clean water on the wicked.

9. *Penetrates easily*; so the Spirit is poured out; floods on the dry ground, Joel 2. 28, Is. 44. 3.

The Way to Heaven.—John 14. 6.

The way to heaven differs from earthly ways in nine points:—

The Hindus call *panth* or way the line of doctrine of any sect followed, in order to attain to *mukti* or deliverance from sin. Way signifies the chief means to an end, and is applied to the Scriptures, Ps. 119. 27, to God's counsels, to God's works. This spiritual way is—(1) *easy* to find, Is. 35. 8; (2) *clean*, no mud of sin; (3) never out of *repair*. Christ the same now as 6,000 years ago;

(4) no *lion* or wild beasts on; (5) *costly*, the blood of Christ made it; (6) not *lonely*, many believers on it, Heb. 12. 1; (7) no *toll*, all may come; (8) *wide*, Christ sends out to the highways and hedges, Mat. 22. 9. The way to the cities of refuge was forty-eight feet wide. The map of the Bible shows this path; (9) the *end* pleasant—Heaven.

The veil that was hung before the Holy of Holies, and which none might pass through, but the high priest once a year, signified to us that there was no direct way to Heaven under the law. "By the law is the knowledge of sin," not the means of deliverance from the power or punishment of sin. And by the rending of the veil at the time of our Saviour's death, was signified that a way was henceforth opened to the penitent unto life eternal, even by the blood of Jesus Christ. In the passage—"I am the way, the truth, and the life," our Lord meant, "I am the way to Heaven." He had just before told his disciples, that he was soon going to leave them, and to prepare a place for them, meaning that he was going to Heaven, and there they should follow, and be happy with him for ever. But his disciples did not quite understand him, and when he said, "Whither I go ye know, and the way ye know," Thomas replied, "Lord, we know not whither thou goest; and how can we know the way?" Christ meant, that he was going to Heaven, and that there was no getting there but through him, just as a way leads to a place, or, in other words, we must follow him, and he will show us the way; for like him we must have holy lives, like him we must pass through the grave, like him our bodies must rise again.

Japan.—A road of 1,000 miles begins with one step.

Urdu.—Who leaves the highway for a byepath will soon lose his way.

Persian.—Travel the highway though it be roundabout.

Christ a Well of Water.—JOHN 4. 14; ZECH. 13. 1.

These words were uttered by Christ when wearied and thirsty in the heat of the day; he drank well-water received from a Samaritan woman—a pariah. Wells were greatly valued in deserts, hence the march of caravans was regulated by the wells, Ex. 15. 27; Lot's and Abraham's herdsmen strove about the possession of a well, Gen. 26. 15. But wells often dry up, or are filled up with sand. Christ the same always: the wicked are compared to wells without water, 2 Pet. 2. 17. *See* Fountain, p. 38.

The Holy Spirit's Influence like the Wind.—JOHN 3. 5–8.

The Holy Spirit's influence like wind in six points:—

We see not the wind itself, but we see what it does, whether when the forest is bowed by some mighty *tempest*, as in a cyclone, or when the corn waves under the gentle *breeze*, soft as the dew, and the flowers of the garden give out their fragrance, as they tremble at its softest touch.

It is thus with God's Holy Spirit. It is mysterious in its coming and in its influence. Unseen itself, it is seen in its effects. The mighty change which the world has undergone, since first the doctrine of the Cross was preached by peasants of Judea, with no human aid to support them, is the work of the unseen but ever-present Spirit, by which the false philosophies and vain superstitions have fallen before the truth, as Dagon before the ark, 1 Sam. 5. 3.

The Holy Spirit like the wind in six points:—

The wind is—(1) *invisible,* though its effects are seen in cyclones, when it travels at 120 miles an hour, so the Spirit's influence in conversion; (2) comes at *God's command;* he gathers the winds in his fist, Prov. 30. 4; (3) *purifies,* drives bad vapours away; so grace does evil passions; (4) *penetrates*, passes through a large city and over hundreds of miles; (5) *various*, the north wind piercing, the south wind warming; so the Holy Spirit rebukes some, comforts others, tempests destroy big ships and large trees; (6) sets in *motion*; we cannot sail across the ocean of life without the wind of the Spirit. Providence has his way in the sea, and he flies on the wings of the wind, Ps. 18. 10.

Atmabodha Prákasika.—The Spirit is in contact with matter without being contaminated by it, just as the crystal permits the colour of the cloth to be seen through it without being in any way defiled by it.

Christ's Yoke easy and his Burthen light.—MAT. 11. 28-30.

Asses or oxen are yoked or harnessed to a cart; sometimes this yoke is heavy, and the burthen of the cart falls on the neck, which becomes chafed; the animal is, however, the property of the owner, who does what he likes. Men are under the yoke of Satan; they are slaves, and Christ comes with the ransom money. Bullocks often, though well-fed, do not like to submit to the yoke, and kick against it, Jer. 31. 18, but must at last submit; so the sinner must bridle his tongue and passions—he must not be stiff-necked.

Reconcile the *easy* yoke with the *narrow* way?

QUESTIONS ON THE EMBLEMS.

BETWEEN the *afflictions* of the righteous and the wicked four points of difference.

Affliction is compared to eleven different objects.

HOPE like an *anchor* in three points.

GOD'S ARM differs from man's *arm* in three points.

What eight *animals* are the wicked compared to?

What three *birds* teach men lessons?

To what two *birds* are the righteous compared?

The *body* is like what the Arabs are fond of, and in three points.

The CHURCH like the *body* in four points.

GOD as a builder differs from earthly *builders* in five points.

The WICKED like *captives* in four points.

The HUMBLE like *little children* in six points.

Christ's second *coming* compared to five different things.

MORTIFYING THE FLESH like *Crucifixion* in three points.

Christ and his work compared to fifteen objects.

COURAGE of the righteous compared to what *animal?*

DEATH of the righteous like a shock of *corn* in eight points.

The HEAVENLY CITY differs from an earthly *city* in five points.

The WICKED like *dross* in six points.

CONSCIENCE compared to five different objects.

DEATH of the righteous and wicked compared to twelve different things.

The DEVIL compared to what five *animals?*

The HOLY SPIRIT like *dew* in seven points.

The meek like a *dove* in four points.

WICKED like *dogs* in ten points.

Double-minded like what three objects.

PRAYING is like mounting on *eagle's wings* in nine points.

ENVY is compared to what is often seen in a *hospital.*

FAITH compared to what four objects?

The FICKLE compared to what the sluggard does not see

GOD like a *father* in ten points.

GOD like a *fountain* in eight points.
CHRIST'S FRIENDSHIP differs from earthly *friendship* in five points.
The CHURCH like a *garden* in seven points.
TRUTH a *girdle* in seven points.
The WICKED like *goats* in four points.
FAITH like *gold* in ten points.
HEARERS, not doers, compared to what vain people like.
HEAVEN compared to seven things.
The HEAVENLY *home* differs from the earthly one in three points.
The RIGHTEOUS like God's *husbandry* in ten points.
HUMILITY like four objects.
HOLINESS compared to seven things.
The HOLY SPIRIT compared to nine objects.
HOUSE, to what part of a, is Christ compared?
HOPES of the world like what is found in a dirty house.
HOPES of the wicked compared to four objects.
The IGNORANT compared to fifteen objects.
EARTHLY INHERITANCE differs from the heavenly *inheritance* in six points.
PRAYER like *incense* in five points.
What INSECT teaches man a lesson?
The IDLE compared to four things.
GOD'S PEOPLE his *jewels* in nine points.
GOD differs from earthly *judges* in four points.
The SPIRITUAL KINGDOM differs from an earthly *kingdom* in nine points.
The RIGHTEOUS like *kings* in six points.
CHRIST'S second coming like *lightning* in three points.
CHRIST'S LEGACY differs from a common *legacy* in four points.
CHRIST like a *lamb* in four points.
Sin like *leprosy* in thirteen points.
LIFE is compared to a thing you do not see at night.
Life is compared to a thing you do not see in summer.
Life is compared to what thieves are fond of.
MERCHANT, the righteous, a spiritual, in seven points.
GOD'S WORD like *milk* in three points.
This WORLD like *night* in four points.
OLD AGE compared to seven things.
HOLY SPIRIT'S influence like *oil* in four points.
PARDON OF SIN compared to three things.
PRAYER compared to five objects.
PROVIDENCE compared to three things.
The RIGHTEOUS like the *palm tree* in five points.
The RIGHTEOUS like a *pilgrim* in nine points.
HELL like a *prison* in six points.

CHRIST differed from other *physicians* in nine points.
PUNCTUALITY taught by what bird?
SIN like a *poisonous serpent* in five points.
God's PUNISHMENT compared to eight objects.
The SPIRITUAL differs from the worldly *race* in six points.
GOD'S INFLUENCE like *rain* in seven points.
The RESURRECTION like what four objects.
REST spiritual differs from worldly *rest* in four points.
RICHES compared to a certain bird.
The river of GOD'S GRACE differs from an *earthly river* in nine points.
CHRIST like a *rock* in ten points.
EVIL PASSIONS like the *sea* in eight points.
GOD'S WORD like *seed* in twelve points.
The RIGHTEOUS like *soldiers* in twelve points.
The RIGHTEOUS *strangers* on earth in five points.
AFFLICTION like *refined silver* in ten points.
The RIGHTEOUS are *servants* in six points.
The RIGHTEOUS like *sheep* in ten points.
The SINNER'S HEART a *stone* in four points.
STORM of God's wrath differs from *earthly storms* in four points.
The RIGHTEOUS shall be like *stars* in five points.
CHRIST like the *sun* in four points.
DEATH of the righteous like *sleep* in four points.
PROVIDENCE like a *good shepherd* in five points.
The RIGHTEOUS like something very valuable got from the sea.
The HOLY SPIRIT like a *seal* in three points.
TIME like to what five objects?
The TONGUE like to what five objects?
WICKED like *thorns* in six points.
RIGHTEOUS like what four trees?
The RIGHTEOUS are *watchmen* in seven points.
The WAY to heaven differs from *earthly ways* in nine respects.
SPIRITUAL like material *walking* in five points.
The HOLY SPIRIT like *water* in nine points.
The WORLD like a *wilderness* in eight points.
The HOLY SPIRIT like *wind* in six points.
WORDS and DEEDS compared to five objects.
CONSCIENCE like a *worm* in three points.
MAN like a *worm* in five points.
WICKED like what is often seen in hot countries.
WORLD'S PLEASURES brief, like what grows of itself.
WORLD compared to a thing found chiefly with the poor.

SCRIPTURE SIMILES ILLUSTRATIVE OF TEXTS.

Adoption, Believers have received the spirit of .	*Rom.* 8. 15.
Arm of flesh, he trusting in, cursed . . .	*Jer.* 16. 5.
Bride of Christ, the Church the	*Rev.* 21. 9.
Blood, woe unto him that builds a town with . .	*Hab.* 2. 12.
Bees, Jews chased by Canaanites as . . .	*Deut.* 1. 44.
Billows of sorrow went over David . . .	*Ps.* 42. 7.
Bucket, nations as a drop of a	*Is.* 40. 15.
Bullocks unaccustomed to the yoke are the obstinate	*Jer.* 31. 18.
Bulls, the wicked compass the righteous as . .	*Ps.* 22. 12.
Bulwarks, salvation of God as	*Is.* 26. 1.
Brier, a bribe-taking judge as a	*Mic.* 7. 4.
Burden cast on the Lord	*Ps.* 55. 22.
Cake, Ephraim is a cake not turned . . .	*Hos.* 7. 8.
Cage full of unclean birds, Babylon is, *Rev.* 18. 2, and sinners are	*Jer.* 5. 27.
Cart rope, sin drawn in as with a	*Is.* 5. 18.
Candlestick of the unfaithful removed . . .	*Rev.* 2, 5.
Cedar, righteous flourish as a	*Ps.* 92. 21.
Crooked nation the Jews, *Deut.* 32. 5; so sinners .	*Ph.* 2. 15.
Crows fed by God, though they sow not . . .	*Luke* 12. 24.
Dead, the wicked twice	*Jude* 12. 13.
Dish, Jerusalem wiped out as a	2 *Kings* 21. 13.
Dream, the wicked fly away as a	*Job* 20. 8.
Drop of a bucket, the nations before God as . .	*Is.* 40. 15.
Drowned in perdition by foolish lusts . . .	1 *Tim.* 6. 9.
Dust, small, of the balance, the nations like . .	*Is.* 40. 15.
Drinking in iniquity like water	*Job* 15. 16.
Dwelling of Christ in the heart by faith . . .	*Eph.* 3. 17.
Enemy, death the last, to be conquered . . .	1 *Cor.* 15. 26.
Fight the good fight of faith	1 *Tim.* 6. 12.

Filthy lucre . . . *Tit.* 1. 7.
Finger of God seen in Moses' miracles . . . *Ex.* 8. 19.
Gaining the world losing the soul . . . *Luke* 9. 25.
Groans of creation for sin . . . *Rom.* 8. 22.
Halting between two opinions . . . 1 *Kings* 18. 21.
Handbreadth, our days as an, before God . . . *Ps.* 39. 5.
Harvest, the, of repentance passed . . . *Jer.* 8. 20.
Heath in the desert, is like trusting only in man . . . *Jer.* 17. 6.
Hedge of thorns, way of slothful as a . . . *Prov.* 15. 19.
Heel lifted up by Judas against Christ . . . *Ps.* 49. 9.
Helmet, the Christian's, the hope of salvation . . . 1 *Thess.* 5. 8.
Hiding-place from the wind, Christ a . . . *Is.* 32. 2.
Hireling, man looks for the reward of his work as an *Job* 7. 2.
Hissing, Babylon shall be as an . . . *Jer.* 51. 37.
Honeycomb, a bad woman's lips like, but her end wormwood . . . *Prov.* 5. 3.
Horn of the righteous shall be exalted . . . *Ps.* 112. 9.
Hosts of angels praise God . . . *Ps.* 148. 2.
Idolatry, covetousness is . . . *Col.* 3. 5.
Itching ears to those heaping up teachers . . . 2 *Tim.* 4. 3.
Lead, Egyptians sunk like, in the Red Sea . . . *Ex.* 15. 10.
Loan to God, the merciful man makes . . . *Prov.* 19. 17.
Madness in the heart of the wicked . . . *Eccl.* 9. 3.
Mother of all is Jerusalem above . . . *Gal.* 4. 26.
Noonday, innocence of righteous manifested as . . . *Ps.* 37. 5.
Nose of Sennacherib, God put his hook in . . . 2 *Kings* 19. 28.
Nursing fathers, kings will be to the Church . . . *Is.* 49. 23.
Ocean depths, the Believer's sins cast into . . . *Mic.* 7. 19.
Oven, day of judgment shall burn as . . . *Mal.* 4. 1.
Path of the just, a shining light . . . *Prov.* 4. 18.
Pavilion, the believer hid in God's . . . *Ps.* 27. 4, 5.
Pierce themselves with many sorrows, the rich do . . . 1 *Tim.* 6. 9.
Plummet, God's judgments laid to the . . . *Is.* 28. 17.
Pillar in God's temple, the believer is a . . . *Rev.* 3. 12.
Rags, our righteousness as filthy . . . *Is.* 64. 6.
Rain of God's fury on the wicked . . . *Job* 20. 23.
Rivers, broad, God as a place of . . . *Is.* 33. 21.
Schoolmaster the law to bring us to Christ . . . *Gal.* 3. 24.
Scroll, heavens will depart as a . . . *Rev.* 6. 14.
Shadow of evening desired by the servant, so death wished for by Christian . . . *Job* 7. 2.
Shining of face by wisdom . . . *Eccl.* 8. 1.
Song, a lovely one, those hearing not doing are like . . . *Ez.* 33. 32.
Strait between life and death . . . *Ph.* 1. 23.
Staying on God, the mind is in perfect peace . . . *Is.* 26. 3.

Sprinkling of the conscience with pure water . . *Heb.* 10. 22.
Store for fire, earth kept as a . . . . . . *2 Pet.* 3. 7.
Stubble before the wind, the wicked as . . . *Is.* 40. 24.
Tooth broken, confidence in the unfaithful as . . *Prov.* 25. 19.
Tower of refuge is God to the righteous . . . *Prov.* 13. 10.
Tree of life, a wholesome tongue as a . . . *Prov.* 15. 4.
Trump of God at last day . . . . . . *1 Thess.* 4. 16.
Vail on the Jew's heart when Moses read . . *2 Cor.* 3. 15.
Vessels of wrath fitted to destruction are the wicked. *Rom.* 9. 22.
Vesture, earth changed as a . . . . . . *Heb.* 1. 11.
Washing their robes in the Lamb's blood . . *Rev.* 7. 14.
Water, as cold, to a thirsty soul, so good news . *Prov.* 25. 25.
Wave shifting, the doubting like . . . . *Jas.* 1. 6.
Wax melteth, so the wicked perish . . . . *Ps.* 68. 2.
Weaned child, David's soul as a . . . . *Ps.* 131. 2.
Winepress of God's wrath, trodden by the wicked . *Rev.* 19. 15.
Witness, conscience a . . . . *Rom.* 2. 15.
Wolves, the wicked inwardly as ravening . . . *Mat.* 7. 15.
Wrestling against the flesh, the devil, and the world *Eph.* 6. 12.

ILLUSTRATIONS IN THE BIBLE OF ORIENTAL CUSTOMS.

Abraham entertains angels under a tree, chapatis or flour cakes prepared	*Gen.* 18. 4.
A wife selected for Isaac by an (*ghatak*) intermediate agent	*Gen.* 24. 4.
A stone anointed by Jacob with *oil*	*Gen.* 28. 18.
Laban refused to marry his *younger* daughter to Jacob before the elder was married . . .	*Gen.* 29. 6.
Esau reconciled to Jacob falls on his knees . .	*Gen.* 33. 4.
Jacob orders his family to *change* their garments before worship	*Gen.* 35. 2.
Water to wash *the feet* of Joseph's brethren . .	*Gen.* 43. 24.
The Egyptians would not *eat* with the Jews . .	*Gen.* 43. 32.
Joseph gave his brethren *changes of raiment* after the feast	*Gen.* 45. 22.
Moses ordered to *put off his shoes* on holy ground .	*Ex.* 3. 5.
First born of man and beast sanctified to God. .	*Ex.* 13. 2.
The Jews *danced* before the golden calf . . .	*Ex.* 32. 19.
The *fire* on the altar perpetually burning . .	*Lev.* 6. 13.
Watering seed with the foot	*Deut.* 11. 10.
Deborah the prophetess lived under a palm tree .	*Judges* 4. 5.
The servant, Uriah, slept *at the door* of the King's house	2 *Sam.* 11. 9.
David, after grieving for his child, *anoints* his body, and changes his garments	2 *Sam.* 12. 20.
The *Idol* Baal said to be *sleeping*	1 *Kings* 18. 27.
Naboth refuses to sell his *father's inheritance* . .	1 *Kings* 21. 3.
Queen Jezebel eaten by dogs	1 *Kings* 21. 23.
A present from the king to Elisha	2 *Kings* 8. 8.
The Jewish women *tinkled* with their feet . .	*Isaiah* 3. 16.
God puts a hook in the nose of the Assyrian king .	*Isaiah* 37. 29.
Women sewing pillows to all arm-holes . . .	*Ezek.* 13. 18.

Pharisees sounded a trumpet on giving alms . .	*Mat.* 6. 2.
Two women grinding at a mill on Jerusalem being besieged by Romans	*Mat.* 24. 41.
A woman poured fragrant ointment on Christ. .	*Mat.* 14. 3.
The *guest chamber* for Christ's Last Supper . .	*Mark* 14. 14.
Christ in a *caravan* when young	*Luke* 2. 44.
Where the *carcass* is the vultures will be . .	*Luke* 17. 37.
Marvel at Christ's talking with a *woman* . .	*John* 4. 27.
Blind man's sins of a *former birth*	*John* 9. 2.
Lazarus' sisters go to his grave to *weep* . . .	*John* 11. 31.
Christ's coat *without seam*	*John* 19. 23.
Peter went to the *housetop* to pray . . .	*Acts* 10. 9.
For Peter and Paul *garlands* were brought . .	*Acts* 14. 13.
Paul brought up *at the feet* of his guru (teacher) .	*Acts* 22. 2.

See also Gen. 15. 4; 16. 3; 24. 11; 33. 60; 29. 18; 43. 34. Lev. 22. 13. Num. 6. 18; 22. 6. Deut. 23. 10; 25. 4. Josh. 15. 8. 1 Sam. 9. 7; 17. 43. 1 Kings 3. 4, 20, 38. 2 Kings 5. 12. Job 24. 16. Ps. 26. 6; 44. 20; 45. 7; 58. 4, 5; 78. 63; 80. 13; 81. 3; 104. 2; 133. 2. Prov. 11. 21; 21. 1. Eccl. 9. 8. Cantic. 5. 3. Is. 18. 2; 32. 20; 45. 3; 46. 7; 60. 4. Jer. 16. 6; 44. 17. Lam. 1. 1. Ez. 9. 4; 23. 40; 44. 25. Amos 5. 19; 6. 11; Mat. 1. 18; 2. 18; 5. 8; 6. 5; 6. 7; 7. 26; 10. 12; 14. 11, 21; 18. 25; 22. 24; 28. 9. Mark 7. 2; 10. 5; 14. 14; 20. 52. Luke 2. 7; 3. 4; 5. 14; 8. 27; 14. 16; 15. 22; 18, 15. John 2. 8; 4. 20; 5. 9; 8. 6. Acts 14. 11. 1 Cor. 10. 25; 11. 6. Gal. 6. 17. Rev. 13. 15.

INDEX.